Strategies
For Change

Strategies
For Change
How to Make the
American Political Dream
Work

Dick Simpson
George Beam

THE SWALLOW PRESS INC.
CHICAGO

Published by
The Swallow Press Incorporated
811 West Junior Terrace
Chicago, Illinois 60613

First Edition
First Printing

This book is printed on recycled paper

LIBRARY OF CONGRESS CATALOG CARD NUMBER: 75-43482
ISBN 0-8040-0696-2

Contents

PART I

A CALL TO ACTION

The Signing of The Declaration of Independence, Courtesy Yale University Art Gallery.

Chapter 1
Political Action

All things are full of weariness;
a man cannot utter it;
the eye is not satisfied with seeing,
nor the ear filled with hearing.
What has been done is what will be,
and what has been done is what will be done;
and there is nothing new under the sun.
Ecclesiastes 1:8

For many years we have lived under a government we neither trusted nor loved. For many years we have known sickness but not the cure. We have seen our weakness but not our strength. We have lost our dreams. We have wanted change but feared failure—feared that our lives might get worse not better.

We once believed that pressure groups and responsible political parties could create a democratic society. We once believed in charismatic leaders and protest demonstrations. But as traditional institutions decayed, as our leaders were shot, as movements fell short of our expectations, we despaired.

To our surprise some people are satisfied with our society. They argue that our political and economic systems are the best the world has known. Often they are successful citizens—businessmen, corporation lawyers, elected officials, foremen, well-paid workers. They believe in waving the flag a little for a country in which they achieved their private dreams.

There are, of course, reasons for being proud. But we find that we cannot be satisfied with a country that is half-just, half-equal, and half-free. We are dissatisfied with America as it is because we see another America. We foresee an America free from discrimination, where talents of every citizen are developed to the utmost. We foresee an America where elected officials are not above the law, where a fair trial is the right of both poor and rich, weak and powerful, Black and White. When we look at our country today, our eyes are not satisfied with our seeing, for we dream of what should be.

Some Americans are dissatisfied because they know that the procedures which are supposed to be followed are openly disregarded. Thus, members of the American Civil Liberties Union, conservative public officials, and citizen watchdog agencies urge return to the procedures outlined in the Constitution or hallowed by tradition. They strive for the protections of "due process." They expose corruption and deceit in government. While it is not true of them all, many guardians of process are completely satisfied if certain forms and procedures are followed in the decision-making process.

A concern for procedures alone fills us with weariness. While important, it is not enough that decisions be made according to certain procedures. It is not enough that public officials do not steal. It is not enough that formal hearings are held. The forms of democracy may make a good society more likely, but they do not insure it. If concentration camps are built legally after full debate in the legislative branch and after approval by the executive and judicial branches, adherence to due process will provide little comfort to prisoners about to be slaughtered. Not only how things are done, but what is done, is crucial to a free and just society.

Other Americans, even some concerned primarily with procedure, recognize the substantive shortcomings—the injustice, inequality, and tyranny of our society. They know the milk is sour and the promised honey now is bitter. They know that the rituals of a democracy are not enough. They know that justice, equality, and freedom require substantive changes. They are the traditional liberals and conservatives whose gentle criticism and conscience impede complete stagnation and prevent greater evils in our country. We, too, were once traditional liberals. But we saw civil rights workers jailed and killed. We saw two Kennedys and King assassinated, and an attempt made to assassinate Wallace. We saw the horrors of the Vietnam War. We heard years of lies from our own government. We know the sorry story of the Joseph McCarthy era and the sordid tale of Watergate. Our hopes have been voted down at national conventions, in city halls, in state houses, and in Washington. With napalm, guns, and false fine words our belief in substantive change through old institutions and procedures has been killed. What must be, cannot be without major substantive changes throughout all America. Gentle criticism and prodding here and there are insufficient to the time.

Finally, there are the reformers. The progressives and populists of an earlier time thought minor structural changes—primary elections for Senators, nonpartisan elections for city officials, antitrust laws, and an income tax—could set this country aright. Socialists believed that more governmental control of business, more public ownership of utilities and industries could provide an economic base for a better society. All these reforms have been adopted and likely our country is better for them. But the poor remain with us, discrimination hangs on, and government is more remote from citizens than it has ever been. Structural reforms alone are not enough.

We differ from satisfied citizens, guardians of process, gentle critics, and previous reformers. We oppose the status quo because *we are dissatisfied with both the procedures and the substance of American politics.* We do not believe that what has been done is all that can be done. We do not believe that what has been must be. We believe that although human nature cannot be changed, still people have a greater potential for good than our institutions allow for. We believe there can be something "new under the sun" —*a new and better America.*

We see our nation faced with a choice between revolution, revision, or repression. We are resolved that America shall not fall prey to violent repression by the government, nor to violent attempts to overthrow the government. We are radicals with a different vision. We are prepared to act to make our vision the new reality in America and to prevent the terrible fate which may otherwise lie ahead for our country.

We are veterans in the struggle to renew our society. We have lost our naive hope of easy victory but we have won important battles. We have stood in civil rights demonstrations and seen restaurants, theaters, and public accommodations desegregate. We have stood in stockholders meetings and seen giant corporations forced to curtail pollution. We have fought in the precincts and consistently defeated the strongest party machine in America. We have fought in the halls of government and forced, step by step, reforms thought impossible by many. But this is the more obvious face of victory. What is more essential and fundamental about these battles, is that we have seen defeated, unaware citizens become dedicated, concerned, and self-confident. We have seen them sacrifice and, most of all, we have seen them *act* to save our country. We join them in pledging our lives to a new America. Together we have accomplished much. Together we have much to do. The bigger part of the task of recreating America still remains.

This book is meant for those of you who share our vision. It is meant for those of you who want to act but do not know how to begin. And it is meant for those of you who have been so busy fighting for change that you have not had the time to consider how best to achieve it. Our purpose is to enable people to reform their own institutions and communities. Major change comes from successful political action. Successful action is based upon strategies thought out in advance and perfected in the doing. We offer what we have learned about effective strategies in the hope that you will be better able to lead the struggle for a new America.

Our Definition of the Problem

> . . . *the definition of the alternatives is the supreme instrument of power. . . . He who determines what politics is about runs the country, because the definition of the alternatives is the choice of conflicts, and the choice of conflicts allocates power.*
>
> E. E. Schattschneider[1]

It is not enough to say we are dissatisfied with America. We must also propose positive alternatives. In setting forth our alternatives we not only assert our own preferences, but, at the same time, we define political conflicts in a manner most likely to bring us victory. "The definition of the alternatives is the supreme instrument of power" because defining the situation permits us to choose our own battleground. Therefore, when we have the power to define the issues, we should define them in a way with which a majority of the people will agree. If our opponents are forced to accept our definition of the conflict, if they must accept a definition of the alternatives which will cause a majority of the people to side with us, then they are likely to lose. Thus, during the depression the Democrats, in contrast to Hoover's policy of inaction, chose to define the critical issue as government action to guarantee prosperity. In the 1952 election Eisenhower chose to define the critical issue as ending the Korean War. Because of their definitions both Roosevelt and Eisenhower won their political contests. To define the nature of the political cleavages is to determine the final outcome of the struggle, even though it may take decades to complete.

Although careful thought goes into making a winning definition, a political situation cannot be successfully defined in an ivory tower—it is defined by action.

Actions change people as well as society. Carmichael and Hamilton in their book, *Black Power*, discuss the consequences of voter registration for Blacks in the 60's:

> The *act* of registering to vote does several things. It marks the beginning of political modernization by broadening the base of participation. It also does something the existentialists talk about: it gives one a sense of being. The black man who goes to register is saying to the white man, "No." He is saying "You have said that I cannot vote. You have said that this is my place. This is where I should remain. You have contained me and I am saying 'No' to your containment. I am stepping out of bounds. I am saying 'No' to you and thereby I am

creating a better life for myself. I am resisting someone who has contained me." That is what the first act does. The black person begins to live. He begins to create his *own* existence when he says "No" to someone who contains him.[2]

People who act out of a redefinition of themselves have already changed their relationship to society. They are already free. They are equal. They are full citizens. They have become makers rather than consumers of history. They determine their own destiny rather than serve as others' pawns.

Thus, *we* define the political situation in America today as democracy vs. repression. In our eyes anyone who stands for war, racism, poverty, or domination by elites prefers a repressive society in which they either rule or receive special benefits from the system. Anyone who fights for peace, an end to discrimination, a guarantee of at least a minimal level of life's necessities, or for a government open to greater citizen participation has joined the struggle to make our society more democratic. We believe that if the choice is between democracy and repression, Americans will choose democracy. This choice between democracy and repression is important to us personally and is critical to the American experiment. We have the chance to prove that men and women can create a just society, that we can rule ourselves rather than being governed by others.

It is not enough to define the alternatives as a choice between democracy vs. repression. We must find actions for ourselves and others which can force acceptance of these terms of battle. We must act as free men and women in the same way that Blacks declared their freedom in the 1960's by registering to vote. This book is meant to help you find your own way of taking action against injustice, against war, against poverty, against tyranny— in short, against repression.

We do not promise that you will win all your battles. But we know that without a clear sense of the alternatives you are certain to lose. We know that defining the situation as a struggle for freedom and greater democracy served our forefathers well. We know that even costly battles in the cause of freedom mean more than easy victories won for lesser goals. We know that a better democracy is worth the fight.

Winning Political Strategies

Change comes from power, and power comes from organization. In order to act, people must get together.
Saul Alinsky

Political strategies are nothing more than plans of action to achieve specific political outcomes. They are a careful answer to Lenin's question, "What is to be done?" The ultimate test of a strategy is its success. Some strategies are clearly better than others because they are more likely to succeed.

A good answer to the question, "What is to be done?" requires careful formulation of the goals, correct analysis of society, and choosing those actions which will work in the existing situation. Effective strategies are born of experience and imagination. We begin with a problem which we have personally encountered—we are cut off from political power by closed parties, or the government adopts war policies despite our protests, or fellow citizens of a different race are excluded from public accommodations, or public schools are so inadequate in the city that we are forced to live in the suburbs, or our university is a bureaucratic quagmire thwarting all efforts to improve education. When we encounter obstacles which create immediate problems, then we are forced to consider alternative strategies.

Our direct encounter with a problem should lead us to reanalyze and redefine our situation. We must ask ourselves, "What is the reality, the context within which the problem exists?" If, for example, we fail to elect a good candidate to office, the fault may not lie only in the techniques we used. More fundamentally, the trouble may lie in a political process controlled by a closed political party. If we study the situation, we soon discover that a few changes will allow us, not only to win a single election, but to win most elections. Once the original problem is seen in this larger context, possibilities for effective action can be developed.

Good strategists, like good artists, look at a situation and see elements which have been there all along but were not noticed before. Impressionist painters see light and shadows and focus our attention on them. Cubists see shapes and forms hidden under the surface. So, too, a Saul Alinsky can see the potential for a people's organization to fell powerful corporations. A Martin Luther King can create a nonviolent campaign to awaken the conscience of a bigoted America and to repeal the segregationist practices of generations. A Martin Luther King can organize people with no resources but their own bodies against a power structure with police, firehoses, vicious dogs, fiery crosses, and bombs, and still these poor Blacks win.

Correct analysis requires a new look at what may seem to be a hopeless situation. It requires foregoing the conventional wisdom which says "you can't fight city hall." It requires foregoing ivory tower idealism which believes that pure democracy will work just because it is a rational way for people to live together. It requires that a strategist study the placement of the status quo's troops so that the troops of change can take advantage of the situation to create a new order, a new reality, a new status quo.

Several concepts are useful for analyzing political situations. We are convinced that *governmental and political outcomes* are always the result of certain *policy decisions* and certain *enforcement decisions* made within strict *structural limits*. Thus, racial segregation exists because of certain policy decisions (namely, local and federal laws) and because of enforcement decisions (namely, decisions by police in forcing obedience to these laws and by institutions like schools and churches in convincing the public of the rightness of these laws). These racist policies and their enforcement are carried out within a structural framework defined by the Constitution and by societal norms. A strategist who would change a particular problem such as racial segregation, must attack the policy-making process, or enforcement, or the structures which uphold both.

After selecting the goals to be achieved and choosing the point of attack, a strategist must still select a course of action. There are basically two types of strategies—pressure strategies and takeover strategies.[3] *The object of a takeover strategy is to gain control*—to put ourselves into positions of policy making or enforcement so that we make the authoritative decisions necessary to gain our desired outcomes. Revolutions and coups are well known takeover strategies. Although we do not often think about them this way, elections are only nonviolent takeover strategies. Whereas the object of a takeover strategy is to gain key positions, *the object of pressure strategies is to force existing policy-makers or enforcement officials to make decisions favorable to our goals.* Lobbying is a common example of a pressure strategy, but riots are another type of pressure.

Effective political strategies, whether pressure or takeover strategies, require mobilizing many people. While individuals can organize or lead groups or point out injustices, strategies in a mass society like ours demand the efforts of many people, not just a few. Without power we cannot force change and without an organization we cannot gain power. In planning a strategy for change we must consider *who* is able and willing to act, *how* many people must act together to win particular goals, and *what* type of organization can best mobilize people for concerted action.

Protectors of the status quo use existing institutions to insulate society from change. Successful strategies of change, must create new organizations to combine the efforts of scattered individuals. Electoral strategies require new participatory institutions to replace old political parties. Administrative strategies require new groups of citizens and administrators to replace old bureaucratic groups and public interest lobbies. Issue strategies require new peoples' organizations in place of old business associations and labor unions. Plenty of people are willing to fight for change; but too few realize that first an army must be recruited, trained, and carefully deployed if protectors of the status quo are to be defeated. "People must get together" before we can create a new America.

In this book we will explore three alternative strategies which can be employed separately or in combination to win significant victories for citizens. In considering these electoral, administrative, and pressure strategies in the next three sections of the book, we will follow the same procedure for each. In the first chapter of each section we will discuss the situation in which the strategies would be applied, we will analyze why other frequently advocated strategies are insufficient, and we will describe our particular strategy and the new institutions necessary to carry out such a strategy. In the second chapter of each section we will explore how the strategy has actually worked when applied in Chicago (or how it would work if applied in the case of the administrative strategy), and we will evaluate the strengths and weaknesses of each strategy. At the end of the three sections examining these particular strategies we will conclude with a final chapter which sets forth eleven propositions for effective strategies and which studies in more depth the basic need to build new institutions if these strategies are to be effective.

Discerning readers will quickly recognize that this book has been written by two authors with very different backgrounds both of whom are advocates for their own point of view. We believe, however, this tension enlivens rather than detracts from our work. Although we each make the strongest possible case for our own preferred strategies, we have readily accepted the insights and corrections suggested by our co-author. Our extensive reviews and modifications of each other's work mean that every chapter is the result of joint efforts; yet the imprint of the original author remains. From this process of mutual criticism and debate each chapter has been improved. Nonetheless, we wish to acknowledge that Simpson is the principal author of Chapters 2, 3, 6, and 7 and that Beam is the principal author of Chapters 4 and 5. The first and last chapters have been so frequently rewritten that both of us fully share the responsibility for the ideas included.

Our purpose is not only to advocate our particular strategies. Our purpose is not only to provide case studies of successful strategies. Our most fundamental purpose is to provide you with a method for analyzing various strategies, the criterion for deciding which strategies to adopt, and ideas about how to create your own strategies and institutions.

A Time to Reflect, A Time to Act

Turning and turning in the widening gyre
The falcon cannot hear the falconer;
Things fall apart; the center cannot hold;
Mere anarchy is loosed upon the world,
The blood-dimmed tide is loosed, and everywhere
The ceremony of innocence is drowned;
The best lack all conviction, while the worst
Are full of passionate intensity.

W. B. Yeats

Our goal is a revised American government, which would encourage greater citizen participation, justice, and freedom. Our fear as we watch the old system fall apart is that either revolutionary or repressive forces will loose the bloody tide of anarchy before a new America can be born. The cycle of violence is already quite advanced in the United States. The apostles of revolution and repression are filled with passionate intensity. Often advocates of nonviolent strategies for change are silenced by fear, are defeated by the slowness of reform, and lose hope.

Nonviolent change requires incredible discipline and sacrifice. Furthermore, such change is slow. But we cannot command other Americans to accept change at gun point; we must convince them by argument and example. Assassinations, guerrilla warfare, and civil wars bring greater violence, bloodshed, and anarchy. Leaders on all sides are killed off to be replaced with authoritarians even less committed to a democratic society.

We seek to come between the violent revolutionary and the despot. We seek to break the cycle of violence and apathy which now encircles our society. We seek to make social change the new reality in America. The old order can be saved only by the birth of the new.

Our country's greatest need is for active citizens who have firm convictions, who have the vision and skills to create new institutions, and who have the courage to lead us in the time ahead. We need activists who can reflect about their actions and thinkers who are not afraid to act. We need citizens willing to assume responsibility for their own and their country's destiny. By turning back the forces of violence and repression, we hope to preside at the birth of a new America. It is for this reason that we study strategies for change, while there is still time.

PART II

ELECTORAL POLITICS

Simpson Aldermanic Campaign, 1971, Peter Williams, photographer.

Chapter 2
A Strategy for Elections

For nearly two centuries elections have provided the standard means of reform in the United States. During the Civil War the electoral process could no longer contain the passions aroused by the slavery issue and a violent struggle for control of the government broke out. And at various times riots by farmers, veterans, laborers, and excluded minorities have exploded when peaceful paths to power were blocked. But for the most part regular elections have permitted orderly change. Thus, one way of bringing about a new America may once again be to use elections to take over positions of government in order to govern differently.

A viable electoral strategy depends upon the degree to which elected officials really make and carry out policies. Certainly office-holders formally adopt laws, approve budgets, and appoint governmental officials. However, some authors like C. Wright Mills claim that our country is run by a power elite of business managers, military leaders, and appointed officials in the executive branch of government. Other analysts believe that elected officials are puppets reflecting the will of their real masters, the capitalists, or that they are severely limited in their decisions because they must rely upon information collected by a biased bureaucracy.

We believe that while some elected officials are only spokesmen for special interests and others are totally dependent on the bureaucracies, elected office-holders still have great power to shape the destiny of this country. Their appointment, budget, and law-making powers are sufficient to control the government. If we want to change America, we might best begin by electing our own officials.

17

Electoral politics is meaningful only if at least one set of candidates is prepared, if elected, to carry out policies different from the current ones. A major struggle is occurring to determine America's future role in world politics and the degree to which new values and customs will be adopted in American society. For the system to be responsive to these demands, new officials who represent movements for change, who understand these contemporary issues, and who desire to protect the dignity, freedom, and rights of all citizens must gain a firm foothold in government. Our electoral strategy calls for electing "new politicians" with new commitments and with the will to change our government's policies.

Electoral politics of one type or another is often advocated and frequently tried. Yet, many concerned citizens have ventured into electoral politics only to be disappointed. Elections, which appear at first an easy answer to discontent, are difficult weapons to use. These strategies, like any other, must be based upon a realistic understanding of the political situation.

The Electoral System in America

Most of us have lived with the American electoral system all our lives. We have known no other, so we have seldom thought about its unique characteristics. We vote without considering that in a different system we might vote for fewer or more officials, that campaigns might be conducted differently, and our votes counted in different ways. Our electoral system establishes precise limits for any electoral strategy. Therefore, those committed to change must know the laws and practices governing elections.

The electoral system in the United States is characterized, first of all, by an incredibly large number of elected officials. One estimate places the number at 521,000 or an average of one official representing every 230 adult citizens.[1] A citizen of Chicago votes for a presidential candidate, two of the 100 U. S. Senators, one of the 435 members of the House of Representatives, 6 state officials including the governor, one of the 58 state senators, three of the 177 state representatives, ten of the 15 members of the Cook

County Board, a President of the County Board, 9 Sanitary District Trustees, 9 University of Illinois Trustees, a Mayor, City Clerk and Treasurer, one of the 50 Aldermen serving in the City Council, and a host of other officials including Circuit Court Judges. The sheer numbers have implications for any electoral strategy. On the one hand, there are so many officials to be elected that it is *relatively* easy to elect oneself or a few members of any particular group. Thus, citizens who are willing to pool their resources can elect a spokesman to insure that their ideas, concerns, and grievances will be heard.

On the other hand, this multiplicity of elected officials makes gaining control over the entire policy-making process nearly impossible, even if you elect dozens of candidates to public office. Therefore, an effective electoral strategy must at first restrict itself to specific goals, which can be met by capturing a few offices. It is unreasonable to pursue an electoral strategy to change national, state, and local policies at the same time because that requires winning more than 260,000 electoral posts. Even at the local level, the proliferation of elected offices demands that a strategy be planned in stages: first, gaining a spokesman in government; second, forming a loyal opposition; and third, achieving majority control.

The electoral system is also characterized by large, single member districts. Unlike systems of proportional representation, we in the United States usually elect only one official to represent a district. We elect a single president, only one congressman from each congressional district, and so forth. Therefore, neither the loser nor his or her political organization gets any voice in government, regardless of how close the race was. Single member districts encourage the dominance of existing parties by making it difficult for new parties to gain a foothold even if many voters support them. Until a new political organization becomes stronger than both existing parties in a district, it scores no victories at the polls and receives no reward for its labors.

Two countervailing tendencies in campaigning must also be remembered in developing an effective electoral strategy. Political parties continue to nominate candidates, provide door-to-door precinct workers, and furnish the expertise needed in a campaign.

At the same time, experts in public relations, computer technology, and mass media are used ever more frequently by major political candidates to overcome the difficulty in reaching voters. Professional campaign managers and public relations firms which specialize in political campaigns sell their candidates to the voters in much the same way that soap is sold. Both political party and public relation efforts at campaigning, however, leave the mass of the people outside the electoral process—they are left as consumers to be manipulated by others. Campaigning means reaching as many eligible voters as possible to present a candidate or at least an "image" of a candidate. Voter contact must principally be made by precinct workers or through the mass media since campaigns rarely involve direct contact between the voter and a candidate. Elections run by political parties and public relations firms, like most aspects of our mass society, have become remote.

In Chicago, new-fangled media and public relations experts have been kept in their place by a party organization which fully lives up to the tradition of big city machines. The Daley machine is organized into 50 wards and 32 townships in Cook County. Its loyal members, more than 35,000 of whom hold patronage jobs, still man 3,500 precincts. Those who carry their precincts each election for the party slate are economically rewarded for their labors. Independents or Republicans must be prepared to defeat the Mayor's standing army of paid precinct captains. Victories do not come easy in a city dominated by a hundred-year history of machine politics. In Chicago, whatever the experience in the rest of America, the party reigns supreme in elections and in the government.

In most of America dependence on mass media has resulted in high campaign costs. Electoral strategies do not come cheap. In 1968 $100,000,000 was spent for Presidential campaigns alone and $300,000,000 for all campaigns. In 1972 costs were even higher. Worst of all, the Watergate hearings have disclosed that in the 1972 Presidential campaign much of this money was spent on bribery and espionage.

Total campaign expenditures in 1968 break down this way: 20% ($58,900,000) was spent on radio and television advertisement and an additional 7% ($20,000,000) on newspaper ads; 17%

($50,000,000) for buttons, stickers, and posters; 8% ($25,000,000) for election day expenses; 2% ($6,000,000) for public opinion polling; and the rest was divided between salaries, travel, headquarters expenses, campaign literature, and postage.[2] Thus, an average of $1.50 per voter was spent in electing over 500,000 public officials, and about $.63 per voter in electing a President.[3] This huge sum was raised by contributions from 8,700,000 people or 11% of those who voted in 1968. Fifteen thousand people contributed over $500, and 414 people contributed more than $10,000.[4]

In Chicago, winning aldermanic campaigns against the Daley machine cost at least $20,000; state representative campaigns, more than $35,000; Congressional campaigns, more than $100,000; and successful city-wide or county-wide campaigns can easily cost from $250,000 to more than $1,000,000. Thus, even local elections require major fund raising. This makes campaigns by poor people virtually impossible. The need to raise large sums of money makes any campaigns by new organizations very difficult. While volunteers can replace expensive media ads and some salaried staff members, a successful campaign still cannot be run without money.

Too much apathy and nonparticipation in elections also characterizes elections in America. Increases in population and in the complexity of government decisions have discouraged citizens from participating and, thereby, alienated them from their government. Over 40% of the electorate do not vote in presidential elections and often 80% or more fail to vote in local contests.[5] Voting is inhibited by the difficulty of registering, by the fact that elections are held on working days, and by similar inconveniences. These barriers might be eliminated by permanent universal registration, voting on weekends, and the development of electronic means for voting from home, although there are problems such as potential vote fraud and higher costs with such reforms.

We also know that more people vote when there is a major difference between candidates, when an election is hotly contested. More voters turn out when they believe that their immediate interests are at stake and that their participation will help determine the outcome.[6] When parties slate only candidates who support existing or noncontroversial policies, citizens stay home. In any case, candidates running for office need not worry about galvanizing support from a majority of citizens in the district. Given the usual level of participation, the support of, say, 30% of the citizens (since no more than 60% vote) is more than enough to win.

The theory of representative democracy to the contrary, the electoral system does not provide for much citizen impact on policy making. There are several reasons why this is true. First, policy making involves many persons over long periods of time. Not only legislators are involved but administrators initiate programs and establish guidelines as well as the judiciary which interprets and enforces laws. Second, stronger forces than elections often affect policy making. Large, well-organized pressure groups, for example, work year round to influence policies. Third, voters often lack information about issues and about candidates' stands on these issues. Surveys of American voters have shown that as many as one-third of the electorate hold no opinion on major national issues and as many as one-half do not know what their government is doing about these issues.[7] Even when a candidate's position is known, campaign promises are not always kept. For instance, President Johnson ran in 1964 on a platform of peace, but after the election he escalated the war in Vietnam. Fourth, another reason why elections seldom determine policy is that many government issues are complex and require information possessed only by technical experts. Deliberations on such issues often take place in committee hearings and in informal meetings between legislators and experts. The end policy is more an outcome of negotiations, compromise, logrolling, and detailed, expert information than of elections. Because policies are often made outside the legislature, because powerful pressure groups exert considerable influence, because information about candidates' positions on issues is often inaccurate, and because technical expertise is valued in decision-making, any direct relationship between elections and policies is almost precluded.[8]

In short, the electoral system is characterized by over 500,000 officials elected in single member districts, by political parties and public relations experts, and by the expenditure of huge sums of money. Elections, furthermore, stimulate only a low level of participation and have only an indirect effect on public policy. As a result most citizens are denied power within their own government and harmful government policies are often enacted.

Inadequate Strategies: Revolutions

Faced with problems in the political system, two frequently advocated solutions are revolution and party reform. For those who believe that our system of government cannot be reformed, revolution is appealing. According to this view, a violent upheaval by oppressed masses under dedicated leaders will displace all current government officials and will break down existing government structures in order to replace them with entirely new institutions and officials.[9] After a brief dictatorship by revolutionary leaders, it is assumed that society will be transformed into a more perfect social system.

Revolution requires a small, secret cadre of leaders to guide the revolution, to educate and prepare the masses, and to fan the flames of conflict by ever more violent acts such as police assassinations and terrorist bombings. Spontaneous riots will set the final stage for revolution. By sheer numbers only the masses can overwhelm the existing government and its defenders. Only when the authority of government is completely undermined in the eyes of most citizens, only when they become desperate for change and take to the streets in massive demonstrations will revolution succeed. Thus, revolutionary leaders are always looking for ways to incite the masses to act, because only mass action can produce a successful revolution.

Several arguments are advanced in favor of revolution in America today. Some argue that social transformation is needed immediately and that revolution is a good strategy for rapid change. Those who argue that revolution is fast do not know the history of previous revolutions. Even if one discounts the decades of effort by early radicals and revolutionaries in Russia, the communist revolution can be directly traced from the establishment of the newspaper *Iskra* ("The Spark") in 1900. In its final stages alone, the Russian

Revolution took two decades. It is reasonable to assume that a revolution in America would take at least as long. *In truth, any program of fundamental reform takes decades to complete.*

Some claim that revolution is a strategy for total change. However, this argument relies too much on the rationality and wisdom of the revolutionaries. Usually, their vision of the revolution is much clearer than their conception of the post-revolutionary society. Major social change is needed in America to eliminate evils in current American government, but there is also much of current society and even more of our heritage which is worth preserving. While change should be in the direction of more freedom, more equality, and more democracy, these qualities already exist to some extent. While American governmental officials have faults, they are willing to abide by the results of elections even when they lose, and to tolerate anti-administration organizations as long as they are nonviolent.

Some revolutionaries claim that nonviolent change will not work. Naive revolutionaries expect instant and easy change. They become more confirmed in their prejudice when their half-hearted attempts at peaceful demonstrations, elections, and community organizing fail. They mistake their faults as strategists for evidence that nonviolent strategies are ineffective.

Those who advocate revolution must remember that the cost is high when measured by the loss of life. It is easy for revolutionaries to say that the current society with its foreign wars and domestic repression already damages and kills. But these existing evils do not give revolutionaries the right to promote riots and civil wars which claim still more lives. Revolution is justified as a strategy only when the existing form of government is so repugnant that it must be eliminated altogether; when the necessary transformation requires that all public officials be replaced and all existing structures destroyed; and when all nonviolent means of achieving these changes are blocked.

In addition to the human costs of revolution, there are several practical problems. Because revolutionaries advocate violence and values counter to existing norms, it is difficult to recruit followers. Recruitment is even more difficult because participants must take great personal risks. Additional problems arise because revolution is always illegitimate, there are few clear guidelines for action, and there is no established timetable for revolutionary tactics. Since no two revolutions are alike, there are few precedents which can be depended upon in planning a revolutionary strategy.

There is no such thing as half a revolution; it must be totally successful to achieve any positive effects. Only by oversimplifying the complex issues of a technological society can a revolt even hope to triumph in this country. As mentioned earlier, most revolutionaries lack adequate solutions for the problems of a post-industrial society even if a revolution would succeed. An unsuccessful revolt, on the other hand, brings in its wake counter repression and authoritarian political control. Finally, another weakness lies in the fact that even a successful revolution involves the manipulation of the masses by an elite cadre. Manipulation of the people is hardly the base from which to build a participatory government, which is the stated goal of most revolutionaries.

Thus, as a strategy, revolution has several shortcomings. The cost in human lives is high. The likelihood of counter-repression is great—jail and death are the rewards to most revolutionaries. Traditional revolutionary strategies are inadequate to transform a technological society. Lastly, the elitism required in mounting a revolution negates the participatory principle that revolutionaries hold dear.

Inadequate Strategies: Party Reforms

Many who reject revolution argue that change can best be achieved by reforming existing political parties. Michael Harrington, for example, has argued quite convincingly that party reform is a more viable alternative than third-party movements:

It would be neater, and ethically appealing, if American politics allowed the Left to make a total break with the past and start a party of its own. And indeed such a strategy might be required. But if it is, the moment will be signaled by the actual disaffection of great masses of people from the Democratic Party. Such a vast shift in political habits cannot be sermonized into existence, a

point which middleclass activists with their philosophic
loyalties and motives do not always understand. Before
raising the banner of a new party, in short, there must be
some reasonable expectation that significant forces will
join it. That could happen in the next twenty years; it
is not presently imminent; and the dispute over whether
it is indeed approaching will turn upon fact and not
morality.[10]

The stability and broad base of support for our current political
system causes most observers to advocate neither third parties nor
new political institutions, but rather reform within the existing
parties.

Within the Republican Party groups like the Ripon Society
push for a more liberal policy orientation and try to attract new
voters. Within the Democratic Party groups like the Americans for
Democratic Action advocate policy changes as well as a restructuring of the party to allow more citizen participation. The McGovern
Commission, established by the 1968 Democratic National Convention, made comprehensive recommendations for fair delegate-
selection procedures. Adoption of these recommendations caused
the 1972 Democratic National Convention to be more open and
more representative of groups which previously lacked a strong
voice within the party. However, the trauma of the 1972 election
caused the Democratic Party to modify these rules. Future conventions will include more office-holders and party bosses and only a
limited number of grass-roots representatives. Despite the efforts
of party reformers, the interim or mini-convention of 1974 neither
brought revolutionary new policies nor a new constituency to the
Democratic Party.

Advocates of party reform argue that political parties are deeply
rooted in American history, having been created in the 19th century; that they perform crucial functions such as recruiting candidates for public office, mobilizing and informing voters about
elections, and assembling power within the government in order to
carry out party policies. Reformers further argue that without
parties our form of democracy would be impossible because ideological and issue clashes between various factions could not be
resolved.[11]

Certainly political parties are useful for making small changes in government. If you want to replace a single elected official or to change a single government policy, party politics is often a practical and simple way of achieving your goal. But if the attainment of your goals requires radical procedural and substantive changes, even reformed political parties are not likely to be sufficient.

Because of the difficulty in creating a substitute for existing parties, many political activists favor party reform. The strategy of party reform assumes however, that parties can act as vehicles for basic substantive and procedural reforms. Can the Democratic and Republican parties be remolded into the modern vehicles necessary to move our society toward greater freedom, democracy, and equality? Can these essentially 19th century institutions be reformed to maximize citizen participation? Can the existing parties provide the mechanism for effective representation and for public accountability by government officials? Can these parties create the radical policies necessary to cope with the foreign and domestic crises which face our nation? These are, after all, the same parties which sponsored the Vietnam and Cambodian Wars, reluctantly enacted inadequate poverty and civil rights programs, and permit only limited citizen participation in party affairs. Their record of progressive programs in recent years does not inspire confidence.

Even strategies which aim at comprehensive party reform will not remedy existing social and political problems. A comprehensive program of party reform is premised, not on the election of a few office holders or isolated policy changes, but on the creation of responsible party government. In contrast to the existing two-party system, responsible party government is characterized by the following features:

1. Elections must involve a clear contest between two or more parties in which major differences are clearly stated and become the basis for decisions by voters.
2. A large percentage of the citizens must actively participate in campaigns in order to present campaign issues to the individual voters in a meaningful way.
3. Political parties must discipline officials they elect in order that campaign pledges can be kept.
4. Within the government there must be clear-cut responsibility

for policy-making so that voters may know whom to support and whom to oppose in future elections.

5. The minority party must offer voters an alternative government composed of different leaders favoring different policies.

This transformation of pragmatic political parties to more ideologically based and responsible parties does indeed require major reforms and would result in significant social changes. Such reforms are difficult, however, (1) because there is no historical precedent in American politics for this type of party, (2) because American political parties are really only coalitions of local fiefdoms of political power, (3) because reform leaders are frequently co-opted, and (4) because political parties, themselves, are fragmenting very rapidly.

American political parties evolved in a pragmatic and not very systematic way, which meant that while issues have often had considerable visibility and importance, they have never remained dominant in the way which they have in the parliamentary systems of England, France, and Italy. The first American political parties grew up as factions or legislative caucuses around two members of Washington's cabinet. The Jefferson faction, known as the Republican Party, was pitted against the Hamilton faction, called the Federalists. The battle for power between the two factions soon spread beyond the Congress and the executive branch to recruit supporters among constituents in order to elect more members of each faction or party to office. While parties were issue-oriented, they seldom were ideological. They were a loose coalition much more than a well-disciplined cadre. Partly because of the American character, partly because of their historical evolution, political parties never became very distinct ideologically. Most often they centered their efforts on a drive for votes by appealing to the broadest possible majority rather than by creating rigorous party platforms.

In America, national political parties are not only non-ideological but they also are only coalitions of local party organizations. Even if reformers capture national conventions or committees, the real power remains with the local party. In major cities like Chicago the party is frequently a closed political machine, controlled by bosses. Likewise many states are really one party states. Even in "competitive" states, party officials are highly insulated from the public, hold office for long periods of time, and have such support from "the regulars" that they are hard to dislodge and totally unaccountable to the national party. Capturing all local party offices in America, like capturing the more than 500,000 government posts, is virtually impossible. Reformers are particularly handicapped in an effort to take over a political party because they are primarily concentrated in major cities and university towns. Usually they are middle class and too often inexperienced political amateurs. As a result most local political fiefdoms and the entire political party structure remain almost impervious to attack. Goldwater's supporters made inroads in the Republican Party in 1964, and the McCarthy and McGovern forces did the same in the Democratic Party in 1968 and 1972. But when the waves of reform subsided, the old political parties re-emerged virtually unchanged.

When party reformers slowly work their way up within the parties, they are too often co-opted by minor reforms or with promises of elected office for themselves. Many reformers achieve personal success while forgetting the reforms which originally motivated them. As reformers meet face to face their enemies in the party, they come to know them as fellow human beings. They learn that most choices involve consequences which they had not fully appreciated when they were outside the government. Mellowed by experience and new friendships, they adopt the attitudes of a professional politician. They don't take time to nurture their reform constituency. Soon they are compromised, cut off from their original supporters, and captured by the old line party organization. They flourish but reform does not.

Even if we could completely overhaul the parties, they might disintegrate before we finish the task. As social and economic changes occur in America, political parties lag behind. Then about every thirty or forty years the political parties leap forward and come to grips with the new socio-economic problems. During the Civil War, and the depressions of 1896 and 1929, there were critical realigning elections which redefined the crucial issues of party politics. Thus, for example, the economic issues of the depression were dealt with by the realigning election of 1932. However, the realigning election which could have been expected in 1964 or 1968 failed to occur. Today we continue to face grave social and political problems for which the major parties offer no adequate remedies. The 1972 and 1974 elections also failed to bring the needed realignment and there is no prospect that future elections will resolve the country's dilemmas. Perhaps we have simply not suffered from a sharp enough blow to the system or a catastrophe sufficient to bring realignment. Perhaps the parties are no longer able to serve as the link between citizen and government in our modern, technological, mass society. In any case the usual realignment of every thirty-two to thirty-eight years has not come.

Instead the party mechanism itself is pulling apart. Walter Dean Burnham in his book, *Critical Elections and the Mainsprings of American Politics,* observed:

A longitudinal analysis of survey results over the past two decades, even at the grossest level, also shows an accelerating trend toward erosion of party linkages in the American electorate, and at two levels: that of voting behavior and that of a normally much more glacial measure, party identification. . . .

There has been a recent and rather sharp increase in independents which has paralleled a sharp decline in the proportion of strong party identifiers—and particularly Democratic Party identifiers—in the electorate. . . .

The political parties are progressively losing their hold upon the electorate. A new breed of independent seems to be emerging as well—a person with a better-than-average education, making a better-than-average income in a better-than-average occupation, and, very possibly, a person whose political cognitions and awareness keep him from making identifications with either old party.[12]

As the old coalitions fall apart, as voters become sophisticated enough to split their ticket on the basis of candidates' personalities and platforms, parties no longer have a monopoly within the electoral process. To expect to woo back dissatisfied voters by reforming the parties is to overlook the need for new institutions altogether. Even if parties could be reformed, there is little evidence that reforms will be brought about by working within the old party structures. Our experience suggests to us that the lever for changes lies outside the traditional parties.

Born in the 19th century, parties are an inadequate vehicle for change, particularly since they are responsible for many of the current problems in our political system. There is no historical base in America for responsible party government. Parties are coalitions of local fiefdoms, which makes it extremely difficult to gain control of the party. Reformers tend to live only in large cities and in college towns, while party organizations which need to be reformed exist all over. Reform leaders are frequently co-opted. Last of all, disagregation is so far advanced that parties may be unsalvageable. If they can be saved at all, it is more likely to be by pressure from new competing institutions than by slow work from within.

Independent Politics

Americans live under a political system which has been loosely labeled a "representative democracy." In truth, it has not been a democracy in which citizens could choose those policies which most directly affected their lives, nor have elected leaders been able to represent adequately the beliefs and ideas of their constituents. Government has become remote, political parties archaic. Independent politics has emerged as an alternative, as a new means of involving more citizens in government, and as a way of making public officials more accountable.

A strategy of independent politics assumes that citizens are capable of governing themselves, that large numbers of citizens will participate in elections and in policy-making, and that democratic leaders can win election to public office. The success of such a strategy depends primarily on the creation of political institutions which differ from traditional political parties in the degree to which they are controlled by their members. These new institutions mobilize citizens, provide the training ground for both them and their leaders, and translate the ideal of participatory politics into a practical, real-life organization.

We are persuaded by analysis and experience that independent politics is a far superior strategy to revolution and party reform. Unlike revolution which inevitably brings further violence and repression, independent politics is nonviolent and is seen as legitimate by existing officials and by the public despite the radical policy changes which independents sometimes advocate. Unlike attempts to reform traditional political parties, independent politics allows for maximum citizen participation and for the formulation of new policies to meet current needs.

Independent politics is not a panacea for all our problems but it is a hopeful strategy for change. It is new, yet firmly grounded in the democratic traditions of our country. It is a positive alternative in a time of despair. In the place of the blood-dimmed anarchy of which Yeats warned, independent politics fosters a new order based on solid human values. This emerging form of citizen politics is founded on the belief that citizens can govern themselves in a freer, more democratic nation.

Concretely, independent politics is a takeover strategy based on electing enough committed men and women to political office to shift policies and to reestablish at all levels a genuine government of the people, by the people, and for the people. As a strategy it requires us to win a large number of elections through issue-oriented, volunteer-run campaigns. Winning these elections, sometimes in opposition to candidates from both parties, requires effective campaign techniques and permanent political institutions capable of launching and directing these campaigns. If enough independent campaigns win and if alternative political institutions are created, then independent politics will either force major reforms on existing office holders and parties, or replace both with able officials and modern political organizations. Therefore, independent politics has a short range goal of immediately electing qualified spokesmen into positions of power and a long-range goal of total reform of political institutions.

Independent politics is based on certain assumptions about the electorate, campaign workers, and political organizations. These differ from the assumptions of revolutionaries and party reformers. What are the independent assumptions about the electorate? We believe that citizens are capable of voting in elections and participating in government without the crutch of party identification. We assume that in hard-fought elections or policy disputes citizens will choose those candidates and policies best for their community and the country as a whole. Obviously, citizens can make such choices only if they are well-informed. Independents know from experience that it is possible to inform the public about candidates and alternative policies through door-to-door, person-to-person contact by volunteer campaign workers.

What are our assumptions about campaign workers? First of all, we assume that at least one percent of the voters in each election will be concerned and informed enough to work in independent campaigns. Since family and job responsibilities prevent the same citizens from working in every election, additional citizens must be recruited for each new campaign. Because of the turnover in volunteers, we must assume that citizens can be taught quickly the necessary skills to be effective campaigners. We further assume that leaders who have the skills will be willing, campaign after campaign, to train and supervise new volunteers. We believe that campaign workers will volunteer not for the patronage jobs promised by party machines, but for the psychological satisfactions of participating in politics. Intense involvement in independent campaigns results in a deeper understanding of the government, a sense of political control, satisfaction in doing our civic duty, and, frequently, the thrill of winning important contests against incredible odds. For all of us, it is psychologically important to be a history-maker rather than a nameless member of the mass. Through participation in our government we become fuller, more developed human beings. We have the ability to become rulers—to share both the freedom and responsibilities of governing.

Citizen campaigns can only be generated time after time by ongoing independent organizations. What are our assumptions about such groups? To be effective they must be permanent, precinct-based organizations whose members are willing to commit large amounts of time and money to independent politics. Just like existing parties, independent organizations must be able to nominate candidates, run election campaigns, keep public officials accountable to constituents, and affect government policy-making directly. Only permanent organizations with experienced leaders and hardworking members can accomplish these tasks.

These independent organizations differ from existing parties in that they require sacrifices of time and money from their members with little material compensation. They can ask for such sacrifices only because real decision-making authority rests with their membership. If independent politics is to bring citizen participation to the whole society, then the independent organizations themselves must be participatory. Learning to govern takes experience which can best be gained through making decisions in our own organizations. When we make wise decisions, our organizations flourish. When we make mistakes, we learn the consequences of our errors. *Thus, independent organizations succeed by being training grounds for democracy, while at the same time providing the means for fundamental social change.*

In addition to our assumptions about citizens, volunteers, and independent organizations we also make some assumptions about government. We share Pericles' view:

> Our citizens attend both to public and private duties,
> and do not allow absorption in their own various affairs
> to interfere with their knowledge of the cities. We differ
> from other states in regarding the man who holds aloof
> from public life not as 'quiet' but as useless; we decide
> or debate, carefully and in person, all matters of policy,
> holding, not that words and deeds go ill together, but
> that acts are foredoomed to failure when undiscussed.[13]

In short, we see government to be the place for public discussion of common problems—the place where private claims may be set aside in favor of decisions which benefit the community. We do believe that we can transcend our private concerns as participants in government. Thus, the first duty of the state is to provide a place and a process which allows government by the citizens. One contemporary supporter of independent politics has put our view rather well:

. . . 'new politics' seeks to re-institute something like the 'polis' of the Greek city-states. That is, it is concerned to make politics a public process in which people participate not only as a civil right and political necessity, but as a function of their lives without which they cannot be fully human. The 'polis' is a public space in which citizens come together as equals to deliberate about matters of common concern and to exercise actual, legal authority over these matters.

But 'new politics' is not only participatory politics. In the conception of the polis the nature of politics itself is understood differently than it is in either the machine or the reform tradition (or in modern liberalism, for that matter). The polis is concerned to maintain some minimal freedom from economic and political necessity; in other words, to seek to transcend the limitations of private politics by simply refusing to accept its quantitative criteria as absolute and by insisting that there be a place in human affairs where men and women can deliberate together with authority about the quality of their common life. . . .

The polis requires its participants at least to some extent to break out of the realm of purely private claims, their own as well as those of others, whether of profit or of simple justice, and to decide in behalf of the whole.[14]

American government today does not foster participatory politics. Rather, the government is becoming more repressive. If our ideal of participatory politics is to prevail, we must be prepared to fight for it. If we lack conviction, if we succumb to the impassioned advocates of revolution or reaction, then all is lost. We must take our case, voter by voter, election after election, if we are to create the widespread understanding and acceptance of citizen politics which are the preconditions of a fuller democracy. Independent politics provides the tools for change but we must supply the vision and the sacrifice.

Chapter 3
How to Win Elections

Independent politics differs from old style parties and campaigns. To understand it better we will look at several Chicago campaigns and a new type of organization, the Independent Precinct Organization. Although reform movements in Chicago have existed since the 1890's, independent political organizations began thirty years ago with the founding of Voters for Victory which has become the Independent Voters of Illinois (IVI). For many years independent politics was confined primarily to the south side, particularly the Hyde Park area around the University of Chicago. However, the McCarthy presidential campaign of 1968 greatly increased the number of citizens in other areas of the city with direct experience in campaigns. Moreover, the 1968 Democratic convention was not a remote event for people living in Chicago. Many of us were in the parks and saw the brutal "police riot," as the Walker Report later named it. On television we saw the liberal wing of the party voted down by the old guard on important issues such as the Vietnam War. Therefore, hundreds of us in Chicago were left with both campaign experience and a desire to change the kind of American politics that we had experienced in the 1968 Convention and in our day-to-day encounters with Daley machine.

In October 1968, we joined together on the north side of Chicago to form the Independent Precinct Organization (IPO). IPO has been able to elect aldermen, state representatives, constitutional convention delegates, and a state senator. We have also effectively supported blue ribbon candidates running for county and state offices. At the same time, the independent move-

36

ment on the south side under the leadership of the Independent Voters of Illinois has continued to elect south-side independents. Because of these successes, an effort is now underway to spread the movement to the rest of Chicago and other parts of Illinois.

Independent Campaigns

Independent campaigns are not easy to win in Chicago. The smallest electoral district, the ward, contains 66,500 people. About 150,000 people reside in state legislative districts, and about 400,000 in congressional districts. In addition to the problem of large urban districts, our principal opposition is the Daley machine —probably the strongest, best funded, and best organized in the nation. Frequently, independents must run against Republicans as well as Daley Democrats. If independents can win elections consistently in Chicago, surely you can more easily win battles in other parts of the country where opposition is less formidable.

How can such campaigns be won? We have elsewhere provided a stey-by-step handbook and a documentary film to give a detailed account of "what is to be done."[1] Our purpose here is to study only the strategy of independent campaigns. After some general remarks about election strategies, we will look at selection of campaign issues, recruitment of volunteers, campaign structure, publicity efforts, and the battle of the precincts which has twice elected one of the authors (Dick Simpson) an independent alderman in Chicago.

Before discussing the details of the campaign, it is worthwhile to emphasize again that the "rules of the game" are well defined in an election. Each stage is regulated by law. Furthermore, because elections occur frequently, the value of new techniques can easily be tested in practice. So, we not only know what is legal, but we can soon learn what works. Much of the uncertainty of other strategies is eliminated. We know exactly the number of signatures required to put our candidate on the ballot, the minimum qualifications to run for office, the day on which the election will be held, the method by which votes will be cast and counted, and which actions, such as buying votes, are illegal. Through experience we know that the most effective contact with voters is person-to-person rather than through mailings or ads in the newspaper. We know how many volunteers are needed and the most likely ways for the opposition to steal the election.

Within this framework, resources and tactics must be carefully matched in a winning campaign. If a candidate has a lot of money but few campaign workers and only a nominal endorsement from the parties, the best strategy is a costly mass media campaign. If a candidate has little money but the backing of a strong party machine, then the best strategy is to let the party run the campaign. Independent candidates have neither lots of money nor strong party support, but because of their superior qualifications and forthright stands on controversial issues, they can attract a larger number of campaign volunteers. It should not be surprising, therefore, that independent campaigns depend on volunteers going door-to-door. Fortunately, this strategy dovetails perfectly with the theme of independent campaigns—more citizen participation in government and better representation by elected officials.

The goal in any election is, of course, to get a majority of the votes for your candidate. Voters will be convinced to go to the polls to vote for your candidate only if you have "cut the issue" wisely. To win elections a campaign must be defined and issues chosen so as to attract both volunteers and voters. Deciding how to cut the issue is a critical choice to be made by the candidate and his or her best campaign advisers. It is not a decision which is made overnight. As the campaign unfolds and the candidate meets with voters, a clearer definition of issues begins to come clear and the differences between opposing candidates becomes more obvious.

To illustrate how independent campaigns are run, we will describe my first successful election as 44th Ward Alderman in Chicago. In 1970 the 44th Ward was gerrymandered to make election of an independent improbable. Ward boundaries had been drawn to include a small population of well-to-do liberals living along the lakeshore, a large number of Latins in the middle of the ward, and in the western section an even larger number of second-generation German working class. The 44th Ward is very diverse with at least some members of nearly every American ethnic group and economic class within its boundaries.

At the early stages of this campaign we projected my image as a pragmatic professor who could "get things done" but who also was an independent, free from machine control. This initial definition was used to attract volunteers. As the campaign progressed, I began to stress three central themes. I promised, if elected:

1. to provide government service for citizens as a matter of right, *not* as a political favor;
2. to represent honestly my constituents and my conscience in the Chicago City Council rather than be just another "Yes Man" for Mayor Daley; and
3. to create a Ward Assembly composed of elected representatives from every precinct and community organization of twenty-five or more people in the ward and open to participation by any citizen. The Ward Assembly would have the power to determine my vote in City Council and to establish projects in the ward. The Ward Assembly would give citizens direct access to government policy making rather than leave such decisions to party bosses.

These pledges were credible because of my past role in independent politics and because I was not a machine candidate. My opponent tried to counter these challenges, but in so doing he was forced to accept my definition of the critical themes of the campaign.

My opponent argued that he could get more services for citizens than I because of his connections with powerful machine politicians; that he would make up his own mind on issues before the City Council despite his party loyalty; and that existing community organizations made a Ward Assembly unnecessary. Unfortunately, his responses did not ring true to the electorate because previous machine aldermen provided city services only as favors, had voted with the mayor regardless of the issues before the City Council, had failed to introduce significant legislation on their own, and had seldom consulted community organizations.

My opponent at one stage late in the campaign attempted a counter-definition of the situation. He charged that since I was endorsed by the Republicans, I would oppose the liberal Democratic reforms of the last forty years such as Social Security. His counter-definition failed because I was endorsed by most liberal organizations in the city, by all four daily newspapers, and by well-known liberal politicians. In addition, I had served as state campaign manager for Eugene McCarthy in 1968 and had founded the Independent Precinct Organization. The conservative Republican label simply did not have credibility and my opponent soon returned to arguing other campaign issues. Had his definition of liberal vs. conservative worked, he probably would have won the election. This is what Schattschneider meant when he said that "the definition of the alternatives is the supreme instrument of power."

In an attempt to reach all 66,500 voters, personal appearances, candidate debates, and hand-shaking at bus stops were all tried. Campaign brochures, buttons, and posters were distributed, but all of these by themselves were insufficient. The mass media had to be used in a special way. Most media campaigns package a candidate like a box of detergent to appeal to "mindless voters" easily swayed by whim and emotion. Regular party candidates use amateurish advertising to achieve only name identification. Independents, on the other hand, employ the media to make their candidate credible, to attract volunteers, and to provide voters information about their candidate's unique characteristics. Because independents do not have the money to buy much advertising, their media effort is based not upon buying ads, but on making news.

My publicity campaign had three stages. In the first stage, news was made when I announced my candidacy and the endorsements I received from political organizations, public officials, and good government groups. Each major endorsement is worth a small news story and sometimes a newspaper photograph or a few moments on television. Each endorsement brings a few more votes, workers, and money from citizens who respect the endorsers.

The second stage was to make news *by doing*. For an independent, news is almost always made by attacking the status quo. During my three-month campaign four actions attracted considerable media coverage. First, my wife and I made a public disclosure of our income and urged that a city ordinance be passed requiring all candidates to disclose their incomes. Second, along with other independent candidates, I called for the use of voting machines rather than paper ballots to insure fairer elections, since Chicago is well known for vote stealing. Third, I introduced a citizen's ordinance into the City Council to limit Mayor Daley's power over school board appointments. This demonstrated both my concern for education and my willingness to oppose the Mayor's almost unlimited political power.

The fourth action which generated news about my candidacy was the initiation of a citizen's campaign against a notorious local towing company. Drivers' complaints of intimidation, damage to automobiles, and actual beatings by towing company employees had become numerous. The news media previously had done exposés and the company had been sued by aggrieved citizens several times, but its practices remained unchanged. My battle against the company's towing practices consisted of a million dollar class-action lawsuit, referral of criminal complaints to the State's Attorney, a public information campaign, and a concerted effort to pass a towing licensing ordinance. This four-point campaign brought changes in company policy, although later loss of the class-action lawsuit weakened the effort. My action against the towing company brought a news story that reinforced my image as a concerned citizen who could get things done, and who was not afraid to challenge powerful interests.

The last stage in my publicity campaign was to obtain endorsements of the daily newspapers. These endorsements not only influence readers directly but were reprinted and distributed as a final argument in convincing voters in the days immediately before the election. Studies have shown that newspaper editorials influence only a small percentage of their readers in most districts.[2] But these votes can easily be the margin between victory and defeat in a close contest.

Good publicity convinces potential campaign workers that the candidate is committed to social change, that this campaign can win, and that it is a critical battle against the party machine. But most volunteers are not brought into the campaign by publicity alone. There must be systematic recruiting. Early endorsements by independent political organizations signify the commitment of many of their members to work in the campaign. These workers, in addition to a candidate's friends and associates, should be sufficient to open a campaign headquarters and to begin the petition drive.

The crucial variable in recruitment is that *the volunteer be asked* to join the campaign. Thus, when the candidate first appoints the campaign leaders each is assigned to recruit his or her friends. When the campaign volunteers go door-to-door for petition signatures, they attempt to enroll the more interested voters in the campaign. When the candidate is shaking hands at a bus stop or supermarket, he or she tries to convert the most enthusiastic greeters into campaign workers. All of these personal pleas bring in workers.

My campaign made great use of "coffees" to recruit other needed volunteers. These gatherings were held at the homes of supporters. Each night as many as five were held, which I personally attended. The idea is simple. Friends of the hosts and residents of their precinct are invited by printed invitation and by phone. Usually, about one third of the hosts' friends and a much smaller percentage of the precinct residents attend. The coffees were chaired by a volunteer who set the group at ease, answered general questions about the election, encouraged people to discuss the problems of the area, and elicited questions to ask me when I arrived. About thirty minutes after the coffee began, I would arrive, be introduced to each guest individually, and talk briefly about why I was running. The coffee chairman would then summarize the questions, and I would respond. Having covered the general points, I then took questions from the floor. A rather frank, if short, discussion of the issues and the campaign occurred. After I left for the next coffee, the coffee chairman would make a strong pitch for volunteers and contributions, explaining why they were necessary to win this campaign and what victory would mean to the community. Successful coffees produce volunteers, money, and new hosts to hold still more coffees. One hundred-fifty coffees and political gatherings were held during my three-month campaign. Campaigns in larger districts necessitate special efforts to increase either the number of gatherings or the number of people attending each event.

The coffee is the secret weapon of our independent campaigns.

Such gatherings allow citizens direct access to the candidate without the intervention of public relations people or party precinct captains. Citizens are converted into volunteers only when they are satisfied by a candidate's answer to *their own questions* and when they are personally convinced that they can trust the candidate. Direct contact with a candidate changes citizens from puppets manipulated by the media to direct participants in government. These voters are personally asked not only to vote on election day but to contribute time and money and effort. They are transformed, if they agree with the candidate, from passive voters into active campaigners. Their commitment, in turn, converts other passive voters into supporters at the polls. Equally important, the candidate is transformed by discussions with thousands of citizens. The candidate's views are broadened by confronting the views of voters. Independents can represent their constituents better after these coffee sessions than can traditional candidates who are relatively isolated from citizen contact. Furthermore, candidates learn from these experiences how to describe ideas for change in a way that gains support, rather than alienates constituents.

Volunteers attracted by publicity, by personal contact with campaign workers, and by coffees must be carefully organized to win an election. Winning an election requires a good campaign structure, a thorough understanding of what must be done, and competent leaders for each campaign function. The structure of an independent campaign is somewhat fluid and must depend to some extent on the personalities and abilities of the leaders, rather than on an idealized organization chart. Nonetheless, the chart on the next page shows the structure used in my 1971 aldermanic campaign.

Most independent campaigns have at least three paid staff members: the campaign manager, office manager, and publicity chairman. The rest of the campaign leadership consists of volunteers who supervise precinct work, set up coffees, plan special events, raise money, budget expenditures, work on publicity, and staff the office. These volunteers give as much as thirty hours a week to the campaign. Paid staff and volunteers who direct key activities often serve with a few experienced campaign advisers as an

Figure 3.1 44th Ward 1971 Aldermanic Campaign Organization Chart.

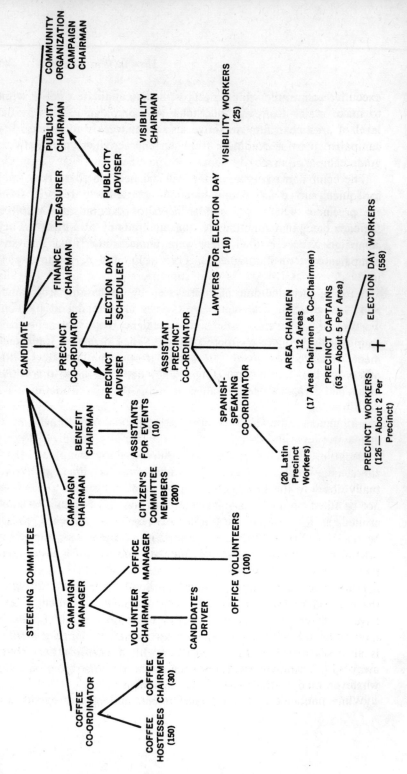

executive committee which meets with the candidate once a week to make major campaign decisions. All campaign leaders at the level of area chairman or above also meet weekly to discuss the campaign, provide feedback from current activities, and help to guide campaign strategy.

The campaign structure is hierarchical because there is a need for quick and exact communication—particularly reports from the precincts. There is a similar need to pinpoint responsibility for each campaign function. As the hundreds of volunteers in my campaign were recruited, they were immediately fitted into the campaign structure, assigned specific tasks, and began to report in.

What the organization chart does not show is that the campaign must also offer companionship and psychological rewards to the workers at all levels. Campaign volunteers are not highly paid employees who can be ordered around. They need the reinforcement which comes from rallies and from social contacts with others working on the campaign. They need to know that their ideas and suggestions are taken seriously by the leaders. They need freedom and autonomy to perform their jobs creatively. They need to meet personally with the candidate to strengthen their own commitment.

Because campaigns are intense, short-lived events, the organization chart cannot adequately describe how all the work is actually done. In the first place, some jobs shown on the chart may not be filled because the person for that job has not yet been recruited. In addition, if the publicity person, for example, cannot be reached during a crisis, the campaign manager or some other official may have to locate the candidate and set up a press conference on the spur of the moment even though this is not his or her formal responsibility. Further, some volunteers may not have the personality for the job they were assigned, or someone may have to leave town for two weeks. Therefore, job assignments have to be shifted despite official titles. In actual campaigns there is always something else to be done with a deadline just hours away. Good campaign workers pitch in and do what must be done whatever their formal role in the campaign.

While publicity, volunteer recruitment, and special events are important, they merely provide the foundation for the all-important precinct work. Effective precinct work is the critical element in winning independent campaigns. Work in the precincts is organized in four distinct stages: (1) petition drive, (2) registration, (3) canvass, and (4) election day. Each phase requires formal training sessions, written instructions, and materials such as poll lists and campaign brochures. Each phase requires accurate reports from the precincts, which are carefully evaluated by the campaign leaders. Each stage provides the base upon which the next is built; each is equally essential to winning.

The petition drive must gather enough signatures to put your candidate on the ballot. In most elections only the signatures of one or two percent of the people who voted in the last election are technically needed. However, the petition drive is also important as an early indication of the strength of your precinct structure—the number of precincts you can cover effectively, the number of voters you can reach. Most of all, the petition drive informs several thousand voters about your candidate and recruits dozens of volunteers. In addition, those voters who sign your petitions nearly always commit themselves to support your candidate.

Stage two, the registration drive, has three purposes: (1) despite the nonpartisan appearance of a registration drive, a whole new constituency favorable to your candidate can be registered to vote; (2) the adequacy of your precinct structure is tested before the final canvass; and (3) formerly registered voters who have died or moved, but who might "ghost" vote, are removed from the voting lists. Independents must mount comprehensive registration drives. Currently registered voters are, after all, the ones who elected the opponents. New voters who have just turned eighteen, who have just moved into the district, or who have refused to vote for candidates in prior elections are likely to be more open to our persuasion. Generally, new voters will register only when motivated to vote for a candidate they like. Thus, if we can get them to the polls, most citizens registered by our precinct workers will end up voting for our candidate on election day.

Accurate reports from precinct workers indicate how many citizens each has visited, registered, and taken off the voting rolls. These reports provide an exact check on each precinct worker's reliability and effectiveness. Where volunteers fail, time remains to replace them, to give them better supervision, or to beef up their precincts with enough workers to get the job done properly. Reports to the campaign leaders are made on designated report nights by precinct workers calling their area chairmen. Area chairmen in turn notify the ward co-ordinators, and ward co-ordinators pass the collected information to the overall precinct co-ordinator. Through this process the candidate and the campaign leaders can tell how effective the precinct structure is before the final battle.

The third stage, the canvass, is a crucial hurdle for an independent campaign. As many voters as possible must be visited by the precinct workers, presented with essential information about the candidate and campaign issues, and politely, but firmly, asked if they plan to vote for your candidate on election day. Many voters can be persuaded to vote for your candidate during this canvass. Voters may be swayed by the personal appearance of your volunteers, by the fact they are working in the campaign because *they* believe in the candidate and the issues, or by the information they present.

More importantly, precinct workers must find out which voters are already favorably disposed toward their candidate. *Precinct volunteers thus function more like public opinion pollsters than like Fuller Brush salesmen.* On their poll lists (lists of those eligible to vote in a precinct) the results of interviews with citizens in each precinct are recorded. A voter who is planning to vote for your candidate is marked as a plus (+). Those who support the opposition are marked minus (−). Voters who refuse to say whether or not they will support your candidate or who honestly are undecided are marked zero (0). Since the canvass is taken within the last three weeks of the campaign, most voters will have made up their minds by then. Thus, winning elections requires not only convincing many citizens to support your candidate, *but it also requires that you know who your supporters are so that you can make sure they vote election day.*

Election day is the fourth and final stage in the campaign. Voters on their way to the polls are handed flyers listing your candidate's endorsements. Inside the polls a volunteer watches to make sure that the election is not stolen. On a poll list your poll watcher draws a line through the name of each person who votes. The list of plus voters identified in the canvass, when compared to the list of those who have voted, is a map to victory. Elections are won when your precinct workers are able to locate favorable voters and to get them to the polls. A "runner" working with your poll watcher visits the homes of all plus voters who have not yet come to the polls to make sure they vote. Because the canvass has already identified our supporters, we win on election day by the coordinated efforts of poll watchers and runners who ensure that all of the previous campaign work culminates in a maximum vote for our candidate.

In conclusion, we can outline fairly exactly what must be done to win an independent campaign. In the 44th Ward of Chicago, with 66,500 residents and somewhat more than 30,000 registered voters, a battle against the Democratic party machine takes, first of all, a good candidate and well-chosen issues. From 300 to 500 volunteers, a paid staff of three experienced campaigners, and at least $25,000 are also required. An incredible number of volunteer hours are needed to visit voters and to get them to the polls. A good candidate, careful planning, enough money, hard work, able campaign leaders, and luck are all needed for victory. We have proven in Chicago that such battles can be won even against the Daley machine. Elsewhere you should win with less effort and less cost; but electoral victories are never free.

An Evaluation of Independent Politics

The most immediate result of independent politics is the election of able men and women to positions of power and authority. At a minimum, they serve as a critical voice explaining our concerns, pointing out flaws in government, and warning when dangerous new policies are proposed. As more independents are elected, a loyal opposition is created to offer alternative policies. As our number increases, we will be able to form a working majority, take control of the government, and implement our policies.

In Chicago the independent movement has reached the opposition stage. In 1955 there was only one independent among the fifty aldermen of the City Council. In 1970 at the State Constitutional Convention a dozen independents, holding the balance of power between Democrats and Republicans, forced through a liberal state constitution. In 1971 six independents were elected aldermen along with enough Republicans and liberal Democrats to bring the potential opposition vote to fourteen. In 1972 an Independent Democrat was elected governor despite opposition by both Republicans and Regular Democrats. More than a dozen independents were elected in 1974 to the Illinois Legislature and, while they do not always hold the balance of power, they are able to affect considerable legislation. In the 1975 city elections, several independent candidates ran for mayor and for a majority of the aldermanic posts. Unfortunately, we lost the mayoralty and won only five aldermanic seats that year. However, we are continuing to build for the 1979 and 1983 elections. If we win in 1979 or 1983 after Mayor Daley retires, we, rather than Machine Democrats, will become the government.

Victories at the polls bring advantages other than electing good people to office. Permanent independent political organizations are formed to support future candidates and issues. To these, money and new volunteers can be added for each specific campaign. The existence of permanent, year-round organizations pressures the dominant political parties to provide better candidates and internal reforms. Party reformers are likely to succeed in restructuring political parties only when independent campaign victories prove to party leaders that continuation of the status quo will be disastrous. If parties adopt the structures, goals, and methods of independents, they may defeat and replace independent organizations. However, they will win only by granting the reforms independents seek or at least by slating better candidates and adopting new platform planks. If parties do not reform, independent organizations may become the vehicles for choosing candidates, aggregating citizen demands, and conducting campaigns. If independents become the dominant power of the future, it will be because they allow more citizens to participate in politics and because they are dedicated to a government of freedom, not repression. Regardless of whether the major parties reform or independent organizations become dominant, independent politics is a major strategy for fundamental change.

To succeed, an electoral strategy must establish permanent political organizations. We know that isolated independent campaigns often fail. We know that we can win few elections on an ad hoc basis. Independent campaigns are won consistently and given meaning by permanent independent organizations capable of launching and directing campaigns year after year. Lone independents, even when they win, can serve merely as a voice in government. Only independents united by a common organization and common goals can transform government and make it more responsive, more participatory, more humane, and more accountable.

What are the strengths and weaknesses of independent political organizations? Obviously, they can win elections. More than this, they pull people out of apathy into community. They join together citizens dedicated to governmental and societal reform. They provide a training ground in democratic participation for their members.

A major issue which we must face, however, is whether these independent organizations will succumb to the same forces which turned earlier political parties into the closed, unresponsive organizations that now dominate politics. Will independents, even though committed now to citizen participation and responsive government, be heir to the fate of the Republican and Democratic parties? Those of us committed to participatory politics need to take seriously the views of Reinhold Niebuhr and other realists who maintain that no institution can be made permanently safe from tyranny.[3]

No independent organization can perfectly live up to its ideals in the real world. They may fall prey to oligarchy, impotence, or irrelevance. It is important to build safeguards against these dangers.

Oligarchy is a danger in any institution. In his classic study of political parties, Robert Michels proposed the "iron law of oligarchy." He maintained that all institutions become oligarchical —no matter how democratic their ideals, no matter how devoted their leaders, no matter how well educated their members.[4] As an organization grows stronger, becomes larger, and hires professional staff, oligarchy increases. Even revolutionary organizations, ideologically most opposed to oligarchy, inevitably fall prey to it.

Several steps, however, can be taken to limit oligarchy. The Independent Precinct Organization in Chicago, for instance, decides policies by a two-thirds vote of the members following a full discussion at open meetings. Further, IPO has only a single staff member, the office manager, who handles the necessary office work. This lack of a large, entrenched staff and the extensive use of volunteers limits oligarchy in the IPO.

All officers of the IPO serve only six-month terms. Even if they are re-elected, no officer, not even the Executive Director has served more than 18 months and no "cult of personality" has developed. These safeguards—open decision-making, volunteer work, and limited terms of office—have thus far proved to be sufficient checks against oligarchy and they have kept IPO a genuinely democratic organization.

Within the IPO the only visible signs of oligarchy are deceit on the part of some candidates seeking endorsement, attempts by factions to manipulate procedures to their advantage, and an over-dependence of the members on the views of officials the IPO has helped to elect. Endorsement sessions require only brief statements on the part of candidates and a short question-and-answer period. Furthermore, the general opinions of IPO members are well known from their previous endorsements. Using this information, a candidate with charisma and the "right" answers can obtain an IPO endorsement. Sometimes such candidates answer questions falsely or simply do not mention opinions with which IPO members will disagree. Thus, candidates can leave a false impression, and the IPO may unknowingly endorse candidates who will not really work to further its goals. Of course, candidates cannot change their past political activities, nor disavow allegiance to the Democratic machine in Chicago and maintain its support, nor avoid direct questions by IPO members. Therefore, attempts to deceive the IPO most often fail.

Another potential source of oligarchy within the IPO is that factions favoring particular candidates may try to stack an endorsement meeting with supporters. But the IPO's membership requirement is that one be a member two months before voting on an endorsement. This rule makes it difficult for partisans to stack meetings with much success. The best protection is faithful attendance at IPO meetings by the whole membership, so there is a high quorum requirement. The fact that IPO meetings decide questions involving work and time for members makes participation important. Because of these requirements and privileges most IPO meetings are relatively well attended.

Finally, elected officials sometimes influence the vote of IPO members on certain issues. Elected officials have prestige, are well known, and are often well informed. They are persuasive spokesmen or they would not have won their elections. However, elected officials do not always get their way. Since there are a variety of independents in office, they do not always agree among themselves. In the last analysis, policies are decided by a two-thirds majority of IPO members, not by vote of the officials.

The danger of oligarchy within the IPO is in many ways less threatening than the danger of impotence. The IPO is better organized in the lakefront, middle class communities of Chicago than elsewhere. If we respond only to middle class concerns, the effectiveness of independent politics will be too limited.

Yet the strength of independent politics is to a large extent a result of its special affinity with middle class professionals.[5] In their work professionals have complete responsibility for what they do. They set their own work schedules and make their own judgments. Independent politics depends on the availability of volunteers with just such abilities to take responsibility, to think for themselves, and to act with only general supervison. An ever-growing professional class with the values and the skills of independent politics should provide new recruits, financial support, and the talent necessary for a strong independent movement.

Although based to a large extent on the professional middle class, independent politics provides the techniques for any group which wants to take over positions of power. Because these techniques can be applied by various groups and classes, independent politics can overcome the class restrictions which might otherwise render it impotent. Yet the process is not automatic. The techniques of independent politics must be translated and adapted to the different circumstances of ghettoes, working class neighborhoods, and wealthy suburbs. The IPO in Chicago is now reaching into working-class and poverty neighborhoods. It has grown from its original 3 wards and 150 members to 15 very diverse wards and more than 750 members.

The movement at this point is restricted primarily to Chicago. Nevertheless, a series of campaigns over the last decade, including the McCarthy, Kennedy, and McGovern presidential campaigns, have brought many citizens into contact with participatory campaign techniques. More and more campaigns for local office in communities across the country embody at least some of the principles of independent politics.[6] From such campaigns many of the ideals of independent politics have spread but often without the institutional structures necessary to sustain this type of politics. For the moment, the IPO remains a special, isolated experiment.

Independent politics is not without its critics. Some critics believe that participatory politics and government are impossible because citizens are not informed enough to make policy choices in a highly technological society. These critics do not believe that many citizens would be willing to forego the joys of family life or the diversions of television to participate in government.

James Wilson in his book, *Amateur Democrat*, argues that even if greater participation were possible in politics, it would be undesirable. Wilson believes that government is not necessarily "more democratic if as many people as possible can participate in the choice of . . . [party] candidates and the writing of . . . [party] platforms."[7] Wilson challenges several of the assumptions about independent politics set forth at the beginning of this chapter:

> An alternative theory of democracy rejects the participatory view as unrealistic. This second theory takes into account the fact that people have many fundamental disagreements which cannot be reduced to two simple choices no matter how elaborate the party system may be; that these people are by and large uninformed on all but the most dramatic and fundamental issues; that many of the politically relevant views of people are emotional and even irrational; and that therefore there is no way—and there *should not* be any way—to arrive at de-

cisions on all important matters or at some conception of the common good by algebraically adding the likes and dislikes of the voters. The implication of this view is that, far from increasing public participation in the choice of candidates and issues, democracy is best served by reducing and simplifying those choices to a single elemental choice—that of the principal elective officials.[8]

The critics are right in maintaining that a nation as large as the United States cannot be a "pure democracy" run by a national town meeting of 220 million people. But independents have discovered some ways for involving citizens more deeply in selecting candidates, in campaigns, and in consulting voters on policy questions. The choice need not be between 100% participation and none. No participation is unacceptable, and pure democracy is not possible. More citizen participation is both necessary and possible.

If citizens are denied the right to participate in their government "[what] remains is a curiously childlike but hardly exemplary creature, for whom the appropriate human scale is not Shakespeare's Hamlet but Kafka's K."[9] Either citizens are evil or incompetent, and therefore must be governed by those few leaders with special capacities and wisdom; or they are responsible, moral, and capable enough to help to make public decisions and to govern themselves.

Despite its pitfalls, we believe that independent politics is an effective strategy for change. *Independent politics work.* The first test of a good strategy is that pragmatic, real results are attained. We have proven in Chicago that independent campaigns can elect better men and women to public office and foster more citizen participation than traditional party politics.

Independent politics does not have the faults of alternative strategies. Unlike revolution, it does not provoke violence and repression. Unlike party politics, it challenges rather than supports the status quo. In taking their case to the voters, independents build a strong base of citizen support for change, rather than depending upon actions by a small elite of revolutionaries or party bosses.

Independent politics encourages new solutions to contemporary problems. Independent campaigns are always issue-oriented. They raise questions and encourage both candidates and voters to consider alternative solutions. Independents generally favor reordering government priorities. They are committed to citizen participation, to experimentation, and to pragmatic efforts to reorganize the government. Because of this, they are more likely to create new institutions and restructure government to achieve effective participation in our mass society, end alienation, and resolve the racial and social tensions which threaten to destroy us.

America today is at best a limited democracy. *Independents seek to alter these limits to allow more citizen participation in government.* Independents believe that candidates running on issues will be supported by enough volunteers and by enough voters to be elected. They believe that local issues can be decided by direct citizen participation and that the electoral process can allow voters to register a judgment on national issues like war, discrimination, poverty, and inflation. Independents are struggling to make the government open to citizen participation and to make citizens capable of self-government.

Independent politics is a desirable strategy because it makes political power available for citizens who have been excluded. Not only minority groups, women, and the young have been excluded from power but, with the exception of the wealthy, party bosses, and top government employees, most Americans have been left out of government. Independent politics allows citizens with limited financial resources to have an effect on government if they are willing to spend their time and talents. The methods of independent politics are available to any citizen and any group willing to use them.

Finally, independent politics is an effective strategy because it can be started with limited resources at the local level, and success at the local level can eventually have profound effects on our national life. Our national constitution was not created out of imagination alone but from experience under English rule and in the new states after independence. So we may reasonably expect that new national political institutions can be built on the experience of local campaigns and local organizations like IPO. The end result may be a new type of pragmatic, issue-oriented, participatory institution and, perhaps, even a new form of democratic government. Independents have already begun to build the local base for change. We need not wait. We need not despair. We are winning victories now in our towns and cities. The elections won by independents in Chicago, as well as primary elections won by McCarthy, Kennedy, and McGovern show that a different kind of politics is possible in America.

Independent politics is a precise, effective strategy already proven in the voting booth. It is a strategy for change which can gradually create the New America. Despite pitfalls and problems, independent politics can change the government permanently. It can make people fuller human beings because they take destiny into their own hands. Through independent politics citizens reassert their citizenship—their right, as equals, to deliberate and to exercise authority over their own government. We, the people, can speak and act for ourselves.

PART III
ADMINISTRATIVE POLITICS

Photograph courtesy of Joseph Sterling.

Chapter 4
Administrative Strategy

There are many aspects of contemporary society which imply the dominance of administrative institutions over electoral processes. To the extent that modern society is administrative, fundamental change requires an administrative strategy. Basic change requires that citizens control administration as the means for controlling political, economic, and military policies. If we believe the world is controlled by electoral institutions, we use an electoral strategy to gain power. If we believe administrative institutions are dominant, then an administrative strategy must be employed.

In advanced industrial nations the significance of administration is increasing in every aspect of life. The key to understanding modern society is the bureaucratic similarities among all industrialized nations, not their ideological differences.

Just as monarchy gave way to parliamentary government, so today electoral institutions are losing ground to the administrative state. The increasing significance of bureaucracy cannot be explained as the result of a conspiracy by bureaucrats nor as the result of incompetent elected officials. Administration has become dominant throughout modern society because administrative rather than legislative processes are better suited to scientific research, technological development, and industrial production. Also, administrative dominance results from the complexity and increasing number of public services—education, housing, transportation, and so on—run by large bureaucracies. Just as the institution for religion is the church, just as the institutions for traditional democracy are parliaments and political parties,[1] so the institution for modern technology, business, and public service is administration.

The contemporary administrative world is exemplified by management, planning, and specialization. Managers play an increasing role in government, finance, education, production, and defense. In all major aspects of modern society managers are increasingly significant, because they are required to coordinate the diverse skills of personnel in large organizations.

Planning takes the place of traditional politics as the decision-making process governing the economy, large-scale production, education, space exploration, pollution control, and the other policy areas which most affect the citizen's life. The rising influence of managers and planning is perhaps most evident within large corporations. While individual stockholders and small groups of stockholders are sometimes still influential decision-makers, managers are, more often than not, the key actors.[2]

Modern production and service require not only managers but also specialists in areas like statistics, metallurgy, physics, and engineering. Specialists cannot attain their organizational positions through elections, but rather they are hired on the basis of test scores, experience, and educational background. Their specialized knowledge and skills can be effectively employed only within the administrative structures which coordinate their separate activities to produce results which no individual can achieve alone.

Throughout the modern world, power is primarily exercised by large administrative institutions. Economic power takes the form of large corporations in which managers exercise major control. Military power is institutionalized not in the platoon of Indian fighters, but in the Pentagon. Science advances, not through the efforts of lone researches in their garrets, but through the coordinated efforts of thousands of scientists and technicians in think tanks, space centers, and research units of business, government, and universities.

Administration is so prevalent in modern society that it is increasingly difficult to find non-bureaucratic occupations. The Socratic teacher has been replaced by the instructor in a large school system teaching a set curriculum to students selected by exigencies of scheduling and available room space. The craftsman in the small shop has been replaced by the machine in the large corporation. In many respects men of money—the Carnegies and DuPonts—have been replaced by experts in international finance. The small town doctor and generous individuals can no longer provide the welfare, medicine, and social services in our mass society. These humanitarians have joined ranks with teachers, scientists, and government officials as functionaries in large organizations. Of course, a few entrepreneurs and craftsmen remain but most of those employed today operate within the rules and structures of the large bureaucracies.

If attention is shifted to the national government in Washington, the dominance of administration is even more evident. Not only has the federal government taken over a steadily increasing number of problem areas, but a huge administrative apparatus deals with these new tasks. The membership of Congress has not expanded much in recent years; but numerous new departments, agencies, and commissions have evolved to carry out the role of the federal government in modern America. The individual congressman can no longer direct the myriad of government services needed by thousands of constituents. The mantle of actual responsibility for government has passed to the bureaucrats.

Government bureaucrats function within huge departments which, as is the practice in all large organizations, are subdivided into various units and bureaus. Organizational charts always diagram in pyramidal form the contrast between the few department heads at the top and the more numerous bureaus and divisions at lower levels. In other words, bureaucracies are not homogeneous and a major separation that affects the powers, functions, and recruitment of administrative personnel is the distinction between the positions at the top and the offices at lower bureau levels.

With the exception of top positions, bureaucratic structures are staffed by personnel selected more or less on the basis of merit. The percentage of government employees covered by merit procedures has steadily increased and, thus, in the modern administrative state, lower echelon bureaucrats tend to be competent in their tasks, secure in their positions, and immune to influence through the electoral process. Extensive patronage appointments provided elected officials in the 19th and early 20th centuries with many offices to fill. Whatever its faults, patronage established a link between the electoral process and administrative officials. Whatever its benefits, civil service has failed to provide such a link.

In contrast to the well-trained civil servants who serve in second echelon bureau levels, department heads and their immediate assistants tend to be short-term political appointees with little relevant training or expertise. Because of the location of expertise, most policy issues are initiated and resolved at secondary levels of administration except in crisis situations.

Bureau chiefs (and other civil servants with long experience, developed skills, and information) emerge, along with senior members of some congressional committees and powerful interest-group spokesmen, as the genuine policy-makers in government. Congress as a whole with its debates and resolutions, political parties competing in elections, and appointed officials at the top of various agencies are more visible, yet they neither formulate nor implement most national policies.

Another manifestation of policy-making as administrative rather than legislative is the tendency for both individual congressmen and congressional committees to increase their staffs. This practice is not just an effort to pad payrolls but it is a recognition that policy-making today requires not only staffs for liaison with the administrative branch, but experts in substantive areas.

Although elected officials appoint department heads, most department heads do not control their bureaus. In addition, Congress does not directly control the activities of individual committees and certainly cannot supervise committee staffs. Whereas most citizens consider policy-making a result of an electoral-legislative process, the fact remains that policies are primarily initiated by administrators and staff personnel within both branches of government.[3]

The case for dominance of administrators over elected officials, while not conclusively proven, is strongly supported by the following facts:

1. Advanced industrialization and technology require administrators to coordinate specialized personnel and to manage the large institutions of modern society.

2. The primary locus of government decision-making is the bureau, which contains knowledgable civil servants who have mastered the details of specific policy issues.
3. The expanding complexity of governmental problems and growing demands on elected officials require them to delegate much of their formal power to those in administrative positions.
4. Even for those decisions they make, legislators and top appointees must depend on administrators and experts to provide policy ideas and supporting facts.
5. Nearly all citizen efforts to influence government are directed at supporting candidates or at lobbying legislators. This myopic concern with traditional forms of political influence leave administrators unknown, unobserved, and free to exercise unfettered power.

While some elected officials are powerful, administrators have considerable, perhaps even predominant, power over many crucial decisions. If we want to change America, we must determine who shall administer our most powerful institutions. Only an administrative strategy can direct this takeover of administrative positions of power which shape the future of America.

The Nature of Bureaucracy

To take over positions of power within a bureaucracy is not as easy as electing public officials under carefully defined rules of electoral combat. An understanding of bureaucracy is as necessary for the creation of an effective administrative strategy as an understanding of electoral laws and voter characteristics is for a successful electoral strategy.

Although we live with bureaucracies in most aspects of our lives, we seldom consider their special features. Unlike other institutions, bureaucracies centralize power in administrative positions, and many of the most powerful administrative positions are at the subordinate levels of the organization. These positions are manned by competent, professionally trained officials fully able to carry out the complex tasks of modern institutions. These massive bureaucracies easily absorb protests and outside pressures for change. At the same time, the rewards bureaucracies offer their personnel are so handsome that they entrap administrators who might otherwise oppose procedures and policies of the institution. We must accept these features of the bureaucratic world if we are to mount a successful administrative strategy.

Why do administrators have power? As we have already mentioned, government administrators have been delegated considerable power by legislative bodies. In large private institutions power has been delegated in a similar manner by boards of directors. While Congress and boards of directors have the legal power of review and even the ability to recall power, this rarely happens. Administrators have developed their powers, however, far beyond what they have been formally granted, because they alone possess the expertise and management skills required by large institutions. The skill and consequent power of bureaucrats make it impossible to do away with them because only they can deliver the needed services. Thus, there exists a degree of power *indigenous* to administrators and their offices. Personnel changes at the top of large institutions do not usually affect the power of the administrators in lower positions, who actually do the work. While presidents, corporate executives, and department heads change and fall like autumn leaves, bureaucrats continue in office as long as the institution remains.

A second characteristic of bureaucracy is that power is dispersed unevenly throughout the organization. Although those at the top have some authority, such as control over rewards and punishments, most of their power depends on the attitudes and behavior of their subordinates. Subordinates persuasively recommend some policies and on their own decide other questions within their own areas, thereby influencing and limiting the decisions of their superiors. Just as it is true that a large organization cannot function without its administrators, so top administrators cannot do their job without the agreement and support of those below them. In short, superiors at the top *are dependent on their subordinates.*[4] Those with authority have it only to the extent that subordinates accept their orders. The existence of the organization is dependent upon the ability of those in higher positions to elicit the contributions of subordinates. Subordinates will contribute their skills only if they consider deference and obedience to be in their self-interest. Otherwise, the organization will fall apart.[5]

In summary:

> (1) the person at the top is in a vulnerable position; (2) subordinates often do not realize the amount of control they actually have . . . ; (3) if the hierarchy is to be maintained, it must be continuously re-established by the person above sending *acceptable* orders to the person below . . . ; (4) the acceptance of orders is always determined in part by self-interest (not only do orders vary in their acceptability, but subordinates vary in their interests and definitions of what is acceptable).[6]

The power of subordinates is evidenced both by the flow of directives and orders down from the top and by the flow of information, facts, and suggestions flowing up to the leaders. Although subordinates theoretically receive policies and do not make them, still they fill out the details and implement policies. In some instances they may nullify them. In actuality, then, those in subordinate administrative positions have an impact on the substance of policy.[7] As a case in point, consider the role and influence of staff personnel in unions:

> Whatever the channels of influence, and whatever the decision, the ways of influence in all unions are strikingly similar: 'crystallize' the policy when the policy is loose, sharpen the definition of the problem when its specificity is low, fill the vacuum when the boss is busy or time is short, use official policy pronouncements as a lever.

> In the final analysis, however, what counts is the cumulative effect of thousands of statements of opinion and fact flowing through all the channels of influence, formal and informal, direct and indirect. 'Most of it is creating a climate,' says one expert, 'and the boss may not even know he's being influenced.' Day by day the

expert articulates trade union aims and aspirations; day by day he invokes the documents (whose content and tone he helped shape) as justification for union action along a broad front. It is plain that the expert supplies the leader with a set of comfortable justifications for union policies and rationalizes the leader's prior beliefs; he also gives some coherence to these policies, and— through a steady influence in the non-bargaining areas— he helps broaden leadership understandings and interests, helps create and sustain leadership views of the role of unionism in a free society.[8]

Anyone who works in a large organization recognizes the key role played by those in subordinate positions. The old adage that the secretaries actually run organizations is folk wisdom rooted in fact. Considering the experiences reported by recent presidents, this adage appears also to apply to the government as well. Commenting on the Kennedy era, the best that Schlesinger can report on the President's power is that although the White House could not do everything, it could do something. In Kennedy's words: "The President can't administer a department, . . . but at least he can be a stimulant."[9] We all realize that being a stimulant is a long way from running a government. If the President doesn't run the government, his "subordinates" have more power than is usually admitted. Watergate only confirms this. The view that bureaucracy can be controlled by appointments at the top is both inaccurate and counterproductive.

Because of their functions, size, and permanency, bureaucracies cannot be defeated, burned down, or eliminated. *Therefore, fundamental change will have to be attained through bureaucracy*. Furthermore, since power in administrative structures does not reside primarily in top positions, strategies aimed at removing, replacing, or pressuring top officials will not result in fundamental change.

The traditional view of activists, calling for an end to large bureaucracies and focusing on board chairmen or school superintendents, results in efforts being directed away from those subordinates with the actual resources to change things.

Another important characteristic of bureaucracy is personnel recruitment on the basis of merit.[10] Recruitment standards determine the training and attitudes of those persons who fill the offices. Knowing the educational and professional background required to become a bureaucrat helps us to answer two central questions for an administrative strategy: Are bureaucrats available for change? What sort of actions are they likely to support?

Because jobs are usually filled by those who pass an exam for competence, bureaucrats possess specific training and skills. They are educated, white collar, and middle class. Therefore, a successful administrative strategy must motivate professional, middle-class bureaucrats for fundamental change, just as the Marxist strategy, premised on the growing power of the proletariat, seeks to motivate lower class workers.

Although bureaucracies recruit professionals, all positions are not, of course, filled with identical individuals. To recruit 100 people with the same professional training is not necessarily to recruit 100 persons of the same party identification, nor even of the same economic origin. This is particularly the case in an advanced, liberal society such as the United States. Here, welfare programs, a generally tolerant outlook, and widespread educational opportunities result in all sorts of professionals. "In a democracy, apart from common technical knowledge, technicians may be found on all political sides of many social fences. The technical knowledge of managers and their relation to production is one thing; their class position, political loyalties, and their stake in the current system is quite another. There is no intrinsic connection between the two."[11] The diverse backgrounds and political beliefs of managers, who share only their expertise in common, suggest that there may be some bureaucrats willing to participate in an administrative strategy for social change.

A bureaucracy is further split by various structural divisions. Some levels are pitted against other levels, some agencies against other agencies, some occupations against other occupations. Each unit in the organization acts to advance and aggrandize itself, which puts it in tension with others.[12]

Bureaucracy is also characterized by its ability to defend itself from outside attack. Activists who have dealt with the bureaucracies of large city schools and modern corporations know that administrators tend to join together to meet outside threats. Sensing that an attack on one is an attack on all, bureaucrats have developed sophisticated and effective defenses against their critics. Paramount is the ability to *absorb protest* by appearing to grant or actually granting concessions while continuing the status quo. The statement by David Rogers in reference to the New York school system is applicable to bureaucracies generally:

> The institution has *organizational defenses* that allow it to function in inefficient, unprofessional, undemocratic, and politically costly ways without evoking more of a revolution or push for radical change than has yet emerged. It has almost unlimited capacity for absorbing protest and externalizing the blame, for confusing and dividing the opposition, 'seeming' to appear responsive to legitimate protest by issuing sophisticated and progressive policy statements that are poorly implemented, if at all, and then pointing to all its paper 'accomplishments' over the years as evidence both of good faith and effective performance.[13]

Another characteristic of bureaucracy with strategic implications is that bureaucrats, like most other Americans, are tied to their jobs. Job dependency is maintained by two considerations, status and money.

Today status depends on one's job. Few can maintain their status outside a large organization. Rapid technological change makes many positions tentative. People in uncertain situations are unwilling to jeopardize their jobs and tend to support the organization. This trend is even more pronounced during times of recession and unemployment.

Most bureaucrats are in debt because of their attempt to meet the standards of upper-middle-class consumption. Because of their debts, they need the income which only their jobs provide. In addition, half the saving done by Americans is through "forced" or "contract" plans such as pensions and insurance programs. Under these plans, savers' contributions are maximized by continuing payments or premiums. In fact, they may lose part of their contributions if they stop payments or leave their jobs. The end result is a desire to keep the job.[14] Thus, appeals to bureaucrats to buck the organization and to risk their jobs are unlikely to be successful.

A Case Study of Bureaucracy: The Chicago School System

Until now we have spoken of bureaucracy mainly in theoretical terms. However, the development of an effective administrative strategy should focus on the particular bureaucracies that daily control our lives if we are to move from generalized understanding to specific action. In this chapter, we have chosen the Chicago school system as a case study. Many citizen organizations have fought the school system, but their gains have been slight. They failed because they did not see the schools as a bureaucracy and, thus, they failed to plan an appropriate strategy.

The Chicago school system is large and expensive. In 1972, there were 552 schools and 556,788 students. Approximately 45,800 teaching, administrative, and service personnel were employed.[15] Chicago schools do not come cheap; the 1973 budget was over $850 million and in 1975 had risen to over 1 billion.[16]

This large and expensive system of buildings, teachers, and administrators is in terrible shape. A recent report by a special state legislative committee charged that the system is close to collapse.[17] Although classes are held and payrolls are met, all evidence indicates that the overall situation for students, teachers, and parents is getting worse. Each year it is reported that students fall further behind in reading and other skills, and that lack of money may cause the schools to be closed for weeks.[18]

Most Chicago schools are located in racially segregated neighborhoods. Furthermore, the trend in Chicago is toward more minority students, which, together with the flight of whites to the suburbs, results in more than fifty percent of the students in schools being Black.

The fact that Blacks make up an increasing percentage of the school population does not imply that they will control the schools. That possibility is reduced by their low economic status and power. Chicago is becoming more Black, not by integration but by the expansion of Black ghettos; and Black ghettos are poor neighborhoods.[19] Thus, neighborhood schools needing the most money are in the poorest areas. Poor areas are the least able, by themselves, to create the strong economic base which would raise their status and increase their clout with the central administration.

The Chicago schools train students to support the existing social system. In addition, the schools must also enforce the status quo by means of truant officers and school personnel who check attendance and keep students in class.[20] Quite clearly, one of the main goals of the Chicago schools is to make sure that young people are kept off the streets and out of trouble. State aid to the schools is even based upon attendance. Social stability is apparently threatened if thousands of relatively dissatisfied youths are left free with nothing to do.

Detention in the overcrowded inner city schools is only part of the problem. Added to this dismal tableau, schools are not safe for either students or staff. It is hard to overstate this aspect of the problem. A telling item was the school board's recommendation for guarded parking lots for staff. It also considered a transportation plan whereby teachers would meet in neighborhoods "posing little or no threat to personal safety" from which they would be transported in groups to and from their schools.[21] This plan was not implemented but its consideration together with extensive budget appropriations for Personnel Security and the use of armed security forces in some schools indicate the extensive hostility between school personnel and some neighborhoods. These rather extreme measures to protect school personnel from the students they are supposed to serve are clear evidence of a breakdown in the schools.[22]

Strategies should be developed in the light of the existing situation. Therefore, a strategy to deal with schools must consider the nature and power of the Board of Education, which formally governs the Chicago school system. The Board of Education is made up of eleven persons serving staggered terms of five years whose names are suggested by the Mayor's Advisory Commission on School Board Nominations. This Commission is not established by law nor is the Mayor required to accept the names suggested by the Commission. Mayor Daley several times has sent names to the City Council for approval which were not suggested by the Commission. In every case, the Council has approved the names submitted by Mayor Daley, just as it routinely rubber stamps the Mayor's other proposals.

The members of the Chicago Board of Education are mostly wealthy, white, and economically powerful. Blacks do not constitute a power bloc, let alone a majority, on the Board even though Black children make up more than half the school population. School Board members appear to be chosen primarily to represent the interests of real estate, labor,[23] and industry. Although there is token representation of Blacks, Puerto Ricans, and the PTA, a majority of the Board as well as the superintendent are under the control of the Daley machine.

School Board members who represent racist unions are unwilling to support an adequate training program for Black apprentices in the trades. Members who represent Chicago real estate interests do not advocate school building and busing policies which threaten the segregated real estate market. Board members who are convinced of the legitimacy of the present social system do not permit the schools to teach otherwise.

The Chicago school system, then, has a governing board subservient to the dominant political and economic forces in the community. In Chicago this means the Democratic machine, racist unions, and corporations. Since the poor, Blacks, and to a significant degree, the middle class do not control politics, unions, nor the corporations, they do not control the school board which speaks for these interests.

School Board members are not all the same, and some very clearly belong in the liberal, reform tradition. But even with increasing representation of liberals, integrationists, Blacks and Puerto Ricans, the Board has not implemented policies adequate to solve the problems of the Chicago schools. Clearly, a majority of the Board is not willing to make the decisions necessary to eliminate overcrowded, segregated, and unsafe schools, which hold students captive but fail to provide them with even the minimal education essential to survival in modern industrial society.

Could the Board by itself bring about the needed changes in

the schools if a majority, or even all members, wished to do so? To put the question another way, if one wanted to change Chicago schools, how much time and effort should be directed toward the Board? Is the Board the lever for change? If the membership of the Board changes, will new decisions bring better education?

These questions raise the possibility that there are sources of power within the schools in addition to the Board of Education. If so, simply changing the Board membership may not counteract these other forces. For example, how integrated would Chicago schools become if all Board members were for integration but real estate interests and financial institutions continued policies of racism and block busting? How much better would students read if all Board members were for quality education but some administrators, principals, and teachers continued their "non-quality" level of education? Although the Board is the most visible authority of the Chicago school system, it is not the only force affecting education. To grasp some of the other aspects of the schools we must examine their budget and bureaucratic structure.

The budget and other official publications of the school board describe the Chicago schools as having a minimal administrative structure. Budget expenditures would appear to indicate that large sums of money are spent for teachers and instruction and only small sums for administration. On page 126 of the 1973 budget, $359,651,249 is appropriated for teachers' salaries whereas $125,113,723 is appropriated for civil service salaries. Almost three times as much appears to be spent for teachers as for civil servants, implying an emphasis upon teaching, rather than administration. The same image is presented on page 126 of the Board's pamphlet, *Facts and Figures, 1972-1973,* which states that in 1972 $444,829,278 was appropriated for instruction, but only $19,755,770 for administration. This ratio of better than 20:1 for teaching over administration would seem to protect the schools from criticism by those who would characterize them as a bureaucracy. The general thrust of all Board documents is that most of the taxpayers' money is spent for instruction and classroom activity, but closer examination of the budget[24] and other Board publications reveal that a great deal of money is actually being spent for maintaining the bureaucracy.[25]

Each line in the school budget is given three code numbers. The first number is the *fund* number, representing "the fund from, or to, which each amount appropriated is to be paid or charged." Examples are teachers'· pension and retirement fund, ·education fund, building fund, and so on. The second number is the *activity* number and "expresses the particular purpose of the expenditure." These purposes of expenditures are grouped into functional categories, such as administration, instruction, operation of plant, and so on. The third figure is the *object* number and it "defines the object or character of the expenditure." Examples of objects of expenditure are teachers' salaries, civil service salaries, commodities, and so on.[26]

There is ambiguity and overlap in these code numbers which permits budget allocations to be described in different and conflicting ways. Consider as a case in point, the budget description of the General Superintendent's salary. The third code number indicates that the object of the expenditure is "teaching salaries." Thus, when the board reports that teachers' salaries in 1972 were over $360,000,000 (about 45% of all expenditures) we must recognize that this figure included $56,000 for the Superintendent. Clearly the Superintendent's salary was paid not to a teacher, but to the system's top administrator. And there are many other personnel listed in the budget whose second code number indicates administration, but whose third number indicates teachers' salaries.[27] In this manner the amount designated for teachers' salaries is inflated to include the salaries of numerous people who are not classroom teachers, but administrators. Thus, by manipulating budget line descriptions, the pay for many administrators is falsely portrayed as salaries for teachers.

Conversely, many administrators (principals, assistant principals, and school clerks) are described by their second number as "instruction" rather than "administration," and their salaries are also incorrectly designated as teachers' salaries. When the Board uses the term "administration," it does *not* mean to refer to all those who administer; and when the Board uses the term "instruction" it includes many who are not teaching. The figures that the Board gives on the cost and size of administration as distinguished from instruction refer only to *administration which occurs in the central office.* In the Board's publication, *Facts and Figures, 1972-1973,* a table which lists 2.6% spent on administration versus 58.7% for instruction required the following explanation: "Administration includes *central office* costs such as professional and clerical salaries [but *not* the Superintendent's salary or the salaries of numerous others paid as teachers], supplies, electricity, telephones, and other services necessary to the *central office.*"[28] The Board would have us believe that there is no administration beyond the central downtown office. Accordingly, the code number for administration does not appear in the budget except on those pages dealing with the central office.

The Board defines "instruction" in the following manner: "Instruction includes teachers' salaries [as well as the Superintendent's and others' who are administrators at the central office], *salaries of principals and other administrators at schools,* textbooks, supplies, telephone expenses, educational equipment, and other instructional aides and services."[29] Thus, the Board is saying, in effect, that teaching takes place in the central office and that principals and other administrators are instructing, not administering. Instructing becomes administering; administering becomes instructing at the whim of school budget-makers who have adopted their own Orwellian "double-think" and bureaucratic double talk.

A brief examination of the budget indicates that much more money is spent on administration than the Board leads the public to believe. Just a few figures from the 1973 Budget illustrate the fantastic cost of administrative personnel for the schools. The Board's President's office, $110,526; Office of the Secretary of the Board, $233,100; Department of Law, $498,375; Department of Curriculum, $3,036,075; Department of Personnel, $1,457,477. In addition, there are many administrators at the area, district, and local school level. Between one-third and one-half of all personnel expenditures are for employees other than classroom teachers.[30]

Examination of the Chicago school budget confirms, among other things, the bureaucratic nature of the schools. Our claim that bureaucracy is a major characteristic of the Chicago school system is bolstered by the huge sums spent on non-teaching personnel and the fact that the system primarily operates, not to educate pupils, but to perpetuate existing bureaucratic positions.

Clearly, Chicago schools are not alone in their emphasis on administration at the expense of teaching; top-heavy bureaucracy seems to be characteristic of all American schools. According to James D. Koener:

> American schools are more lavishly administered than any in the world. The educational system of no other nation can come even close to matching the number of full-time, non-teaching school administrators that run our local school systems. The administrative hierarchy of some of our big cities' systems is larger than that of entire ministries of education in countries like England and France. . . .[31]

Although the bureaucratic nature of the Chicago school system is evident by the large sums of money spent on administrative procedures and personnel, the situation is fully revealed only when we understand that most teachers are also bureaucrats. Because of the daily demands or paperwork, most teachers in a large system find it almost impossible to function except as professional bureaucrats. Supplies must be ordered, grade and attendance records turned in, a detailed curriculum followed, and faculty-administration meetings attended. Although many conscientious teachers work hard to serve their students, in most instances creative teaching is obliterated by bureaucratic imperatives.

What is the major force for preserving this state of affairs in the Chicago schools? Having argued that bureaucracy is the dominant characteristic of the schools, it follows that neither school board members nor the superintendent can be the key power wielders.[32] The school board as the formal governing body of the Chicago schools certainly exercises some power. Nevertheless, the Chicago school system is a 45,800-person bureaucracy faced with a complex array of problems which individual board members do not have the training nor the time to solve. Consequently, they defer to the superintendent and the staff to provide the expertise and facts upon which policy can be based.

Although greater than the power of the board, a superintendent's power is much less than the combined power of other school administrators and teachers.[33] Imagine the consequences if an Ivan Illich were made Superintendent of Chicago schools but nothing else were changed. We can be absolutely sure that no matter how fine his qualifications nor how noble his intentions, Illich would not overcome the massive bureaucracy. Opposed to his will would be the will of thousands.

The American educational graveyard is strewn with repeated failures to reform school systems by a few appointments at the top. In Chicago a citizen campaign dumped Superintendent Benjamin Willis in 1966 and replaced him with James Redmond, but schools have remained segregated and education continues to worsen. Now Redmond has been replaced by Joseph P. Hannon but there is little hope that this change alone will solve the Chicago school problems. Around the same time that Chicago was getting rid of Willis, significant appointments at the top of the Philadelphia school system also brought minimal results. In 1965 a change-oriented Philadelphia Board of Education along with a new President of the Board replaced status quo officials. Mark Shedd, a young reformer, was made Superintendent in 1966. Shedd proceeded to appoint Harvard grads and other quality educators to his staff. Yet, these highly trained, well-intentioned people in the top formal positions of power were unable to bring significant change to Philadelphia schools.

> The new team had come to Philadelphia with the hope that enough of the 'right' people working for change at the top could really have an effect on the entire school system, that they would be able to counteract not only the inertia resulting from decades of neglect but the fragmentation of the city as well. Even by the end of Shedd's first year in office, however, all the talk of revolution seemed like naive pipe dreams. Shedd and his assistants, many of whom began to look for other jobs, were apparently no better at working miracles than anyone else who had promised to end (or win) the urban war.

> After almost two years of Mark Shedd and a full three years of the new Board, the Philadelphia public school system remained essentially the same institution that it had been before the battle began.[34]

The Chicago and Philadelphia experiences, which have been repeated many times in large school systems, prove that superintendents are powerful only to the extent they become a part of the administrative reality of the existing system. The power of superintendents depends on their ability to tap the resources and support of other professionals in the schools: the principals, teachers, and civil service personnel. It is the will of these professionals which predominates. Superintendents win when they act in accordance with the preferences of other professionals; otherwise, they are ineffective.

The power of professionals is not limited to the local school systems. Federal and state bureaucrats and officials of professional educational organizations join local administrators to set the tone and direction of education. According to Koerner, ". . . the main currents of American educational development are flowing mostly away from the ordinary citizen and toward a new coalition of specialists—school administrators, class room teachers, academicians, federal and state education officials, along with an assortment of other kinds of specialists (foundation, testing, accrediting, and manufacturing-publishing executives). . . ."[35]

Who really controls the schools? From our examination of school budgets, the limited power of those in formal positions at the top, the failures of Chicago and Philadelphia reform superintendents, and the absolutely essential expertise of professionals and specialists, we conclude that controlling power resides in the subordinate positions of the large school systems. This fact indicates that *only a strategy which includes the efforts of professional educators—both teachers and administrators—stands any chance of success.* As Koerner observes, ". . . parents and the body politic are normally effective in American education only when they support the local school administrators."[36] Citizens who are concerned with quality education or with the effects of other large bureaucracies must find ways of working with the professionals in programs for change. Strategies must be premised upon reality, namely, that power resides in subordinate positions in large institutions.

The failure of past strategies does not prove that they could never succeed. A strategy may be premised on an accurate assessment of the situation but fail because too few people support it. However, if a strategy is inconsistent with reality, its failure is assured, no matter how many citizens join the struggle. Until now, strategies to reform Chicago schools have failed primarily because they were not premised on the administrative realities of the school system.

Faced with a major bureaucracy like the Chicago school system, the most frequently advocated strategies are 1) to support professional organizations or unions in a fight for change within the school system or 2) to establish parallel institutions to replace existing schools altogether.

Inadequate Strategies: Professional Organizations

An example of the first strategy has been to support the National Education Association, the major professional organization for teachers. Until recently, the NEA was an organization of teachers and administrators which lobbied in national, state, and local governments. The organization of the NEA separated teachers from administrators and even sub-divided various types of teachers. Thus, the organization did little to bring various sorts of educators together on the substantive issues of education. Instead, high school principals, elementary school principals, math teachers, and so on each pressed their particular interests. The end result was an organization for the development of various professional interests. The primary goal of the group was not to change education radically. It was a protectionist organization that pitted professionals against students, parents, and other lay persons interested in educational issues. As such, it was not a viable alternative for those who wanted fundamental change in the schools.

Within the NEA, school administrators traditionally have been a numerically small minority, yet they filled many of the top leadership positions. Today, the NEA has become primarily a movement of teachers. Administrators have become disaffected as the NEA has developed an ever clearer identity as a teacher's organization with teachers' goals and perceptions predominating. One group, the National Association of Secondary School Principals (NAASP) has completely cut its ties with the NEA.[37]

In many respects the Parent Teachers Association suffers under handicaps similar to the NEA. Whereas the NEA excludes parents and laymen from membership, the PTA excludes administrators. Although there have been instances in which local PTA groups have brought about needed changes in schools, the general picture is one of PTA collaboration with the school administration in support of the existing state of affairs.[38]

At the local level, the PTA normally does little more than supplement school programs by holding social events, by buying books for the library, or by pressuring elected officials for traffic signs around the school. The by-laws of the Burley School PTA in Chicago explicitly rule out activity that might be seen as critical or disruptive. They declare one of the purposes of the Burley PTA to be: "To refrain from encroaching on the administrative functions of the school."

Neither NEA nor PTA strategies lead to fundamental change. Neither combine the skills and professional talents of teachers and administrators with the zeal and concern of parents and students for improved education.

Inadequate Strategies: Unions

Of course, many seeking changes in education today do not look to the NEA, the PTA, or other such groups. They look to unions as the instrument of change. Although effective in attaining higher salaries and better working conditions, unions will not improve the education provided by the schools. A major reason why teachers' unions cannot bring about fundamental educational reform is because unions, like the NEA, pit teachers against administrators, parents, and students.

Furthermore, trade unions are not organized to create a new state of affairs. They attempt to ameliorate harmful effects in bad institutions, but do not attack basic causes. In other words, teachers' unions do not aim for fundamental change, but seek higher wages and material benefits for their members. For example, each time contracts for Chicago teachers expire, the union is quick to publicize its concern for quality education and integration. But when the dust settles, the contract issue is ultimately reduced to a dispute about salary. Whether or not the teachers will agree with the school board on a new contract is never a matter of creating a new school system for Chicago, but always a matter of more money for the union's members.[39] This is not to say that higher wages and better working conditions are poor goals, but only that the attainment of such goals does not guarantee quality education. To achieve quality education within large, bureaucratic school systems requires a quite different strategy.

Organizing teachers to the exclusion of all administrators, all community people, and all students, dooms unions as a base for fundamental change. Since union membership is restricted to certain occupations, the only grounds for agreement are wages and other occupational benefits. Because of its occupational base, unionism cannot unite those teachers, administrators, community people, and students who wish to deal with fundamental educational problems. Instead, unionism pits such people against each other. To the extent that quality education requires joint efforts of educators and citizens, unions are a negative force.

The drive for community control, for instance, usually conflicts with union priorities, which are wages, job rights, and status. Community control over hiring and firing teachers precludes union control of these matters; and thus, true to its trade unionism, the union fights all such attempts to reform education.

Those who have seen the need for basic change have always had doubts about the ability of unions to deal adequately with substantive and system-wide problems. Even Albert Shanker, the trade unionist who heads the New York teacher's union, hinted at the same weakness. Shanker has written that ". . . both teachers and students are being destroyed by a rotten system . . . That system can be changed only if parents and teachers enter into a partnership for educational revolution. . . ."[40] But not even Shanker's union includes non-teachers as members or full partners; and the record of his union regarding school desegregation and decentralization shows that it is not engaged in "educational revolution;" rather, it supports the "rotten system."[41]

Other activists are also uneasy about the ability of teachers' unions to bring major educational change. The Teachers Action Coalition (TAC), formed within the New York City ' United Federation of Teachers (UFT), sees the UFT as a reactionary force opposed to community control, acting more in the interest of the school board than in the interest of parents, teachers, and students. Paul Becker, head of TAC, has argued that the UFT has betrayed the parents and all those who fought for better schools in New York. He said the actions of union leaders in the face of monetary crises may constitute "one of the most colossal sell-outs of any union in recent memory."[42]

The union often gets caught between the school administration on the one hand and the community on the other. In Newark, the teachers union has satisfied neither the school board nor the more critical elements in the community. True to its trade unionism, the first objective of the Newark union is occupational benefits, not educational reform. The Newark teachers' union, ". . . has been criticized—and its effectiveness limited— for not having made demands to involve the community in the running of schools, for concentrating more on the union and work conditions than on improving conditions for school children, for having made demands which could be prejudicial to the student (e.g., more security guards and psychological testing) and for not strongly confronting racism in its white members."[43]

The teachers union in Chicago is no different than the unions in New York and Newark. Although thousands live in poverty, the union demands and wins middle class salaries for its teachers. Although well-trained teachers for ghetto schools are lacking, the union fights transfers of experienced teachers to these schools.

What is needed? We need organizations or movements that *bring together* administrators, teachers, students, and community leaders who agree on priorities and goals. These organizations must include professionals in the second echelon positions of power because only those with such positions possess the essential resources to create a new reality. It is clear that trade unions and professional organizations are not the basis for such movements; the further question is whether community organizations are better able to solve school problems.

Inadequate Strategies: Community Organizations

Without taking time to analyze separately all the pressure group tactics, demonstrations, and school boycotts mounted by various community organizations in Chicago during the last decade, we simply conclude that only partial success at best has resulted from these efforts. Such strategies may effectively pressure top officials but do not result in the attainment of the more crucial power positions beneath the pinnacle and, as we have argued, only those who have these positions of power have the means to remedy basic educational problems. Not being able to attain institutional power positions, the reformers are limited to monitoring school officials already in power.

Careful follow-up and monitoring is difficult to sustain over long periods of time by those outside the school system. Yet, their only recourse is to maintain pressure on school officials who make and implement school policies. But members of community organizations and the public at large have other more personal and more immediate interests than schools. Consequently, after a pressure strategy forces a change of policy, support and interest tend to wane and the new policy statement tends to remain just that—a policy *statement*.

In addition, because moderate action by community organizations does not alleviate basic school problems, more militant groups begin to make demands which those in power refuse to meet. In the face of these new demands, school officials cling more strongly to established policies, causing militants to push ever more extreme demands. This increasingly separates them from moderate segments of the community. The militants, having lost community support, attain none of their educational goals, which further reduces their influence. The end result for both moderate and militant pressure strategies is the same. Although they focus attention on special school problems and force a few minor reforms, they fail to alleviate fundamental problems.

Inadequate Strategies: Parallel Institutions

The failure of pressure strategies has caused some people to search for other means to cope with the Chicago schools. Rather than acting against the school power structure, some citizens have chosen to establish their own schools and thereby control the quality of education received by their children. Establishing new schools is a constructive program which can be supported by people who are unwilling to engage in direct action against those with legal authority.[44]

There are, of course, already established private schools in Chicago; some are associated with religious organizations, such as the Catholic Church, and the Black Muslims, and one of the most prestigious is affiliated with the University of Chicago. But many parents dissatisfied with the Chicago public schools have either financial, religious, or ideological reasons for not sending their children to these private institutions. Thus, a group of parents established the Parents School on the north side and another parallel school, Co-operative School No. 3, was created in the South Shore neighborhood.[45] These schools, and a few other experiments in parent-controlled education, are usually supported in part by volunteer work from the parents and in some instances tuition is assessed depending upon a family's ability to pay.

Legally, it is easy to start a school in Chicago. Certification depends only upon the fulfillment of state health and safety requirements. But financial and ideological difficulties often hamper the growth and effectiveness of parallel schools. The Parents School, for example, has been plagued by disagreements among the parents. Ideologically, the parents range from liberal to radical and disagree at times about the functions of the school

—some seeing it as a revolutionary institution, others as simply a practical alternative to more expensive private schools.[46]

In addition to the conflicts that arise in any cooperative enterprise, building parallel institutions is a poor strategy because the people who most need better schools are often the least able to establish and maintain parallel institutions. First, money is a factor. The poor do not have the resources to support *two* schools. They are already assessed through taxes for existing schools and do not possess additional money for tuition to another school. Furthermore, most people have neither the inclination nor the skills required to sustain a parallel school. Parallel schools probably cannot be created everywhere. Conservative white ethnic families may not even see the need for different schools. Furthermore, schools like the Parents School are a product of those who participate—in the Parents School major participants are writers, artists, and lawyers. Other neighborhoods characterized by poverty, racial oppression with its consequent psychic damage, and substandard education usually cannot sustain independent schools.

Parallel schools, community organizations, unions, and professional groups have not been able to transform Chicago schools. Nor have these strategies resulted in a large number of students getting a better education. The failure of these strategies is due in large part to the disjunction between them and existing reality. Chicago schools are fundamentally a bureaucracy, and successful strategies must be developed in light of that reality.

To deny the bureaucratic nature of Chicago schools is to fail in our efforts to provide quality education for our children. To deny the bureaucratic nature of many critical institutions in contemporary society is to doom our efforts to create an America of freedom, justice, and citizen participation. A successful strategy for changing the Chicago schools or any of our mammoth bureaucratic institutions must be an administrative strategy. Only an administrative strategy recognizes bureaucratic reality and charts a course of change based upon that reality.

Chapter 5
How to Take Over Bureaucracies

We have thus far defined the Chicago school system as a bureaucratic structure, described insufficient educational strategies, and discussed some characteristics of bureaucracy which must be considered in the construction of an administrative strategy. Unlike professional, union, parent, or community organizations, which represent a limited self-interest point of view in opposition to school administrators, the strategy we advocate joins all of these groups in a common movement for change. Unlike parallel institutions which provide education for only a few children, our administrative strategy changes education for all children.

Successful strategies follow from accurate theory. But the construction of a new theory that fits the reality of contemporary America has been slow in developing. As Schaar and Wolin argued:

> Over the course of its first ten years, the New Left failed to create the new radical theory beyond both liberalism and socialism which the Port Huron Statement had called for. Although the New Left gradually has moved away from the single-issue, basically reformist outlook of the early sixties over toward a general indictment of the system, that movement was not powered or accompanied by an increasingly coherent and comprehensive theory. Rather, it is a mood, a feeling of rage and revulsion, which is increasingly impatient with theory or

even thought and argument. The anti-intellectualist strain which was present in the movement from the beginning has triumphed. Theory in the New Left is now reduced to the vulgar Marxism and Maoism of Progressive Labor or to the Weatherman view of white radicals as a suicide squad providing cover for black urban guerrillas, the true vanguard of the revolution.[1]

Writing a year later, Hannah Arendt, speaking of the student protest movement, agreed that the movement is hindered by theoretical sterility:

> At the moment, one prerequisite for a coming revolution is lacking: a group of real revolutionaries. Just what the students on the left would most like to be—revolutionaries—that is just what they are not. Nor are they organized as revolutionaries: they have no inkling of what power means, and if power were lying in the street and they knew it was lying there, they are certainly the last to be ready to stoop down and pick it up. That is precisely what revolutionaries do! Revolutionaries do not make revolutions! The revolutionaries are those who know when power is lying in the street and when they can pick it up! Armed uprising by itself has never yet led to a revolution.
>
> Nevertheless, what could pave the way for a revolution is a real analysis of the existing situation such as used to be made in earlier times. To be sure, even then these analyses were mostly very inadequate, but the fact remains that they were made. In this respect I see absolutely no one near or far in a position to do this. The theoretical sterility of this movement is just as striking and depressing as its joys in action is welcome.[2]

This theoretical sterility has meant that most recent political actions have been premised on old theories or else done on an ad hoc, experimental basis. Models of reality which may have been accurate in an earlier age prescribe actions which are not effective in today's administrative world. Consequently, time and effort are misdirected, and the results are correspondingly limited.

What is needed is a definition of the situation which directs attention toward the dominant administrative reality and limits the area of concern so that time and energies are not wasted.

Definitions are important not just because they limit areas of concern, but also because acceptance of a common definition leads to the creation of a group whose members act out the new strategies. A successful strategy to control administrative institutions depends on bringing into existence a new group, whose members accept an administrative definition of reality and are prepared to act along those lines.

This new *movement* is not a *coalition*. A coalition is comprised of groups which have agreed to work together to achieve particular goals. Each group that joins has previously defined itself differently from the others. Attainment of coalition goals is always, therefore, made more difficult by each group's insistence that its own identity and existence not be threatened by any of the coalition goals or actions. Consequently, coalitions can be held together only by the lowest common demoninator— hardly the basis for fundamental change. Staughton Lynd's first-hand experience with coalitions is instructive on this point:

> The greater the degree to which the "umbrella organization" is built from pre-existing smaller organizations, the greater the likelihood that it will be ideologically flaccid and united only in mechanical ways. The so-called national peace movement, for instance, has existed for six years as an agency for setting dates for one-shot demonstrations. Were it to undertake anything more ambitious, it would instantly fall apart.

> Pretty much the same thing is true of the local organization I worked on, the Calumet Community Congress. In the time-honored manner of Alinsky organizations, the CCC drew into its founding congress the parish councils, conservation clubs, and organized what-nots of the community. That founding congress was an impressive affair: 1,000 delegates from five organizations, the picket captain at the Memorial Day Massacre as chairman, a stirring anti-corporate keynote speech by one of

Ralph Nader's associates. When the dust had cleared, however, the new organization soon gravitated away from anti-corporate issues toward the staple of lowest-common-denominator politics, the corruption of the elected officials.[3]

Instead of coalitions of existing organizations, new definitions bring into existence a new movement with a membership cutting across old organizational and class divisions.

It is imperative that our situation be defined in such a way that a winning movement for fundamental change is possible. To some extent the world is as people see it. The situation in a post-industrial society must be perceived as an administrative one. Second, bureaucratic institutions must be recognized as including at least some administrators who can be enlisted on the side of fundamental change.

To use Schattschneider's words, new definitions must "blot out other issues." By making irrelevant older definitions, our new definition will provide a foundation upon which we can build a new movement.

> *The substitution of conflicts is the most devastating kind of political strategy.* Alliances are formed and reformed; fortresses, positions, alignments and combinations are destroyed or abandoned in a tremendous shuffle of forces redeployed to defend newer positions or to take new strong points. In politics the most catastrophic force in the world is *the power of irrelevance which transmutes one conflict into another and turns all existing alignments inside out.*[4]

An effective definition of the school problem does not make the administration the enemy. Rather, it calls attention to the needed, crucial power of administrators, calls attention to the goal of quality education, and defines the primary enemy as those administrators, teachers, and their outside supporters who perpetuate the sad state of affairs in Chicago schools.

An administrative strategy creates a movement of parents, students, teachers, and administrators who take over and use the key positions of power beneath the pinnacle in order to provide better education. It is a positive strategy for the attainment and redirection of bureaucratic power.

Sidney Lens has argued that ". . . there are only three ways of effecting social change: through persuasion of the men who hold power in the existing system, through a conspiratorial *coup d' etat,* or through the open mobilization of the people against the prevailing order. The first is the technique of liberals, the second of one type of anarchist, the third of most other radicals."[5] Our argument here is for the development of a fourth strategy, a strategy premised not on *persuading* those who have power to act in a particular way, but to gain power ourselves; a strategy premised not upon a *conspiracy,* but upon the legitimate and open struggle for power; a strategy premised not upon organizing the people *against* the power-holders, but upon recruiting powerful bureaucrats into a movement that uses their positions of power to make and implement new policies.

By way of summary, the following are what we believe to be the ingredients of an effective strategy to deal with the Chicago schools and other bureaucratic institutions:

1. The existing situation must be accurately analyzed. In modern society such an analysis centers attention on administrative structures, actors, and processes.
2. The situation must be defined so as to attract a sufficient number of administrators who have the power necessary to bring about fundamental change.
3. Given the reality of administrative dominance, a successful strategy requires the existence of a new movement, not a new coalition.
4. This new movement must be made up of both insiders and outsiders. Insiders possess institutional positions of power and outsiders provide support. Successful administrative action for fundamental change is assured by their unity in the new movement.
5. Our goal is to attain power. Consequently, our appeal to action is based upon the likelihood of victories, gains, and success, rather than losses, martyrdom, and defeat.

Unity of inside and outside action is the primary prerequisite for an effective movement for change. Only if we are able to use the institutional resources of some insiders and the support of some outsiders, is fundamental change possible in an administrative world.

Inside Strategy

The argument for an inside strategy can be summarized succinctly. First, a good administrative strategy depends upon insiders as well as outsiders. Second, we need not organize the support of every insider, but only those who want quality education. Third, there are many insiders who believe in quality education and who would be willing to join a movement dedicated to that goal. Fourth, an association of insiders must be created before individuals can do much to further our goal. Fifth, insiders must use their power as insiders if the movement is to succeed. Sixth, we must not be deceived into believing that structural change within the bureaucracy is a primary goal or in any way a prerequisite for real changes in the schools. Seventh, while economic security must be guaranteed, psychological rather than material rewards provide the real reason for insiders' involvement. Last of all, bureaucracies are more susceptible to change than is commonly believed. Their permanence is assured only by acquiescence of subordinates and outsiders.

Michael Harrington has written, ". . . the fate of the poor hangs upon the decision of the better-off."[6] His insight can be applied to citizens in an administrative world; the fate of the citizen depends to a large extent upon the decision of the administrator. Enough resources and power for basic change reside with insiders. This is why action by those inside an administration is crucial to any effective strategy. Change results from the action of those with significant power. When an elite group uses its power to cause institutions to adopt new policies, change occurs. Outsiders, the poor, racial minorities, the ill-trained, manipulated, and oppressed of our country do not have, by themselves, the ability to generate fundamental change.

What is essential is a unified movement of both insiders and outsiders. The establishment of quality education is a complex matter, not to be adequately handled by one person, one group, or one type of experience. What is needed is the unity of interests, knowledge, and insights of all those who can contribute to good education—administrators, teachers, parents, interested community people, and students. Any school strategy which does not attract members from all these groups will fail. Any strategy which organizes teachers but not administrators or organizes teachers and administrators separately will fail. Any administrative strategy which is more than action against, must include administrators. Their inclusion in the movement means we can move from protest to control.

Our future depends upon what insiders do. That has been true in the past—it is even more true today. An effective administrative strategy depends on insiders, but not on all of them. In fact, a major weakness of many strategies is that reformers often assume that all of those who happen to share the same class, the same jobs, or the same social characteristics hold the same opinions. There is, however, much diversity within occupational and social groups. Although they carefully guard the point of entry into the bureaucracy, most institutions still admit people with a wide range of backgrounds and interests. This is especially the case in larger institutions such as urban school systems, leading corporations, and the military. Since insiders disagree about many things, a successful strategy taps the resources of only those insiders who share the same objectives. Our task is to define the situation in such a manner that a significant number of insiders can be mobilized in support of specific goals.

The question then becomes whether or not there are enough administrators and teachers in the Chicago school system who agree that the schools need to be changed fundamentally *and* who agree on how quality education might best be achieved. There are numerous insiders who want fundamental change in the schools. Periodically, newspapers report the views of some teachers who wish to reform the schools. On the basis of his study of the New York schools, Rogers concluded that "many school officials sincerely want to improve conditions in ghetto schools as much as some parents and activists."[7] We are convinced that many insiders will support movements for improved education because their training in college stressed the value of quality education. Inside action for quality education does not conflict with the socialization of insiders and, therefore, a significant number will be available to act for change.

Insiders bring about fundamental change only if they are organized into a movement for coordinated action. Insiders come together, not because they are of the same level, status, or occupation, but because they agree that unless they act together *as insiders* to bring about a more humane reality, business will continue as usual, ending eventually, in either greater repression to save the status quo or rebellion to destroy it.[8]

What is required are men and women throughout the school administration who as insiders control the resources of the school system. According to Lewis Mumford, we need:

> . . . to insert active human agents trained to register human responses and make moral decisions at every point in the process; people capable of answering back, of halting the smooth flow of automatism, of sending the printed directives back to headquarters when they do not make sense, or when human life or human values are endangered. We need audacious, self-respecting people ready, as the Quakers say, to speak truth to power, able to intervene in every automatic process, to turn off the juice, or to reverse the direction of movement, or to change the goals, when the automatic mechanism threatens to limit our freedom or to deform our lives.[9]

Organizing individuals as "active human agents" within the larger bureaucracies is our main task. The basis for a movement is acceptance of a new definition of the situation. Both the definition and the movement then provide self-esteem, identity, and support for participants. A lone bureaucrat may follow Mumford's moral code, but he will surely be replaced, superceded, or sabotaged by other bureaucrats. Change does not flow from the individual acting alone but from individuals acting as a group. Only insiders who act together with support from outsiders can turn around a runaway bureaucracy. Shifting the Chicago school system from a course of self-perpetuation to one of quality education for all children cannot be the work of one lone person. We need a committed group—in short, a movement for change.

The first rule for insiders, even those organized into a movement, is that they must act as insiders. Too often, insiders who have agreed that change is necessary and who have agreed on the direction of change, have acted as outsiders. This happened not too long ago when the Federal Employees Against the War in Vietnam was formed. As federal employees they were insiders, they ran the government. Yet, they planned a series of actions in no way related to their positions as insiders. They scheduled a *rally* in front of the White House, presented a *petition,* and ran a full-page *newspaper advertisement* opposing the war.[10] None of these actions took advantage of the particular power which belonged to their jobs with the government. To the contrary, these insiders chose activities which properly belong to outsiders—signing petitions, holding rallies, and so on. Spending their time on protests and petitions, they failed to use their unique resources as insiders to oppose the war.

Those insiders who "tell all," who oppose the government, who work for new policies and goals *after* they give up their positions of power, choose to be moral only *after* they have forsworn the very power needed to achieve their moral goals. Hubert Humphrey, for instance, supported the war and gave no hint of opposition when he was vice-president of the United States, that is, when he was second in command of the world's greatest power. But, when he no longer had the resources of the inside position, then he told us how bad the war was and that it must be stopped. If he really was opposed to the war all along, then the more effective strategy would have been to use his inside position to end the war. In fact, if he had acted while he was vice-president, he might have won the presidency in 1968 and changed the dismal direction of American politics.

In other words, effective strategy in an age of administrative dominance depends on insiders who desire fundamental change and who are prepared to act *as insiders*. If no insiders are available or if no strategies can be devised to effectively use their power, then repression or rebellion are our only alternatives. To put the matter plainly, our only hope to avoid repression or rebellion is for liberal insiders to put their power on the side of change. Expressions of concern, opposition against, and the other examples of moral purity, are not enough. Insiders must act as insiders. They must use the intrinsic power of their inside positions.

Some reformers recognize the crucial need for action by insiders only to fall into the common trap of believing in structural change as the key to quality education. Rogers, for instance, after arguing that there are school officials in the New York system who desire to improve conditions just as fervently as some parents and activists, goes on to say that these officials have not been successful because they ". . . are hamstrung by the bureaucratic structure." Consequently, Rogers concludes that "changing that structure must be the system's top priority."[11] These reformers emphasize structure far too much. Structures do not create power or change but only reflect shifts which occur. Those who already possess power mold structures to attain their goals. We know, for example that the existing structures of Chicago and New York schools do not "hamstring" all groups nor restrict them equally. The same structure which enables status quo groups to attain their goals would probably permit many changes suggested by reformers. Changing structures will not, of itself, bring needed changes in the schools[12] because *much more important than formal structures is the distribution of power between those who wish change and those who do not.*

Although the need for insiders is clear, a question arises as to their availability. Is it possible to develop a strategy which can tap the resources of a significant number of insiders, who publically favor a movement for change? Under what conditions can such movements be established?

Traditionally, the strategic dilemma has been that those citizens most available for social action are the very people who have not "made it" in the existing system. But those who have not made it do not have the resources to win. On the other hand, those citizens who are better equipped to solve our problems are the fortunate professionals who have made it in the existing system. But they will not act for fundamental change if their action jeopardizes the benefits they have as winners in society. The strategic dilemma has been, therefore, that in trying to bring about fundamental change, only the losers have been available. The Marxist solution to this dilemma calls for organizing the workers, the oppressed, the exploited. This may have been sensible as the means of organizing the Russian proletariat of 1917 or the Chinese peasants of 1940, but it is obviously inadequate in post-industrial America. Our administrative strategy instead calls for organizing the *winners*, the administrators with the power, skills, and status to tackle the complex problems of our contemporary society and to build the new institutions necessary for a better America.

Insiders who see the necessity for fundamental change must define themselves differently in order to *free themselves for action*. After all, as winners most of their restrictions are self-imposed. What we need is a self-definition which infuses the positive psychological aspects of the popular dissident movement of the 1960's and 1970's into our administrative movement. The student, anti-war, and civil rights movements emphasized the need for individuals to think for themselves and to act on their beliefs. Protestors of the 1960's taught us that individuals should define themselves as free persons, able to establish a new social reality for us all.

Effective inside action today, no less than the movements of the 1960's demands that we consider the psychological needs of the participants. Individuals must be free for new action, but they will not risk new action if they are captivated by old ideas and blinded by old definitions. Like protestors of the 1960s, insiders need to see the existing situation as one of crisis—a crisis that affects them. A sense of the personal immediacy of the situation is needed to spur action.

Psychological security is also necessary for insiders to act freely. Willie Smith, head of the Neighborhood Youths Corps in New York who got into difficulty when he demonstrated for more summer jobs for blacks, concluded:

"For a Negro to work for the administration but remain independent of it requires considerable self-confidence.

A man's self-esteem cannot be built on his bureaucractic role, but on who he is. Only if your ultimate commitment is to yourself can you be free to act. There are a lot of guys who make penultimate concerns ultimate. They think their job or their car or their apartment is the most important thing. But if they do that, they're through."[13]

Like most individuals, administrators get tied to their jobs through status and monetary rewards. Effective inside action requires loosening these ties by changing how individuals think about themselves, their jobs, and the social problems which face us all. Effective administrative strategies contain, therefore, an educational ingredient. Through educational efforts which develop a "human" rather than "class consciousness," insiders free themselves as individuals for creative action.

Just as high salaries and status can be incentives for compliance and conformity, so also can they produce the material security for independence and innovation. Surely it is true that the hungry outcasts of society lack greater opportunities for successful social action. Many people with money and status fail to act as free men and women, not because they are *in fact* less free than others, but because they choose to define the good life as dependent on more and more money, status, and security. So, what is required for a successful movement is for insiders to accept a different definition of themselves and their society; a definition which places much less reliance on material and status rewards. Our argument is *not* that effective inside action requires individuals to give up their positions and accompanying rewards, rather that they no longer be captivated by the desire for money beyond that required for health and happiness.

The real need of insiders, the winners, the ones who have enough status and money,[14] *is solutions to the larger problems which destroy the lives of others and make hollow the material rewards won by insiders.* Our argument is *not* that effective inside action requires individuals to give up their salaries, but only that they risk future big raises. Salary increases and promotions should not be essential for insiders' self-respect if they have a strong self-image and a human approach. When a raise or promotion is no longer necessary, insiders are freer to act. Insiders already have money and status, they already have the resources for food, clothing, shelter, and even some luxuries. Participation in the movement for change need not be a hardship. A rethinking about money and material needs, and also a rethinking of status and identity is required. We must replace a concern with status and job with a new identity based on our role in the movement.

It is not enough that individuals think in a particular way, it is also necessary that the group be able to win its battles. But winning will not be easy. We know that insiders in the movement who free themselves for creative action will have to take risks. Indeed,

> If the individual is to carry on social action in and through his job, he may have to call into question the established and revered goals of the very organization for which he works. Others holding key positions in the organization might well take a dim view of his efforts.[15]

Since most people depend on their jobs to provide the necessities and nicities of life, it is unreasonable to base our movement on the premise that to join the movement is to lose one's job. In other words, an effective administrative strategy must choose a course of action which achieves social goals while permitting insiders to continue to hold their jobs. As a movement of real people with real needs and legitimate fears, we must protect the jobs of our members. Our strategy must convince insiders who wish to act for fundamental change that if they act, they can win. They must also be convinced that they can act for the new goals without paying an undue cost. There are not enough saints for a successful social movement. On the other hand, there are enough "people of good will" as Dr. King called them —there are enough men and women willing to take reasonable risks in the cause of freedom.

Insiders who pursue an administrative strategy have a greater chance for success than is usually recognized because the continuation of any bureaucracy in its present form is always a tentative matter. The simplistic popular view that bureaucracies are solid within themselves and have an inertia which keeps them as they are has become an unquestioned belief. But this is an in-accurate description of large bureaucracies. The supposed complexity, power, impenetrability, and facelessness of modern organizations provide an excuse for inaction which encourages citizens to accept their powerlessness.

Contrary to popular belief, the fact is that large organizations are susceptible to change. Their continuity is in large part a result of the repetition of organizational processes and the acceptance of new orders by subordinates. *Subordinates, not those at the top, thus become the key actors in maintaining the status quo or in bringing change.*

> At any moment in time, there are possibilities inherent in the information on which an organization operates which, if noticed and actualized, can undermine the workings of the organization. There are always mutations which affect the workings of the organizational processes. These mutations occur continuously. Any process is always being diverted, modified, undone, simplified, or made less orderly. It is never true that a process simply unfolds time after time. Instead, in order for the process to unfold at any moment in time, its components must be reinstated, reaffirmed, and reaccomplished. Failure to do so can produce an irreversible change in the way the process unfolds. . . . Processes are repetitive only if their repetitiveness is continuously accomplished.[16]

Just as the bureaucratic process is dependent on its reinstatement by the actors involved, so policy outputs likewise result from the acquiescence of those involved in decision-making. Bureaucratic processes and policies depend more on the compliance of administrators in subordinate positions than on the power of those at the top. Compliance and cooperation are not foreordained, nor necessary, nor inherent in the structure of the organization. Whether or not an organization continues its present procedures and policies depends on the attitudes and actions of numerous individuals throughout the structure.

In determining whether policies will remain or change, effective inside action must, therefore, be based on how subordinates define authority and how much support they have.

Chester I. Bernard's discussion of the nature of authority is helpful in this respect. Bernard argues that authority does not reside in those giving orders but in the acceptance of orders by those who receive them. If they do not accept an order, then the order has no authority. Thus, it is up to subordinates to grant or not to grant authority to orders from above.[17] Because subordinates make indispensable contributions, they have power which can be used for change. But subordinates who fail to perceive their power will unconsciously grant authority to the established directives and procedures. The more higher ups rely on rewards and coercion to force compliance, the greater the need for subordinates to have their own support for independent action. When subordinates exercise their discretion to grant or not to grant authority to decisions and procedures, they must be able to keep their jobs.

Two conditions are necessary for the effective exercise of independent action by subordinates. (1) They must have sufficient power to have at lease a 50-50 chance to win. (2) They must be willing to accept personal responsibility.[18] That is to say, administrators must make firm decisions for which they are willing to assume full responsibility. While the status quo assumes its staying power from the anonymity of the bureaucrats who perpetuate it, change must have an acknowledged father. Administrative change is possible only if some officials are willing to assume responsibility for the new state of affairs they seek to create. Only those who are willing to bear the burdens of responsibility can take the forceful action necessary to win.

The effectiveness of inside action is conditioned by the power available to the dissidents. As already noted, their power is partly a matter of how insiders define and organize themselves. Their power is also a matter of outside support. Tullock calls bureaucrats with inside and outside support, "Barons." Barons are distinguishable from Tullock's "Courtiers" "who are almost wholly dependent upon the favor of their sovereigns [superiors] for their current positions and for their hopes of advancement."[19]

Since the effectiveness of the insiders depends in part in outside support, we need to consider how this support can be organized.

Outside Strategy

Insiders do not act alone. Current institutional leaders who perpetuate the status quo rely on outside support to prop up their power. Thus, the superintendent of schools, school board members, and top school administrators are actively supported by business interests, labor unions, and political leaders.

> A first and fundamental source of power for administrative agencies in American society is this ability to attract outside support. Strength in a constituency is no less an asset for an American administrator than it is for a politician, and some agencies have succeeded in building outside support as formidable as that of any political organization. The lack of such support severely circumscribes the ability of an agency to achieve its goals, and may even threaten its survival as an organization.[20]

Thus, administrative insiders willing to work for change must be supported. They must be able to incorporate the community's strength into their own.[21] The greater the desired change and the more extensive the opposition, the more important outside support becomes.

Outsiders alone cannot often bring administrative change. Either their leaders will be coopted or the bureaucracy will delay administrative and hearing procedures until the outside pressure group dissipates. Therefore, outsiders should not be organized separately from insiders in an administrative strategy. What is needed is a new movement combining the support of outsiders with the knowledge and skills of insiders. As we have said before, this new movement cannot be a coalition of existing groups but must be an entirely new organization based on a new definition of the situation. We must unite insiders (some school administrators, and some teachers) and outsiders (some parents, some interested lay people, and some students).

Contrary to most outside groups which pressure against the insiders, a primary role of outsiders in the administrative strategy to support movement insiders. The movement is a unity of insiders and outsiders which depends upon outside participation in *all* aspects of the strategy. In addition to support, outsiders provide stimulus, identify problems, and contribute their particular information and abilities.[22]

The power of subordinates, when joined with the support of outsiders, insures the success of our administrative strategy. Speaking of the New York schools, Jason Epstein put it this way: "A bureaucrat's power over his subordinates, and thus his strength within the hierarchy, is partly determined by whether these subordinates will carry out his orders. If enough of them resist or passively ignore what they are told to do, and if they are supported by forces . . . over whom the system has no control [outsiders], then the responsible officials are likely to retreat. . . ."[23] Whether one is for minimal reform, fundamental change, or the status quo the fact remains that the continuance or destruction of an administration is a consequence of inside and outside power.

In the absence of any actual instances of an ongoing movement of insiders and outsiders to change the Chicago schools, it is impossible to be very precise about what ought to be our specific actions. While successful strategies follow from adequate theory, experience is essential to develop the details of organization and action. Only theory tested by experience can provide winning responses to the question "What is to be done?" In the absence of concrete experiences, the following propositions provide at least general guidelines for the development of an administrative movement.

Fact 1:

   Administration is prevalent throughout all aspects of modern life and has brought into existence a new power reality which is not contained within established institutions nor controlled by the electoral process.

Proposition 1:

   Because this new administrative reality cannot be adequately controlled by groups, parties, or coalitions based upon the older, electoral reality, a new movement must be created. Only a new movement based upon a definition of the situation as administrative can be an effective force in an administrative world.

Fact 2:

Lone individuals in the bureaucracy speaking and acting for fundamental changes usually fail to obtain their objectives and, in many cases, lose their jobs.

Proposition 2:

Insiders who wish to be effective agents for change must band together for mutual support.

Fact 3:

The power of administrators flows from the resources they command; resources which are theirs to use because of the *positions* they have in the bureaucracy. In an administrative world, power is a consequence of one's organizational position.

Proposition 3:

Insiders must act as insiders and enlist the resources of their positions on the side for change. Inside action is administrative action; it is action which uses the power inherent in administrative positions for the attainment of new goals and priorities.

Fact 4:

Specific structural arrangements in bureaucracies, although they aid some groups in attaining their goals and hinder others, can be used by diverse groups to attain a wide variety of policies.

Proposition 4:

The attainment of power with the consequent ability to use existing organizational resources is the first objective of the movement, not structural changes. After one has power, the structure is frequently changed to make one's power more secure, but structural change is not the route to administrative power.

Fact 5:

Large organizations are susceptible to change and can continue unchanged only as long as those in subordinate positions comply with directives from the top and only as long as they cooperate by contributing the resources of their position for the achievement of organizational goals.

Proposition 5:

Organized lower echelon insiders who use the resources of their positions for change and for the attainment of new organizational goals can succeed.

Proposition 5a:

Insiders have many possible courses of action. They can *refuse* directives from above, destroying the authority of superiors, and they can refuse to contribute the resources of their positions. They can *initiate* new policies and procedures.

Fact 6:

All large organizations require outside support if they are to implement their policies. Even large institutions can be blocked by other institutions, by the government, and by powerful groups in society. To act effectively, organizations and their leaders must have some outside base of support.

Proposition 6:

Outside action consists primarily of support for movement insiders rather than pressure against nonmovement insiders. Support may take the form of public demonstrations, grants of money, positive publicity, statements of endorsement from high-status members of society, technical and legal information from experts, or laws passed by sympathetic public officials.

Fact 7:

In an administrative world in which major resources reside within large bureaucracies, outside action alone is seldom sufficient to bring major changes in organizational policies and procedures.

Proposition 7:

Outsiders must be organized together with insiders in one unified movement.

Fact 8:

Major problems in contemporary society are complex matters which can be solved only by combining the ideas and work of numerous persons. To solve major problems large organizations must utilize the talents, knowledge, and concern of people at various levels within the bureaucracy and within the constituency served by the institution.

Proposition 8:

Outsiders are not coalition members who only serve insiders; they are full members of the movement contributing a range of information and perspectives on the problems at hand. Outsiders aid in creating policies and strategies; there can be no winning movement without them.

Fact 9:

Large institutions are run by committees, by groups of men and women, not by individuals. The very size and complexity of large urban school systems and other massive bureaucracies necessitates pooling and coordinating the expertise of many people in the organization where committees are important to the original institution, for these reasons, committees are not equally powerful. Some determine policies, others simply contribute needed information; and some have no real impact.

Proposition 9:

A movement insider should be willing to serve only on those committees which can make final decisions on issues on their agenda.

The most basic strategic concept in all of these propositions is that insiders have organizational power which, when united with outside support, can be effective for creating new policies and procedures. In all large organizations power is in the hands of subordinates and is dispersed to many committees and individuals, throughout the hierarchy. Only coordinated efforts by many people can keep the organization on its present path and only coordinated efforts by many movement insiders can change its direction and priorities. It is critical that movement insiders not let themselves and their organizational resources be used. Since the organization needs their expertise, they should put a price on it. Their contributions should not be free in the organization; rather, the price for their contributions is power. In addition to serving only on committees that can resolve their own agenda, there are undoubtedly other techniques by which their power can be increased if insiders are organized and refuse to contribute freely their needed resources.

Power can be centralized at the top of an organization only when those below agree to spend their time working in groups without real power. Refusal to participate in these powerless groups forces a greater decentralization of power and, thereby, results in greater power for insiders below those in top positions.

Institutions which pursue wrong policies do so primarily because subordinates and the public have acquiesced. Change comes only from a vision and an agenda. It is not enough for insiders and concerned outsiders to refuse to acquiesce. Together we must initiate, propose, and fight for better policies. It is not enough for insiders to refuse to serve on powerless committees, even their participation on the powerful committees must be directed toward common ends. In short, our movement must have a positive, clear agenda for change. We must carefully define our ultimate goals, our short-term objectives, and the specific policy and personnel changes necessary to achieve these objectives. Every time personnel are appointed, budgets are adopted, and even minor policies are set, we must be able to shape them to fit our agenda for change.

An Evaluation of Administrative Strategy

Unlike the strategies discussed in other chapters, the administrative strategy outlined here cannot be specific because, to our knowledge, it has not yet been tried. However, we have set forth an analysis of why strategies attacking bureaucracies have failed and we have presented the principles of a successful administrative strategy. Whereas our other strategies have been refined through first-hand experience, for this one we lack direct experience to guide us.

In common with the other strategies we advocate, the administrative strategy depends on creating a new organization. In this case, a new movement is needed to unite both insiders and outsiders in a common effort to achieve quality education for children in the Chicago schools.

We believe that our administrative strategy would be effective because it is realistic in its recognition of the power of large institutions and of the administrators who run them. It wisely marshalls the resources of both insiders and outsiders. It creates a new movement, puts new people in power, and permanently changes the vast bureaucracies which control our lives. Rather than create small institutions which only a few privileged students can attend, we seek to transform all schools for all children. Rather than fighting *against* impenetrable monoliths with vast resources, we seek to attract both those insiders and outsiders who are willing to work together for change.

An administrative strategy avoids the pitfalls which so greatly limit most alternative strategies. Professional organizations and unions pit one group against another. They organize *against* existing power but not *for* new institutions and new goals. Salaries and status are goals too narrow, too private, and too self-centered to promote radical reforms. Parent groups are even weaker. PTA's allow parents to be easily co-opted by administrators and set parents at unnecessary busywork far from the centers of power. Parallel institutions serve too few constituents to bring fundamental change for most children. Community organizations which directly attack bureaucracies are doomed to failure because corporate rather than personal responsibility make it impossible to locate a real villain. Whatever its faults, an administrative strategy is not irrelevant, not quixotic, not self-centered. Administrative strategists do not organize against the current reality, but rather they create a better reality.

Our administrative strategy is premised on the realistic assumption that significant power resides *within* administrative structures. Participation in our movement by administrators and other insiders is essential if fundamental change is to be attained. Although almost everyone agrees that major power resides within large organizations, other strategies have failed to enlist the participation of insiders. Instead, they have relied solely on outsiders. It is therefore understandable that their strategies have not brought about fundamental policy changes nor altered significantly the distribution of power.

Our administrative strategy has an advantage similar to independent politics in that it puts good people in positions of power.

If the movement is successful, insiders who favor change will be advanced within the bureaucracy; others opposed by our movement will find their promotions blocked. More importantly, the creation of such a movement transcends individual victories. As a permanent organization created around a concrete agenda, our movement has the potential of organizing subordinates and outside supporters into an overwhelming force for obtaining important public, as well as private, goals. Currently, the large institutions of America are run by elites who implement specific policies to which we and many other Americans object. For example, parents of Chicago school children would not, if they were in control, perpetuate schools which are unable to educate their children. Our movement, by taking over the positions of district superintendents, principals, and directors of special programs, could easily redirect the teachers' energy to teaching and better utilize the positive role which parents and students can play in education. By creating a permanent self-conscious movement dedicated to quality education, we believe our strategy is not only realistic, but hopeful. Finally, our movement seeks to gain control over large institutions in order to foster a better life for most citizens. We oppose continuing the high life for the few and the impoverished life for the many. Not only do we seek to change institutional leaders, but by controlling the subordinate key decision points, we seek to lay the foundation for a new America.

Of course, we must be honest concerning the difficulties faced by any strategy which confronts the large administrative structures of modern society. The first problem which must be overcome is that most citizens do not define large bureaucracies as the locus for their primary attention and effort. Therefore, it is an uphill fight just to have an administrative strategy accepted as a strategy to be pursued. Although many citizens are convinced that large bureaucracies are not only powerful but also wasteful and corrupt, still they believe that some form of electoral or pressure action will remedy the problems. Thus, most citizens fail even to see the need for an administrative strategy.

Second, the implementation of an administrative strategy is further hampered by the absence of established procedures and rules. In other words, an administrative strategy must be started from scratch, whereas the party organizations, voting procedures, district lines, and legal means for attaining office already exist for those pursuing an electoral strategy.

Third, large bureaucracies appear to be very complex, and most citizens do not feel competent to bring them under control. The bureaucratic mode of operation, its weaknesses, and the nature of its power remain mysteries to most citizens. Even those who are members of a large bureaucracy often do not understand its unique characteristics. To a large extent, the bureaucracies appear complex because citizens simply have not been educated about them as they have, for example, about elections. Children in third grade learn how to vote for class president, but few ever learn about bureaus and administrative decision-making. The electoral system in the United States is a very complex apparatus, but it does not appear so to most citizens because they are familiar with it. But, regardless of the reasons the fact remains that bureaucracy is perceived as complex, and thus most people do not have the information and training to undertake a successful administrative strategy.

Finally, attempts for fundamental change will be difficult because the extensive resources commanded by the large bureaucracies provide them with very substantial means to sustain the status quo, even in the face ·of attack. When in difficulty, large organizations can buy off, repress, or manipulate both its inside and outside agitators. This does not mean that an administrative strategy cannot win but only that the task is not easy. The existing power elite is a formidable opponent.

One of the most attractive aspects of an administrative strategy, given the obstacles which must be overcome, is that it *can mobilize resources sufficient to defeat the status quo.* By uniting insiders and outsiders, our administrative strategy has the advantage of bringing together those very groups which possess the specific resources each needs to be effective. Outsiders need to tap actual power in the large organizations. Otherwise they will never be part of a movement that *attains* power, but instead, always reacting against those who hold power. Insiders, on the other hand, require the support and contributions of the outsiders to exercise power over long periods of time. The unity of insiders and outsiders means that participation in the movement is not restricted to the "elite" insiders, but rather an active role for outsiders is equally important. Since outsiders are unified with insiders, they are part of a movement for the attainment of power. Their participation becomes more meaningful for them because it is more successful. They see their ideas translated into practice.

An administrative strategy is also desirable because it opens up major areas of citizens' lives for social action—their occupations. Too often formulas for civic participation have designated only leisure time or evening hours for social action. Most citizens spend the major part of their waking hours within the large organizations. To preclude civic responsibility during these hours is to make the social life of citizens peripheral when, in fact, our civic activities should be central. While independent politics or pressure strategies may allow citizens to be active after work hours, our administrative strategy allows citizens to be *citizens in their work.* It makes what we do with most of our lives—not just our free time—valuable. It gives meaning and purpose to work which too often has had only an economic reward. As we have stated before, we believe citizenship and the assumption of responsibility for our community to be essential to the full human life. To open up our vocation to responsible social action is to increase the scope for personal growth. Our present state of affairs did not come about as the result of part-time and after-hours efforts of those with dominant power. Neither can it be corrected by such means. Thus, there are both personal and strategic reasons to adopt an administrative strategy.

As we see it, administrative strategy is needed to solve the problems which face citizens in an administrative state. The difficulties must not deter us from creating movements necessary for citizen effectiveness in a world of large bureaucracies. Only thus can we, as citizens, once again direct our own lives. To attempt to create a democracy which ignores large bureaucracies is to create only an illusion. A movement which controls large institutions is the precondition for a modern, free society.

PART IV

PRESSURE POLITICS

Dr. Martin Luther King in Chicago, Stef Leinwohl, photographer.

Chapter 6
Nonviolent Issue Strategies

Nonviolent issue campaigns are pressure strategies quite unlike the takeover strategies discussed in previous chapters. Pressure strategies depend neither upon the outcome of elections nor on the goodwill of administrators. Instead, they force officials to enact our policies and to enforce them properly regardless of their predispositions, goodwill, or party affiliation.

By themselves, both administrative and electoral strategies limit the scope of citizenship, which is more than just electing others to govern us. Full citizenship embraces more than power moves within large bureaucracies. Pressure strategies are an integral aspect of democratic politics because they allow us to dictate an agenda for change on the whole range of human problems which both politicians and administrators must honor and fulfill. A successful pressure strategy can obtain immediate redress of grievances and can prove to citizens who feel hopeless that they can affect their own destiny.

The civil rights campaign of the 1960's proved the effectiveness of pressure strategies. More than a decade after the Montgomery bus boycott, sit-ins, and the march on Washington, we witness the passage of civil rights legislation, equal opportunity programs, and the election of Black officials. These slow steps toward full equality were the product of the original civil rights demonstrations. Without these efforts segregation would have remained unchallenged and unchanged. Before these demonstrations there was no open struggle. Oppression went unrecognized and unopposed except by lone individuals. Electing a Dr. King as mayor of Atlanta or as United States congressman would not have been nearly as effective as boycotting segregated facilities. Appointing a Dr. King as Secretary of Health, Education and Welfare would have been even less effective. Pressure in the case of civil rights meant more than a takeover of a few governmental posts. The government and private sector were transformed, not by changing personnel, but by forcing a major change in policies.

America has a host of bad policies which cannot be changed by electoral and administrative strategies alone. Nonviolent issue strategies are needed to change detrimental policies which favor the military, big business, and other powerful interests. Rampant discrimination against Blacks, Latins, and women continues. The basic human dignity and rights of these citizens are still denied. American foreign policy favors American business interests over the lives and rights of people living in undeveloped nations. Pollution and a major energy crisis threaten us all. Watergate hearings demonstrate the contempt of the powerful in America for the rights of those who might challenge their power. Lying, wiretapping, burglary, and bribes have become official government policy. Discrimination, a war-oriented foreign policy, destruction of our environment, squandering our natural resources, defrauding citizens, and direct lies of the government—these are some of the policies which cry out for change. These are some of the issues around which nonviolent campaigns can be built.

Power in America

In Chapter II we explored the nature of the electoral system and suggested that great power lies in the hands of elected officials by virtue of their ability to make policy, determine appropriations, and appoint other government officials. In Chapter IV we described bureaucracies and suggested that great power also resides in the hands of bureaucrats. Administrators in subordinate positions have power because of their control over information and their ability to initiate and implement policies. In this chapter we will argue that signficant power also lies in the hands of elite businessmen and their political allies. These influentials operate within a conservative social system in which societal norms and formal laws support the status quo and are biased against fundamental change. It is this view of reality upon which nonviolent issue campaigns, particularly Alinsky campaigns, are based.

For twenty years social scientists have debated the nature of local community power structures. One group has maintained that power resides primarily in a small unified elite (usually businessmen),[1] and the second group has argued that the power structure is more pluralistic.[2] As the debate has worn on, it has become increasingly clear that some cities are informally controlled by a single elite and others are governed by several competing elites, each with their own arena of control. In each city the powerful are heads of larger industries and financial institutions, local political leaders, executives of major institutions such as hospitals, and to a much lesser extent, leaders of civic organizations. These powerful figures comprise less than one percent of the population. In most cases, their informal power is bolstered by their formal positions such as mayor or president of a large corporation.

This is not to say that all members of the local elites inevitably oppose all change. Indeed, there are people at all levels of society who wish to build a better America. Mobilizing support from among the powerful can be a significant component of a successful strategy. In general, however, most members of the various elites will oppose fundamental changes because it often endangers their power.

As activists at the local level, we are faced with a power structure of a hundred or so key leaders and several hundred lesser officials who head business, political, governmental, and social institutions. These leaders have formal positions of authority, high social status, and considerable informal power. They know each other personally. Even in a competitive power structure, these leaders often support each other and the status quo when faced with the demand for radical change.

The powerful in local communities join with one another in major ventures, whether revitalizing the downtown business district or putting down violent attempts to bring change. Usually, members of the elite possess a similar background and have frequent reinforcing contacts at their clubs and social gatherings.

However, the fluid nature of the social and political elite in America allows for able members of other social classes to be brought into the inner circle of power; thus, continually replenishing their pool of talent. This diverse nature of local elites may allow for liberal or even radical allies within the power structure.

Power in America is not as rigid as a permanent aristocracy. But neither are the resources of power—wealth and formal positions—numerous enough to allow most citizens a chance to wield power. Faced with a power structure which takes a slightly different form in different communities, faced with major intractable problems festering unresolved, we search for new methods to change society. Unlike many other societies, ours is a seemingly liberal and tolerant one, a society which is governed not by a single evil figure but by several sophisticated elites which share power. Local and national elites are, nonetheless, quite real and citizens are converted unknowingly into an apathetic mass public. This subtle repression and manipulation goes unnoticed. America's durable power structure, hidden behind the facade of representative democracy, rules.

Even if we understand the general nature of power in America, we need a much more precise understanding of where power lies in each community if we are to formulate effective strategies. To be effective in Chicago, for example, we must understand Chicago's power structure. As with other cities, political leaders, businessmen, heads of major institutions, and, to a lesser extent, civic leaders, possess the most power. A diagram of this power structure and how major projects get done in Chicago is shown in Figure 6.1. In Chicago civic groups, community organizations, and even the crime syndicate can occasionally influence particular decisions by appeal to political leaders. More frequently, however, heads of major corporations and major institutions either act directly with their own resources and authority (Decisions D and E in the diagram) or they cause the political leaders to act on their behalf (Decisions A, B, and C).

In other words the power structure in Chicago is such that political leaders act as a funnel for many decisions, but they do not control all actions by the business community and major institutions. The details of this decision-making structure are best spelled

Figure 6.1

A Model Of Power And Decision-Making In Chicago

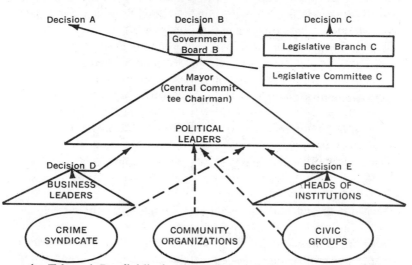

out in Edward Banfield's book, *Political Influence.*[3] He suggests that in the face of an incredibly decentralized *formal government*, political heads such as the mayor and the governor use their *political party organizations* to centralize decision-making in order to get things done. Institutional executives and key businessmen usually propose major new projects for Chicago which can only be carried out by the Democratic party leaders, who can force the proper government agency to authorize the action. Given the nature of Chicago's power structure, if businessmen, institutional executives, and political leaders agree, government acts. If they disagree, a stalemate results and projects are blocked.

As Figure 6.2 demonstrates, Chicago is unique in that Mayor Daley has almost complete control over all units of government through his control of the Democratic Party. Nearly 100% of the mayor's proposed legislation in the City Council was passed in 1971 and there never were more than 14 dissenting votes among the 50 aldermen. On the other hand, only 8% of the major legislation of the mayor's opponents passed, although occasionally the city administration will steal an idea from their opponents and reintroduce it in the name of the mayor.

Figure 6.2 Major Legislation in the Chicago City Council in 1971

Sponsor	Number Pieces of Legislation Introduced	Number Not Reported Out of Committee	Number For Which Rules Suspended Or Committees Reported	Number Pieces of Legislation Passed	Percentage Passed of Legislation Introduced
Mayor	117	2	115	115	98%
Minority Alderman*	122	107	15	10**	8%
Majority Alderman	49	35	14	14	29%
City Council Committees***	22	0	22	22	100%
Other	33	21	12	12	36%
Total	343	165	178	173	50%

Source: Dick Simpson, *A Proposal for Reform of the Chicago City Council* (presented to Chicago Home Rule Commission, Sept. 1972).

*13 Alderman who voted against the city administration with some regularity.

**Minority legislation passed included 7 resolutions related to state and federal legislation; two resolutions about the CTA and one ordinance prohibiting peddlers in the 50th ward.

***City Council Committees frequently handle for the mayor legislation which needs to pass quickly without being first introduced in the City Council. Only rarely do committee chairmen with a lot of "clout" introduce their own legislation and even these ordinances must be cleared with the mayor.

In most cities, political leaders would like such extensive control over the government but fail to achieve it. As Mike Royko's *Boss* and other books on Chicago politics have shown, Daley's control comes from his power as mayor and as Chairman of the Democratic Party Central Committee.[4] Patronage jobs, executive authority, and powers of a party boss are combined in one leader. Other cities which have less monolithic power structures still have political figures with considerable muscle.

Thus, in Chicago and much of America we are confronted with very strong and reasonably stable power structures. In such situations it may not make sense to attempt takeover strategies in direct opposition to the status quo. Because business and institutional leaders have power to make and implement many decisions on their own, pressure strategies aimed at these officials may be effective. In addition, political officials are sometimes willing to implement policies with which they may disagree if their formal positions of authority remain unchallenged. Under these circumstances, our movement for change can organize successful pressure strategies which bring major policy changes without replacing existing officials in the power structure.

Inadequate Strategies: Riots

Pressure strategies other than nonviolent issue campaigns have often failed to bring the comprehensive changes which we believe necessary. The strongest alternatives to issue campaigns are various forms of violence and legislative lobbying. In the late 1960's we witnessed a spiral of violence beginning with confrontations on college campuses, escalating to riots in major cities, terrorist bomb tactics, and kidnappings, before dissolving back to a deeper citizen apathy and despair. Lobbying, of course, we have with us always. But lobbying usually favors the status quo or, at best, incremental development. Neither violence nor lobbying has brought much change.

First let us discard terrorist tactics. Terrorism is a meaningful tactic only if it is part of a revolutionary strategy. In Chapter II we have already given our argument against revolution as a feasible strategy in America today.

Even if revolutions are discarded, what about other violent strategies? Tom Hayden in his book, *Rebellion in Newark*, defended the Newark riot with these arguments:

> The riot is certainly an awkward, even primitive form of history-making. But if people are barred from using the sophisticated instruments of the established order for their ends, they will find another way. Rocks and bottles are only the beginning, but they cause more attention than all the reports in Washington. To the people involved, the riot is far less lawless and far more representative than the system of arbitrary rules and prescribed channels which they confront everyday.[5]

Riots involve acts of violence by frustrated citizens and fearful authorities. While violence is often limited to bottle throwing, property burning, and looting, people are often killed in riots.

Authorities usually respond in one of two ways. Either they contain the riot within a given area, keeping violence to a minimum, and let it play itself out; or, in the words of Mayor Daley, they "shoot to kill." A third response, namely, meeting just demands of the rioters, is rarely chosen since it requires a partial abdication of power and authority. Furthermore, riots in progress do not provide the best conditions for judging specific demands or for meeting them.

Riots are generally spontaneous outbursts triggered by a specific incident, such as an act of police brutality or the assassination of a popular figure.[6] Riots may be encouraged and enlarged by militant leaders, but they are not organized in the same way as more deliberate strategies. As a consequence, they are often not aimed at critical targets and their short duration fails to provide the long-term pressure required to create and implement sweeping policy changes. It is true that riots may call attention to the gravity of a problem which policymakers have ignored. For example, the Watts riot may have brought public and private assistance programs into the community by focusing attention on residents' difficulties. But poverty and racial discrimination in

Watts and in the country as a whole remain fundamentally unchanged by that riot and by all the riots of the late 1960's.

Thus, riots which are not part of a revolution have only the limited effect of calling attention to problems. No matter how grave the injustice, riots by themselves cannot provide a solution. They can be understood as acts of frustration and despair, they can offer a temporary catharsis, but they can provide neither immediate cures nor even a realistic hope for the kind of sustained effort necessary to bring fundamental change. Worst of all, because they are uncontrolled, riots become mob action—action which may destroy property, lives, and yesterday's leaders of the mob.

As we have stressed throughout, evaluations of strategies should consider the costs as well as likely benefits. The costs of riots are high. Almost invariably a number of lives are lost. Surveillance and repression by the government increase. Legitimate avenues of change may be blocked and a spiral of rebellions and repression may set in. Good strategies achieve their goals at reasonable costs. Riots usually fail to achieve positive goals, and their costs are great.

Finally, riots are simply an inappropriate response to complex issues. Pollution, inflation, the energy crisis—none of these lends itself to a riot. For example, it is hard to pinpoint the specific enemy causing environmental destruction, inflation, or the energy crisis. While the problems are real and may bring sickness, hunger, or even death, they are too complex and too remote to spark a riot unless, for instance, people are literally dropping in the streets around a particular plant which is polluting a neighborhood. Many of the problems in our technological society are just too complicated to be solved by riots.

Inadequate Strategies: Confrontations

If we reject riots as an effective strategy because they are unwieldy, cumbersome, and costly, what about their more controlled and directed cousin, confrontation? Some of the more important confrontations during the last decade include the attempted student takeover of Columbia University in 1968, battles in Chicago's Lincoln and Grant parks during the 1968 Democratic Convention, and the nation-wide college strike in 1970.[7] As a rule, such confrontations occur in stages. Demonstrations and mass meetings are transformed into confrontations when participants take over a physical space (park or building) and claim it for themselves and "the people." Rules governing the use of the space, such as closing hours and authorized activities, are ignored by the demonstrators. Inevitably, spontaneous actions by some participants result in clashes with police. It is at this stage that confrontations take on many of the characteristics of riots. As a result of the takeover of public space and damage to property (destroying files, etc.), officials often conclude that they cannot tolerate this challenge to their authority. They order police to remove the demonstrators.[8]

The immediate effect of a "successful" confrontation, as with a riot, is that it brings attention to a serious problem such as the war in Vietnam or the poor quality of college education. As a strategy, confrontation elicits countermeasures by the police which expose the repressive nature of the political system and radicalizes people so they will participate in more militant actions.[9] In the "police riot" at the 1968 Democratic convention, both demonstrators and innocent bystanders were beaten and jailed by the police, frequently in front of national TV cameras. Demonstrators and bystanders are often radicalized by such experiences and, what is more, millions of television viewers and newspaper readers are presented with visible documentation that protestors' charges of repressive government are at least partly true. The overreaction of the police inadvertently creates a larger, more radical group of citizens alienated from their government.

Thus, the central purpose of confrontations is to expose the repressive nature of government and to radicalize people. As part of a revolutionary strategy, confrontations may make sense. By themselves, they are not an effective strategy. As with riots, officials may make a token response; but the long-term pressure necessary to make major changes is lacking. Often the demands and goals of confrontation activists are too general and too radical to be granted by existing authorities.

The national college strike after the Cambodian invasion of 1970 demonstrates the confusion of goals which accompanies confrontations. Often both symbolic and material demands are made. *A symbolic demand is one which requires a response in words or symbols,* such as a declaration that a government official is in favor of ending a war. Lyndon Johnson, for instance, as a candidate in 1964 said that he was in favor of ending the Vietnam War, while Goldwater stood for escalating that war. Of course, after Johnson was elected he did *not* end the war, but his statements during the campaign can be seen as a symbolic response to voters opposed to the war. *A material demand is one which requires a specific material change.* A labor union, for instance, strikes to force a wage increase.

In addition to confusing symbolic demands with material demands, the college strike of 1970 also pursued simultaneously local and national objectives. This mixture of symbolic and material, local and national demands made it difficult to find either a single target to which student energy could be directed or a single tactic capable of achieving all demands at the same time. According to *The Daily Strike,* a newspaper published briefly by the Chicago City-Wide Strike Committee, the demands of the student strike were primarily:

1. U.S. Out of Southeast Asia—NOW!
2. Troops Off Campus—Stop Suppression of Political Dissent!
3. ROTC Off Campus!

The only truly local, material demand was that ROTC be removed from campus. It was a demand for a specific policy change at each university. The demands for troops off campus and an end to suppression of dissent were more rhetorical and symbolic. Students were looking for a statement by universities or the national government that troops would not be used. Although troops had been called in at Kent State, they are rarely ordered onto university campuses. Thus, it was hard to know if a material demand about the use of troops was being met or if there was simply no need for them. Finally, as far as university administrators were concerned, the demand to pull U.S. troops out of Southeast Asia was clearly symbolic. While the national government could grant this student demand, it is unclear how college students refusing to attend class could force the government to comply.

Not surprisingly, the demands of the strike changed as the strike continued. More immediate demands took precedence over the more abstract demands with which the students were sympathetic. As the strike progressed, the question of grades became more important. It was possible to appeal for support from faculty and administrators to change grade policies in order that students would not be penalized for participating in the class boycott. This demand could be granted without putting the university in opposition to other powerful institutions such as the military. The student strike thus brought *concrete material victories concerning the grading system but neither symbolic nor material victories concerning national war policies and ROTC*. In short, confrontations, like riots, often have confused goals and employ tactics which fail to create long-term pressure for policy changes.

Inadequate Strategies: Lobbying

What about lobbying as an alternative strategy? For long-term pressure, legislative lobbying is a time-honored and accepted method of influencing government policy in America. Liberal organizations like Americans for Democratic Action, good government groups like the League of Women Voters, traditional interest groups such as labor unions, professional associations, and business organizations engage in full-time, year-round efforts to influence legislators. The more powerful the legislative body or administrative agency, the more lobbyists to be found there.

Lobbying is so exhaustively covered in political science literature[10] and in the press that we need consider it only briefly here. The most effective method of lobbying is to support candidates in agreement with our self-interest issues. It is easier for a legislator than for any outsider to solicit other lawmakers for their votes, to keep track of bills as they move through committees, to introduce helpful legislation and to block harmful laws, and to press their cause within other branches of government. In short electing people to public office, as we explained in Chapter II, can play a major role in bringing change. Because election campaigns cost a lot of money, lobbies (particularly business and labor) make large contributions to many candidates—and thereby leave them indebted and willing to help the lobbyist's cause if elected.

Other lobbying techniques include drafting legislation, providing technical information, suggesting arguments for or against bills, bringing public pressure to bear on issues, and offering gifts or bribes. If applied well, these various techniques can cause the passage of laws favoring a particular group.

Fundamental policy changes, however, cannot be achieved through lobbying. New Deal legislation, for example, was the result of a depression and the full commitment of the president. Lobbyists for the poor, labor unions, and all good government groups combined could not have forced the national government to regulate business and to develop the welfare state as the New Deal did. Similarly, a redistribution of wealth and power in the United States will not be achieved by lobbying, no matter how skillful. *It must always be remembered that business has the most powerful lobby and business will oppose any radical changes!* Moreover, lobbying involves one piece of legislation at a time— small gains here, an amendment there. But the changes we seek cannot be encompassed in even a dozen pieces of legislation. We seek a more open, more participatory, more just society. Lobbying is not a proper instrument for so fundamental a change.

Lobbying also occurs in bureaucracies. Frequently, government agencies and the groups they are supposed to regulate are tied together. Personnel for both tend to have the same background, the same technical training, and the same ideals. The Farm Bureau, for instance, has immense power in the Department of Agriculture; and large contractors have easy access to the Department of Defense. Administrative decisions can be influenced by lobbying in much the same way that legislative decisions can be influenced. Although it is less open to public scrutiny, administrative lobbying has the same strengths and weaknesses as legislative efforts. Administrative lobbying can be effective on day-to-day operations of agencies and result in fluctuations of policy, but to achieve fundamental policy reforms other strategies must be employed.

Nonviolent Issue Campaigns

An effective pressure strategy for fundamental change in America must be nonviolent. There are two justifications for this: one is philosophical, the other pragmatic. Martin Luther King's philosophy of nonviolence, for example, rested on an ethic of love, which assumed that social change begins with individuals. Dr. King believed that only love can overcome the hate and fear in each heart. He believed that conscientious nonviolence brings human dignity and individual freedom to participants, whereas violence only perpetuates and inflames hate and fear. Whoever wins by violence cruelly represses the loser, but by so doing lays the foundation for future violence. Only love has the unique ability to overcome hate, thereby laying the foundation for a new society of equality, dignity, and freedom. Strategies derived from the philosophy of nonviolence are based on winning the hearts and minds of one's enemies. Because the philosophy of nonviolence views all men as infinitely precious, it calls for a permanent transformation of both participant and foe through the personal sacrifices of participants in the movement. Dr. King put the case most eloquently:

> When for decades, you have been able to make a man compromise his manhood by threatening him with a cruel and unjust punishment, and when suddenly he turns upon you and says: 'Punish me. I do not deserve it. But because I do not deserve it, I will accept it so that the world will know that I am right and you are wrong,' you hardly know what to do. You feel defeated and secretly ashamed. You know that this man is as good a man as you are, that from some mysterious source he

has found the courage and the conviction to meet physical force with soul force.

So it was that to the Negro going to jail was no longer a disgrace but a badge of honor. The Revolution of the Negro not only attacked the external cause of his misery, but revealed him to himself. He was *somebody*. He had a sense of *somebodiness*. He was *impatient* to be free. . . .

Nonviolence had tremendous psychological importance to the Negro. He had to win and to vindicate his dignity in order to merit and enjoy his self-esteem. He had to let white men know that the picture of him as a clown—irresponsible, resigned and believing in his own inferiority—was a stereotype with no validity. This method was grasped by the Negro masses because it embodied the dignity of struggle, of moral conviction and self-sacrifice. The Negro was able to face his adversary, to concede to him a physical advantage and to defeat him because the superior force of the oppressor had become powerless.[11]

The philosophy of nonviolence advocated by Dr. King often required civil disobedience—deliberately breaking a law to protest its injustice. Yet an act of civil disobedience does not destroy society; it reaffirms society. The participant recognizes the right of society to have laws but makes an unequivocal protest against a specific unjust law. The participant does not attempt to avoid punishment; rather, punishment is accepted to demonstrate to the community the unfairness and injustice of the law. As Dr. King expressed it:

One who breaks an unjust law must do so openly, lovingly, and with a willingness to accept the penalty. I submit that an individual who breaks a law that conscience tells him is unjust, and who willingly accepts the penalty of imprisonment in order to arouse its injustice, is in reality expressing the highest respect for law.[12]

Saul Alinsky, on the other hand, justified nonviolence pragmatically. Nonviolence was to be used because a violent strategy would fail. His basic premise in organizing the poor was: "The opposition is always stronger than you are and so his strength must be used against him."[13] In an all-out war with tanks, planes, and guns, a "people's organization" is certain to be defeated. What is required then is "mass ju-jitsu" in which your opponent's strength and overreactions help to build your organization, create your allies, and cause powerful institutions to intercede in your favor. Suppose, for example, the issue of a people's organization is pollution from some utility company in the neighborhood. If the people attack the utility head-on, they probably will fail. Alinsky suggests causing trouble in those banks which handle the company's accounts. For example, a thousand people in one day might open $5.00 savings accounts and then close them the next day. As Alinsky points out, the banks belong to the same power sector as the large utilities and "if their banks . . . start pressing them . . . they listen and hurt." The savings accou t tactic ". . . could well cause an irrational reaction on the part of the banks which could then be directed against their large customers, . . . the polluting utilities."[14] While Alinsky favored tactical nonviolence, he did not advocate passivity. He used anger and friction to create new, more equitable relations between groups. For Alinsky, compromise could only follow controversy and conflict.

Unlike King, Alinsky did not expect to shame or to change his opponents. Nor did he expect "people of good will" to intercede to resolve disputes. He began from what he believed to be realistic principles of human motivation:

> In the world as it is, man moves primarily because of self-interest.
> In the world as it is, the right things are usually done for the wrong reasons, and vice-versa.
> In the world as it is, constructive actions have been reactions to a threat.[15]

Given his understanding of human motivation, Alinsky did not emphasize the need for people to make sacrifices in the spirit of nonviolence. Rather, he avoided violence because it could only bring an attack from better-armed opponents. Nonviolence was a pragmatic necessity for victory.

Real discipline is required in a successful nonviolent campaign. It is well understood that discipline is required in the military. The drill, maneuvers, and strict penalties for disobeying orders are standard procedure. What is less understood is that discipline is equally important to the armies of nonviolence.[16] The status quo can be altered only when a large number of people take direct action. But to be effective direct action requires planning, training, and careful execution. In major demonstrations, for example, there must be marshals to control demonstrators so as not to give police an excuse to attack. In negotiations there must be one unified set of demands or the enemy will play one faction off against the others. Even in simple citizen activities like letter-writing campaigns, letters must arrive at the same time to put significant pressure on public officials. While spontaneous action may be a meaningful component in some issue battles, victory depends upon a group's ability to organize mass pressure at a single point. Without disciplined action by followers, no threat by leaders is credible.

Boycott and Civil Disobedience

Nonviolent issue strategies can be more fully understood by studying in some detail the boycott and civil disobedience tactics of Martin Luther King and the pressure tactics of Saul Alinsky. Both are examples of valid nonviolent issue strategies but they use slightly different methods.

The logic of boycott tactics is simple: they cut off a basic resource such as money or labor. Strikes are the most common examples of this strategy. A business must have workers to produce its products. If auto workers go on strike, they can paralyze the productive capacity of even Ford or General Motors. If a company like Ford or General Motors can no longer produce cars, it loses money. Like any other company, General Motors is forced to settle with the workers before production and profit-making can continue.

A strike, however, is not the only type of boycott. Good organizers can develop a variety of ways to cut off resources. The sit-in movement in the South, for example, prevented customers from buying food at lunch counters that discriminated against Blacks. In Nashville the 1960 sit-ins were so effective that nearly the entire downtown shopping area became a ghost town. Needless to say, the lunch counters in Nashville were soon integrated after that demonstration of black economic power. Northern economic groups like Operation Breadbasket in Chicago successfully picketed grocery stores in the Black community to force better hiring practices and services. The largest boycott of recent years, however, was organized by the United Farm Workers against non-union grapes and lettuce. It brought pickets to stores in the north as well as to growers in California and affected millions of dollars of produce. These boycotts have focused not on the production process but on consumers who refused to purchase the products. They have been effective, not by cutting off labor but by cutting sales.

Dr. King suggested four basic stages for an effective boycott[17]:

1. Collection of the facts to determine if injustices exist
2. Negotiation
3. Self-purification
4. Direct action

As King suggests, boycotts begin as an attack against a specific injustice such as racial discrimination or low wages. Although an injustice may be rooted in basic economic institutions or the mores of the larger society, a specific target—the enemy—must be identified. Certain chain stores which fail to serve minorities, certain manufacturing companies which discriminate in hiring can become the target of a boycott. Before the issue is isolated, defined, and pointed out, there is no issue, only the injustice. Defining the situation and focusing on specific demands from a particular target make public what was previously private and hidden. The whole point is "to make an issue" out of an unjust situation in a way that allows us to ask for support on the broadest possible base.

In picking an enemy, the issue should be put so that the overwhelming majority of people will be on our side. We want to attract citizens in a fight against big business, for instance, because the number of *big* businessmen is far fewer than the number of consumers and workers. Or we recruit honest citizens in a battle against a corrupt political machine, because there are more citizens than politicians. Thus, our definition of the situation, of ourselves, and of our opponents helps to build widespread support.

Issues must also be dramatic. Some issues are inherently more dramatic and important than others, but in every campaign a way must be found to dramatize the issues. For instance, an Alinsky organization in Chicago concerned with rat control dramatized their issue by dumping dead rats at city hall. This action publicized their problem and placed the blame in a way hard to forget.

Besides dramatic issues, it is necessary to identify some immediate citizen action. The time for action must be now, not in the future. If action is postponed, participants will lose interest and, just as important, the enemy will have time to strengthen his position. Immediate action taps the resources of aroused citizens, keeps the enemy off balance, and thereby fosters success for the movement.

Defining an issue as an injustice requiring immediate action is not enough. The issue must be personalized. Our enemy must not be "the system," it must be a flesh and blood person. Whether police chief, mayor, or company president—a single individual must be pinpointed as both the cause and solution to the problem. Frequently, specific enemies nominate themselves by their overreactions to early demands and demonstrations. Police Chief Bull Conner set dogs on Southern demonstrators, Mayor Daley ordered the police to attack 1968 Democratic Convention protestors, Lyndon Johnson and Richard Nixon escalated the Vietnam War. In each case they emerged as enemies to citizen groups.

Although boycotts can be very effective, they are very demanding. Before undertaking this type of action, we ought to consider all the potential problems. First, a boycott can be successfully undertaken only by a strong, well-organized group willing to work for months or even years. Second, boycott participants must be prepared to picket and to take part in nonviolent demonstrations.

Most citizens have never participated in protest demonstrations. They may be afraid to become involved in a strategy which seems alien to middle class politeness. Even if participants' inhibitions are overcome, boycotts require a considerable sacrifice of time, and there is a real possibility of jail or violence. Third, a boycott will be successful only if the margin of profit of the institution we are fighting is small. For example, will a five percent of sales loss force our opponent to negotiate a settlement? Fourth, if the community is going to be asked to refrain from buying products or services from one source, the same products or services must be easily available elsewhere at a reasonable price. Thus, a boycott should be directed at only one institution at a time. Focusing on a single target, correctly calculating how much business can be cut off, and providing alternative sources of supply are absolutely essential to a successful boycott.

Boycotts often require civil disobedience. In order to protest unfair policies inside a store or restaurant, it may be necessary to enter private property and to refuse to leave until the demands are met. Failing to leave private property when ordered is against the law and can result in arrests. Civil disobedience is a serious choice, to be made sparingly and with judgment. As Dr. King warned:

> When we speak of filling the jails, we are talking of a tactic to be flexibly applied. No responsible person would promise to fill all jails everywhere at one time. Leaders indulge in bombast if they do not take all circumstances into account before calling upon their people to make a maximum sacrifice. Filling jails means that thousands of people must leave their jobs, perhaps to lose them, put off responsibilities, undergo harrowing psychological experiences for which law-abiding people are not routinely prepared. The miracle of nonviolence lies in the degree to which people will sacrifice under its inspiration, when the call is based on judgment.[18]

A willingness to break laws and to go to jail is often—although not always—needed, because our laws frequently protect established interests.

Creative Pressure Tactics

Saul Alinsky has proven that successful nonviolent issue campaigns are not limited to boycotts and civil disobedience. Creative pressure tactics include pressure against an enemy's vulnerable points in such a way as to overload his system. The company's phone lines are clogged with calls or a hundred demonstrators crowd into the president's office. According to Alinsky, there is an endless arsenal of pressure tactics available to the creative organizer:

> For an elementary illustration of tactics, take parts of your face as the point of reference: your eyes, your ears, and your nose. First the eyes; if you have organized a vast, mass-based people's organization, you can parade it visibly before the enemy and openly show your power. Second the ears; if your organization is small in number, then do what Gideon did: conceal the members in the dark but raise a din and clamor that will make the listener believe that your organization numbers many more than it does. Third, the nose; if organization is too tiny even for noise, stink up the place.[19]

The key to a successful nonviolent issue campaign is the ability to think up new pressures to put on the enemy. New tactics continuously are required because the opposition always learns to counter any particular form of pressure. Effective pressure can usually be generated by undermining the enemy's image. Business and political leaders prefer to "act in the public interest," and they prefer a reputation for beneficence, not villainy. This concern for reputation is an Achilles heel. Its vulnerability can be exploited by forcing leaders to meet an enraged constituency, making their demands in person. Direct confrontations with citizens or customers are usually experiences for which leaders are personally ill-prepared. They become flustered and make themselves look silly, or else they overreact and make themselves look unreasonable and undemocratic.

Creative tactics often employ institutional ju-jitsu, which pits major institutions against each other, keeps the enemy off balance, and encourages him to meet our demands. Ju-jitsu can cause opponents to overreact in ways which win sympathy and support for our cause, create further conflicts within the power structure, and draw more members into our organization.

As Alinsky continually preached, tactical improvisation must be based on experience and understanding of human dynamics. Successful issue campaigns cannot be created from books or ideologies alone. Rather, a winning campaign must be built upon a realistic assessment of human nature and a practical knowledge of the tactics which have succeeded and failed in prior campaigns. Only imaginative, pragmatic organizers build effective issue campaigns:

> One thing I've learned in spades—though I didn't want to accept it for a long time—is this: organization doesn't come out of immaculate conception. It takes a highly trained, politically sophisticated, creative organizer to do the job. . . .

> [Water pollution is] a good issue but I can't tell you what tactics [an organizer would] use because in organizing you are always improvising. For instance, The Woodlawn Organization—TWO—in Chicago got Mayor Daley to deal with them after they threatened to tie up all the rest rooms at O'Hare—keeping all the booths occupied. O'Hare is one of Daley's sacred cows. . . .

> The only thing that the poor have as far as power goes is their bodies. When TWO has a bunch of housing complaints they don't forward them to the building inspector. They drive forty or fifty of their members—the blackest ones they can find—to the nice suburb where the slumlord lives and they picket his home. Now we know a picket line isn't going to convert the slumlord. But we know what happens when his white neighbors get after him and say, 'We don't care what you do for a living—all we're telling you is to get those niggers out.' That's the kind of ju-jitsu operation that forces the slumlord to surrender and gets repairs made in the slums. . . .

> It's very hard to try to get across how an organizer

works—being loose and free, not really knowing himself what the issues are going to be. He knows that in life you go with the action and that you consciously look for hooks and handles that you can grab hold of, that you can twist and turn and pull and get the reaction that is so important in building a power organization.[20]

The Alinsky approach requires full-time organizers to devise radical, new tactics. The organizer is not the spokesman for the group—a legitimate member of the community serves as spokesman—but the organizer analyzes the situation and mobilizes a large section of the community around the current battles of the organization. The willingness of an organizer to do the preparatory work rather than to be a spokesman in the spotlight, a tactician rather than an orator, a behind-the-scenes worker rather than a star on center stage, requires a personal commitment to this special role. It is analogous to being a campaign manager rather than the candidate in electoral politics. Finding and training organizers is essential to stimulate broadbased issue campaigns.

Professional organizers like King or Alinsky usually began their organizational efforts with groups which already exist in the community—churches, clubs, gangs, and neighborhood organizations. Existing groups form a single organization around either a community (The Woodlawn Organization) or an issue (Campaign Against Pollution). These larger community organizations are built through countless conversations with the leaders of smaller groups to convince them that coming into the larger organization will not destroy their limited power but will provide a better vehicle for the attainment of some of their goals. After the organizer has been accepted by the community and a new group begun, the organizer meets with these subgroup leaders again to choose goals and enemies. Locating leaders of existing organizations, bringing them together, and selecting an issue campaign which can be won are the principal early tasks of the organizer.

It would be a mistake to think of these community or issue organizations as similar to social clubs with temporary leaders, loose structures, little cost, and democratic procedures. In fact, they are more like an army than a social club. Like an army they are expensive; it costs \$10,000 to \$100,000 a year to fund a successful organization. In building community organizations, Alinsky required that a community already be organized enough to issue an invitation to the organizer and to raise enough money to pay the first year's operating expenses.

No matter how much money is available or how skilled the organizer is, an effective organization cannot be created without good issues. In Alinsky's words, an organization must "pick the target, freeze it, personalize it and polarize it."[21] Issues give an organization purpose, concrete goals, and a specific enemy. As Alinsky commented, the issue "must be *this* immortality of *this* slumlord with *this* slum tenement where *these* people suffer."[22] Moreover, the issue must be cut as completely black and white as when our forefathers characterized the war against England:

> Jefferson, Franklin, and others were honorable men, but they knew that the Declaration of Independence was a call to war. They also knew that a list of many of the constructive benefits of the British Empire to the colonist would have so diluted the urgency of the call to arms for the Revolution as to have been self-defeating. The result might well have been a document attesting to the fact that justice weighted down the scale at least 60 percent on our side, and only 40 percent on their side; and that because of that 20 percent difference we were going to have a revolution. To expect a man to leave his wife, his children and his home, to leave his crops standing in the field and pick up a gun and join the Revolutionary Army for a 20 percent difference in the balance of human justice was to defy common sense.

> The Declaration of Independence, as a declaration of war, had to be what it was, a 100 percent denunciation of the role of the British government as evil and unjust ... in no war has the enemy or the cause ever been gray.[23]

Nonviolent issue campaigns are like wars. Troops cannot be raised for any cause less than justice nor will they fight an enemy who is less than bad.

Most issue campaigns begin, not with direct negotiations between the organization and the enemy, but by indirect communication through nonviolent protests. According to Michael Lipsky,[24] protestors frequently cannot pressure their enemy directly; so their protest is conveyed by the media to reference groups (other corporation heads, political leaders, or social contacts) who then influence the enemy. This is another example of the institutional ju-jitsu which Alinsky advocated. When the enemy's reference groups cut off financial resources or bring social pressure to bear on the enemy, the enemy responds with either symbolic or material rewards sufficient to pacify the protestors or at least the reference groups. Thus protests communicate to important sectors of the power elite who pressure the enemy and force capitulation.

Nonviolent issue campaigns may also include direct negotiations. These are not polite conversations, formal debates won by rational argument, nor friendly discussions among equals. They are the opportunity to present demands and force a response. Here are eight rules for effective negotiations:

1. Negotiate only with chief decision-makers who have the power to grant demands on their own authority.

2. The first demand is always for official meetings with these decision-makers. This has the additional benefit of granting formal recognition and official status to your organization.

3. In the beginning your demands should be stated as absolute, although a later compromise on details may be necessary.

4. Demands of the organization must be legitimately derived and supported by the whole membership, not just the leaders.

5. Demands must be accompanied by a threat of what will happen if they are not met. Having several hundred members of the organization present outside the negotiation room will help make the demands and the threats more credible.

6. Negotiators must know what is non-negotiable and what is negotiable in their organization's demands, so that they do not compromise *too much* and destroy their own base of support.

7. Leaders should first show their organization's strength by either boycotts or protests before beginning negotiations.
8. Whether a handful of leaders or thousands of protestors are present at negotiations, there should be only one or two spokesmen to present the organization's case. Everyone else must back up their spokesmen. If this is not done, the enemy will use the world's oldest tactic—divide and conquer. If offers are made or questions asked which spokesmen cannot confidently decide on their own, it is easy enough to recess negotiations until they can caucus with the entire organization. *The unity of the organization must be preserved at all costs if anything is to be gained from negotiations.*

Thus, we come full circle from the creation of an organization to negotiation of the terms of victory which, in turn, strengthen and enlarge the organization so that it may take on new struggles.[25]

Pressure strategies will not place new officials in either government posts or at the top of private corporations, nor will they solve all the nation's problems. But under the leadership of a Dr. King or a Saul Alinsky, the have-nots of our nation can force giant corporations and remote governments to make and enforce policies which meet their needs. The battles for equality, for less discrimination, for more liveable cities, and for a cleaner environment can be won by clear-cut issue campaigns. People *can* control those policies which affect them most directly, and they can do it quickly. When they win early victories, they can form permanent organizations dedicated to change and strong enough to get it. The long journey to freedom and justice can begin with just such issue campaigns in local communities across this country.

Chapter 7

How to Win
Issue Campaigns

Chicago is a tightly-run city. Every study of power in Chicago has concluded that big business, political party machines, and a few leaders of major institutions run the city. Chicago is an outstanding example of old-fashioned, benevolent tryranny. Yet Chicago is also the city of social experimentation *par excellence*. Dr. King came to Chicago to bring the civil rights movement north and Operation Breadbasket (later PUSH—People United to Save Humanity) grew from these seeds. Saul Alinsky and the organizers he trained created numerous peoples' organizations in Chicago such as the Back of the Yards Council, The Woodlawn Organization (TWO), Northwest Community Organization (NCO), and the Organization for a Better Austin (OBA). These citizen organizations have had remarkable success in fighting the power structure in Chicago, and the movement for change continues vigorously.

Chicago spawns such organizations largely because its power structure is tightly closed and will not assimilate critics. Anyone who presses for even minor changes must operate outside the established institutions. Because the dominant political, social, and economic institutions in Chicago will not assimilate their critics, they create their own opposition. As a result of the rigidity and blindness of the present power structure, many problems in Chicago are not ameliorated. They fester. They become dramatic in their extreme stages and such issues then spawn new organi-

139

zations. So Chicago, the city of clout, the city of machine politics, also is the city of creative social movements. Faced with such entrenched power, only the most imaginative organizers can win in Chicago.

The Chicago Anti-Pollution Campaign

In 1969 two things happened which made pollution an issue around which a successful strategy could be built. First, a dramatic event made pollution even more visible and dangerous. In November Chicago suffered a severe temperature inversion which trapped polluted air over the city for more than a week. Chicagoans suffering from respiratory ailments were particularly hard hit. The pollution was visible in the air and could be smelled. Increased sickness, dirty air, and the smelly fumes of that November week drove home the pollution problem to Chicagoans.

Second, a citywide coalition under trained leaders was put together to fight polluters. Although the 1969 inversion dramatically exposed the problem, harmful inversions had occurred before but nothing had been done about pollution. This time, however, concern with the environment was growing into a major national issue, even something of a fad among the young. The largest single polluter was, of course, the automobile. But carbon monoxide was not the most dangerous pollutant; and, certainly, cars could not be banned from Chicago. On the other hand, sulfur dioxide was a dangerous pollutant and 65.58% of the total sulfur dioxide emmission in Chicago came from one company, Commonwealth Edison. The inversion had made Edison a household name. But it and other large corporations with their well-financed public relations programs had weathered citizen concern before. The inversion by itself was no guarantee of a successful campaign against a politically well-connected corporate giant. Yet the inversion caused anti-pollution groups to proliferate rapidly and mobilized citizens who had never before participated in an issue campaign.

Three groups were particularly important to the anti-pollution campaign as it developed in Chicago during 1970. They differed from each other but each made their own distinctive contribution. Businessmen for the Public Interest (BPI), now renamed Business and Professional People for the Public Interest, provided a public interest lawyer, Joe Karganis. He had previously handled cases for citizens against a polluting asphalt plant and had experience with regulatory agencies such as the Illinois Commerce Commission. Through BPI, Karganis had contact with many of the more traditional citizen groups such as the League of Women Voters. He was able to draw these groups into planning public events such as Earth Day, which demonstrated broad support for regulating polluters. BPI was not, however, a mass organization. It provided expertise but not many activists. Other groups would have to provide the thousands of people needed to win.

The Tuberculosis Institute, which has since been renamed the Lung Association, founded a coalition of organizations concerned with pollution. This coalition, the Clean-Air Coordinating Committee (CACC), was comprised of leaders of both established civic associations and new pollution groups. Most activities were carried out by a twenty-member board of directors, although CACC had a much larger mailing list of supporters who were interested in anti-pollution activities. CACC brought a lot of doctors, lawyers, scientists along with a cadre of concerned housewives into the battle. CACC concentrated primarily on educating the public and organizing testimony before the Illinois Commerce Commission. They also worked with BPI to make Earth Day a success. John Kirkwood from the TB Institute's staff provided the key leadership for CACC. The Institute not only provided financial backing, staff, and meeting rooms for CACC, but also did the printing for CACC and many of the smaller pollution groups around the city.

In addition to BPI and CACC, a third, more radical organization was founded in January, 1970. The Campaign Against Pollution (CAP), later renamed Citizens Action Program, was created as a mass-based Alinsky-organized group with the explicit purpose of confronting Commonwealth Edison and its political allies. Because of its willingness to take mass actions and to push confrontations with company officials and political leaders, CAP soon emerged as the most visible and best known anti-pollution organization in Chicago.

These three parallel and frequently competing organizations undertook a series of actions which improved the air breathed by Chicagoans.

The Chicago battle began even before the inversion. In June, 1969, Mayor Richard J. Daley retreated from the air pollution problem by introducing into City Council an ordinance extending Commonwealth Edison's exemption from standards controlling sulfur dioxide emissions. The company told the mayor that they couldn't get enough low sulfur coal to meet the city's standards. The mayor's ordinance was passed without hearings the same day it was introduced. However, fourteen of the fifty Aldermen voted against the exemption—the largest vote against the mayor since he had taken control of Chicago fifteen years earlier. To add to the mayor's troubles, at the very next meeting of the City Council Alderman William Singer offered a strong anti-pollution ordinance with strict standards which would eliminate the sulfur dioxide problem.[1] True to the Chicago tradition, Singer's ordinance was buried in Committee. But it remained there ticking like a timebomb. If public pressure became too great, this bomb would explode and end the comfortable relationship between Commonwealth Edison and an overly friendly city administration.

Then came the November pollution inversion. In their outrage concerned individuals and groups turned first to the Illinois Commerce Commission, which happened to be holding hearings on a proposed Commonwealth Edison rate increase. I.C.C. hearings are traditionally held in a small hearing room at the State of Illinois office building across from City Hall. The room was too small for the crowd which wanted to testify against proposed rate increases. Many citizens couldn't get in the room even after climbing nineteen floors of stairs. This fight to attend I.C.C. hearings provided the first direct action of the anti-pollution battle of 1970. Stimulated by Alinsky-trained organizers from the Industrial Areas Foundation, these frustrated citizens formed the base for the Campaign Against Pollution.

Recognizing that the I.C.C. hearing alone could not win the

anti-pollution battle, CAP began the hard work of merging individuals into a single force with common anti-pollution goals and strategies. In December, 1970, the Boul Mich Bar and Restaurant directly underneath the Industrial Areas Foundation offices on Michigan Avenue became the site for regular meetings of community and anti-pollution leaders from throughout the city. From these two dozen leaders a steering committee was formed to plan the first public meetings of the new citywide CAP. During this early period students from the Industrial Areas Foundation worked hard to build a mass base for action.

CAP's first public meeting, held on January 15, 1970, was chaired by an Episcopalian minister, Rev. John Penn. Penn was a good choice. As a man of the cloth, he was reassuring to the middle class from which the movement would have to draw its support. This first meeting attracted several hundred people. CAP's program of action included 1) participation in a final hearing before the I.C.C., 2) a drive to obtain individual and institutional pledges to cut off payment of electric bills if Commonwealth Edison did not reduce its pollution, and 3) an effort to obtain sufficient stock and stock proxies to gain admission for thousands of people to the April stockholders meeting of Commonwealth Edison. From the perspective of building a mass organization, the least important of the three tactics was continued participation in I.C.C. hearings. When BPI and CACC planned for an enlarged citizens hearing, CAP had to participate. Its major emphasis, however, stayed with direct action.

Immediately after the I.C.C. confrontation and the January meeting, CAP began direct negotiations with Commonwealth Edison. Thomas Ayers, president of Commonwealth Edison had previous experience with union negotiations and saw meetings between management and its opponents as natural. When the president of Commonwealth Edison recognized CAP as a legitimate pressure group, it couldn't be a subversive organization. This public identification of CAP as the official anti-pollution group speeded the mobilization under CAP's banner and fostered new branches in many Chicago neighborhoods. Had it ignored CAP, Edison might have squelched the movement before it began. On the other hand, had Edison granted CAP's minimal demands for a timetable for ending the company's sulfur dioxide pollution, the dramatic issue would have been eliminated and CAP would have been impotent. But once officially and publicly at loggerheads, CAP became a formidable threat to Edison.

During January and February, 1970, the pollution battle centered on negotiations with the utility and on community meetings where Edison officials tried to sell the public their company's policy on pollution. February 26, 1970, brought the first direct action against the company. It was a classic example of institutional ju-jitsu. CAP members went to the First National Bank of Chicago, which occupied the ground floor of the building where Commonwealth Edison had its offices. Protestors stood in line to get pennies in change for various sums of money. The pennies were then scotch taped onto flyers, saying that Commonwealth Edison spent only pennies to eliminate its air pollution. Forty demonstrators, several wearing gas masks to dramatize the issue, went to the front of the building, which served as entrance to both the bank and the elevators to Edison's offices. Incoming patrons were handed the flyers. The hope was to tie up the bank enough to cause its president to call Commonwealth Edison and complain that our demonstrations were harming his business. Institutional ju-jitsu was used to draw the First National Bank into the battle because it had more influence with Commonwealth Edison than CAP did. The attempt to use the bank's power against Edison was based on manipulating the bank's own self-interest, not by an appeal to idealism. After distributing all of the leaflets the crowd went upstairs in mass to meet with Byron Lee, a Commonwealth Edison official, to demand a timetable for pollution control.

This demonstration had several virtues. It pitted the bank against the company. Moreover, it provided a good introduction to direct action for CAP members who had never been involved in demonstrations. No one was arrested, no one was hurt. The action was novel and fun, and broke the routines of housewives, students, and professionals. It provided citizens, who had never expressed their frustrations and anger, the satisfaction of telling off company officials. The failure of most civic projects stems

from endless, dull talk which gets nowhere. In contrast, participants in "the great penny bank raid" came away enthusiastic
enough to recruit others for later skirmishes.

The demonstration at the Commonwealth Edison office forced
company officials to face a large number of unhappy customers.
The confrontation with Byron Lee disturbed the normally efficient office, as both secretaries and executives came to see what
was happening. Finally, this demonstration set the stage for further battles because CAP members learned first-hand that the company's uncompromising response to citizens' reasonable requests
served to expand and arouse a constituency ready to press for
even stronger action.

In March, the focus of anti-pollution groups switched back to
the Illinois Commerce Commission with BPI and CACC taking
the lead. Notices were sent to CACC's wide mailing list. Ads
were taken in local newspapers to publicize commission hearings.
A training session was held at the University of Illinois, so that
experts could brief citizens on facts about pollution and suggest
realistic demands to be made of the I.C.C. CAP also joined the
effort and helped to get witnesses. With this preparation, several
hundred witnesses appeared at a special I.C.C. citizen hearing
on the evening of March 10th at Northwestern University Law
School. Despite vigorous cross-examination by the lawyer for
Commonwealth Edison in an attempt to discredit witnesses, the
public outcry for pollution control was unmistakable. Three
months later in rendering its decision, the I.C.C. granted Commonwealth Edison's rate increase *only* on the express condition
that the new revenue be used to install anti-pollution devices.
This decision partially vindicated BPI's and CACC's confidence
in the I.C.C. and the regulatory process. However, effective pollution control could not be gained by appeal to the I.C.C. alone.

After the March hearing, CAP looked for another target. Negotiations and demonstrations at the company headquarters were
not producing results. An intermediate target was needed to bring
more pressure on the company and build the organization before
the stockholders meeting a month off. Signing pledges to withhold
payment of bills was a good organizing tactic, but too few had

been collected to make an actual boycott successful. A new target was needed. CAP strategists chose the City Council and Mayor Daley as the focus for the next action.

Meetings were held with aldermen and Democratic ward committeemen in various wards. The most colorful, and perhaps the most important, were two meetings with Alderman Kuda of the 23rd Ward. He represented a conservative, white ethnic ward on the southwest side. It was significant that he became the target of his working class constituents, who suffered directly from the fumes of a nearby Commonwealth Edison plant. Mayor Daley could ignore liberal troublemakers from the upper middle class area along the lake but not white ethnic voters who, along with Blacks, were the backbone of the machine.

Father Leonard Dubi led several hundred southwest side residents in the two confrontations with Alderman Kuda. At the first meeting Father Dubi and CAP supporters pressed the Alderman to get them an appointment with the mayor so they could demand his support of legislation to regulate Commonwealth Edison's pollution. They returned two weeks later, only to have Alderman Kuda present spokesmen from Commonwealth Edison and city agencies to explain why there was no pollution problem and, even if there was a problem, why it couldn't be easily solved. CAP members had already sat through several earlier meetings with Edison apologists. Enraged at the alderman's duplicity, they marched out of the meeting several hundred strong while Alderman Kuda frantically denounced them as S.D.S. revolutionaries.

CAP members also met with Alderman Wigoda (49th Ward), Alderman Kerwin (46th Ward), and Democratic Ward Committeeman Korshak (5th Ward). These lesser officials were quick to call the mayor to tell him that they were receiving unprecedented pressure from their voters on the pollution issue. Because of these events, an ordinance, similar to the one introduced by Singer the previous June, was introduced in the City Council under the mayor's name. The mayor's ordinance was introduced on April 8, and CAP was granted an audience with the mayor on April 13th. Alderman Wigoda, who helped arrange the meeting, had expected a delegation of twenty-five. CAP neglected to tell him that in addition to the twenty-five leaders they were also bringing five hundred supporters to wait at the mayor's office door during their meeting. Clearly CAP had no strength unless they represented voters. So they brought people with them as a living testimony to the power of the anti-pollution issue. Angered by this mob of people, the mayor refused to meet. So CAP supporters, after an hour-and-a-half wait, marched back to Commonwealth Edison's offices and began the battle directly with the company again.

The city's political leaders had been drawn unwittingly into the arena. The mayor and his aldermen were on the spot. They had been publicly asked to protect people from air pollution. Now they were taking the heat for Commonwealth Edison. It is one thing to help out a friendly company like Edison, but to lose votes just to protect them was asking too much. Politicians could not publicly support the company against the voters for long. Again, tactics of institutional ju-jitsu were being applied. Pressure against political leaders caused them to push the company for a change in policy. A few demonstrations at company offices might be borne by the company, but pressure from the city government which regulated them, granted their franchise, and allowed them a continued monopoly meant that some accommodation had to be made.

While CAP confronted aldermen and the mayor directly, CACC and BPI joined with a dozen other civic organizations on April 22nd to participate in national "Earth Day" demonstrations. Under the leadership of Joe Karganis and John Kirkwood, several thousand people rallied at the Civic Center. The political speeches were mostly platitudes, but the significance of a gathering of several thousand "respectable" people in the Civic Center was not lost on the mayor and officials in City Hall across the street. Clearly these polite demonstrations held at many different locations in Chicago as well as in other major cities across the country on "Earth Day" signaled smart politicians that they needed to find ways to ride this bandwagon. Thus, pressure for government action continued to build.

Alinsky might term these Earth Day demonstrations examples of unpointed action. And, in fact, across most of the nation Earth Day brought little concrete results. Similarly, Earth Day organizers might say that CAP confrontations frightened citizens. Taken together, the direct action by CAP and the respectable rallies by BPI and CACC provided a greater combined force than either of them could provide separately.

The final trump was played by CAP at the April 27, 1970 stockholders' meeting of Commonwealth Edison. Company management had several hundred thousand proxy votes to insure continued control. Despite appeals to the Security Exchange Commission, Edison had prevented CAP from breaking down large blocks of stock into separate proxies for each CAP member. So, only a few hundred CAP supporters were allowed inside the stockholders' meeting. While some churches and universities supported CAP, most Edison stockholders remained primarily concerned with profits, not pollution. But outside the meeting, two thousand CAP members were demanding a change in company policies. CAP members inside the meeting were able to put their demands before the stockholders and the meeting's agenda was suspended to allow discussion of the pollution problem. When CAP demanded an immediate program to eliminate Edison's sulfur dioxide pollution, the chairman simply adjourned the meeting without acting upon the demands.

Had CAP failed? The same officers still controlled Edison. CAP didn't have nearly enough votes to dislodge them. CAP hadn't even been able to get most of its supporters into the meeting. Although the stockholders had discussed the company's sulfur dioxide pollution, the meeting was adjourned before any official action was taken on the issue. There would not be a stockholders' meeting for another year; there would be no second chance. This meeting had been the principal focus for CAP from the beginning. Now it was over. Did it mean the end of CAP, the end of the anti-pollution battle? Did it mean defeat?

Fortunately, this nonviolent issue campaign was won, not lost. There had never been any hope of outvoting the Edison board of directors. This was not even CAP's intent. The stockholders' confrontation had been only another way of escalating the campaign. The "have nots" and "have littles," as Alinsky called them, never have the money or the votes by themselves to win a direct contest. What they have is their bodies, the justice of their demands, and their willingness to put unbearable pressure on decision-makers to force decisions in their favor. CAP, CACC, and

BPI were right about sulfur dioxide pollution harming every Chicagoan. They were right that the principal polluter was Commonwealth Edison. As they dramatized their demands, as they raised the public consciousness of the problem and possible solutions, they began to mobilize massive support. This support was visible in public demonstrations.

The combination of public support in the meetings with aldermen and the mayor, huge Earth Day rallies, and several thousand people at the Edison stockholders' meeting forced governmental action which the company dared not oppose. On April 29, 1970, Alderman Singer's revised ordinance, now known as the Mayor's Ordinance, to curb sulfur dioxide pollution, passed the Chicago City Council and became law. It was much more restrictive than the ordinance from which the mayor had exempted Commonwealth Edison less than a year before. It caused industries and homes alike to switch to low sulfur coal, to change energy sources, to phase out old furnaces, and to develop new anti-pollution devices to clean all emissions. It was total victory in this first battle against air pollution in Chicago.

The Chicago City Council has since gone on to pass a series of ordinances to protect the environment, including outlawing phosphate detergents and establishing an automobile testing program to reduce carbon monoxide pollution. In 1970 the city reached a major watershed in control of pollution; and very concrete changes have been made to lessen air, water, and noise pollution since then. As a victory of citizen organizations against the combined power of Big Business and the Chicago Democratic Machine, this anti-pollution battle is proof of what can be done in a well-run issue campaign. Although the three groups involved had somewhat different ideologies and strategies, they focused on a common target and applied enough pressure to win a very sizable victory.

Perhaps the most important result of the anti-pollution battle was to build enlarged and strengthened organizations. BPI has continued to file important lawsuits in the public interest. CACC has continued to push pollution regulatory agencies, particularly at the state level. Several of its leaders have been appointed to state and federal posts within new government anti-pollution agencies. CAP has had the most remarkable growth of all. It soon changed its name from the Campaign Against Pollution to Citizens Action Program and embarked on campaigns against steel companies which pollute the water, against the Chicago school board which neglects education priorities, against developers and local government which fail to preserve the lakefront, and against an unnecessary Crosstown Expressway. From the victory against Commonwealth Edison, CAP gained the resources and popular recognition to launch a variety of other campaigns on behalf of a more aroused citizenry. In a real sense this is the foremost goal of a nonviolent issue campaign—to create a permanent, viable citizens' organization capable of undertaking new battles. In this sense, especially, the anti-pollution battle in Chicago was extraordinarily successful.

Lessons From the Anti-Pollution Campaign

The anti-pollution battle in Chicago and the writings of Martin Luther King and Saul Alinsky suggest the following steps to be followed in a nonviolent issue campaign:

1. Organize people and community groups together in an organization focused on immediate, practical, gut-level, self-interest issues with an identifiable, visible enemy. Paid organizers and researchers will have to be used to pull people together and to propose a strategy.
2. Make demands on the enemy so that his overreaction provides a basis for further organization. It is important that demands be phrased in terms of justice and that they be so costly to the enemy that they can not be granted lightly.
3. Gain official recognition from the enemy by direct negotiation or confrontation. This is crucial to give the group new stature as a legitimate negotiator.
4. Organize imaginative nonviolent demonstrations to back up demands, to gain publicity, and to hurt the enemy's image. Often status quo institutions and their leaders sur-

vive entirely on unjustified reputations for power or benev-
olence. By standing up to bullies and by demanding that
good talkers do good works, you can either get opponents
to act in your favor or you can undercut their base of support while enhancing your own.

5. Attack allied institutions so that they will put pressure on
   the enemy to settle the dispute in your favor. In the Chicago anti-pollution battle, other institutions like the First
   National Bank and city officials were pulled into the action
   arena against their will and forced to pressure Commonwealth Edison.

6. Keep up the attack until you win your demands or at least
   enough of them to declare a victory. Organizations which
   do not win at least some battles within their first year usually go out of existence.

7. Follow up to make sure that the promised policies are carried out by the enemy. If not, attack your enemy again for
   going back on his word.

8. Locate a new enemy for your now enlarged citizens group
   to attack. By now you should have an experienced cadre
   of activists, enough credibility, and good leadership to take
   on bigger battles.

Most successful nonviolent issue campaigns are carefully nour-
ished by skilled organizers.[2] However, they do not usually begin
in totally unorganized communities. In the case of the anti-pollution campaign in Chicago, there were already many civic and
church groups concerned about the problem. The trick was to
bring them together to plan a common program, to develop agreement on the type of direct action to take, and to pool all members and resources in a concerted attack.

As Alinsky has said, "An organization needs action as an individual needs oxygen."[3] The early confrontations at the I.C.C.
hearings gave oxygen to the Campaign Against Pollution, and
laid a foundation for CAP's further growth. Citizens will act only
if they get excited. When people are aware of their troubles, anx-
ious about a problem, and angry, they will act. As Alinsky has
pointed out:

The organizer dedicated to changing the life of a partic-

ular community must first rub raw the resentments of
the people of the community; fan the latent hostilities of
many of the people to the point of overt expression. He
must search out controversy and issues, rather than
avoid them, for unless there is controversy people are
not concerned enough to act.[4]

Organizers do not placate, they agitate with a purpose. They
seek to direct popular dissatisfaction into an organization which
can eliminate injustices. In the film "The Troublemakers" Tom
Hayden talks about the effort of organizers to channel anger into
action and to overcome the doubt and despair in the Newark ghetto:

What they [the organizers] argue is that united action
might build power. If people come together, decide what
issues they want to attack and how best to attack them,
an effective movement for change might begin in the
neighborhood. . . . If so many angry people can come together, maybe something can be done. But if that anger
is not focused on an action, meetings become repetitious,
nothing is decided, people get discouraged, and stop
coming.[5]

Anyone can call a meeting, but meetings alone cannot build a
citizen's organization. Mass meetings are useful to plan for actions
and to finalize decisions. But neither endless meetings nor un-
directed action can create organizations. Successful organizing
requires channeling discontent into constructive action; thereby
strengthening the organization so that its goals can be attained.

A nonviolent issue campaign requires direct action but it also
requires building, person by person, a strong membership organization which can sustain months of demonstrations. A single demonstration brings attention to a problem but by itself solves nothing. Numerous demonstrations are often necessary to force
compliance from a strong opponent. So the key task, on which
the success or failure of everything else depends, is not to put together a one-shot demonstration but to create and maintain an
ever-growing citizen organization capable of action over a long
period of time. Organizations with enough strength and staying
power usually need paid, full-time organizers to research oppon-

ents' weakness, to help plan meetings and demonstrations, and to do the myriad communication and logistical work required for effective action and growth.

Seldom are these citizen organizations completely democratic in their internal procedures. They are democratic in that members are not forced to participate but do so because they want to fight a common problem. Members can also reject leaders, if they think them unfit. They can suggest ideas and are frequently asked, as individuals, what they think should be done. In addition, they can always reject tactics and refuse to participate in unwise demonstrations.

On the other hand, the fact remains that an effective organization is an action organization, not a discussion group. Success often means that decisions must be made on the spot, and seldom is there time for debate. An effective group adapts immediately to changing situations. It votes quickly, often "with its feet." Winning requires acting on the quick choices made by leaders. If their judgment is faulty in one battle, they can be replaced before the next.

The Chicago anti-polution campaign also teaches us how to plan successful demonstrations. First, a demonstration must fit within an overall strategy. Tactics, whether they be demonstrations, press releases, or campaign speeches, must conform to an overall plan of attack. A successful campaign must cut the issue and define the situation consistently. Effective tactics are pointed at a particular opponent and designed for a final victory.

Second, a demonstration requires demonstrators. This means convincing potential participants to join the action. Few demonstrations involving five or ten people are successful; most require at least fifty people. In Birmingham Dr. King at first led only 67 people, although hundreds later participated. The early CAP demonstration at First National Bank began with about forty to fifty people.

Ultimately, a successful pressure strategy may require several hundred or even several thousand demonstrators. They will not appear by magic. They must be asked, and they individually choose to participate. Each one must be contacted and encouraged to join. Remember the poster: "Suppose they gave a war and nobody came." Wars can't occur without soldiers. Peaceful struggles for freedom and justice can't either. But there are no standing armies for freedom. They must be recruited each time. Participation can never be safely assumed or taken for granted. Each confrontation must be larger and more exciting than the last. Selecting the right enemy, planning exciting demonstrations can help, but each person still must be asked individually to participate.

Third, in addition to fitting tactics into an overall strategy and getting demonstrators, organizers must also consider physical factors. For example, the geographical and logistical aspects of the site should be studied in advance. Where should the picket line be to cause the maximum number of customers and workers to respect the boycott? How many people are needed to fill an official's conference room? Picket signs, arm bands, name tags, and other props need to be prepared and distributed at the right time to the right people.

Fourth, actions must be coordinated. Training sessions are needed to instruct demonstrators as to what they must—and must not—do. In the civil rights movement, participants were trained by playing the roles of demonstrator, policeman, and hostile bystander. Through these sessions, they gained the self-confidence to act nonviolently even in the face of violence. The anti-pollution campaign in Chicago was much less demanding. But organization spokesmen had to be identified and marshalls made sure people got to the proper place at the proper time, were encouraged to speak up, and were restrained from foolish actions. Participants should always be trained and guided for maximum effect.

Thus, demonstrations should be planned in accordance with an over-all strategy, several hundred people should be asked to participate, the physical arrangements should be studied in advance, and demonstrators should be trained and carefully coordinated. There are dozens of other decisions—whether or not there should be singing or chanting, who will serve as group spokesman for the occasion, and so on. We wish only to stress that demonstrators do not find their way to the First National Bank by accident. Like most everything else, a good demonstration is the product of perspiration as well as inspiration.

An Evaluation of Nonviolent Issue Campaigns

Is a nonviolent issue campaign an effective strategy for fundamental change? We believe that it is for several reasons: 1) It directly involves a large number of people in actions which they can take to solve their own problems; 2) it focuses on specific, achievable goals as opposed to vague, unobtainable ends; 3) it may bring tension, frustration, and public demonstrations, but it stops short of violence, thus avoiding repression, which violent tactics so frequently bring in their wake; 4) it allows direct action to be taken immediately on a problem. We do not have to wait for an election, which may be years away, nor for the issue to come up on the agenda of some bureaucracy; 5) determined minorities who can arouse general public sympathy with their cause can win battles when they do not have the numbers to win elections nor trained members to compete inside the power structure.

Participatory strategies, such as nonviolent issue campaigns, are naturally preferred by those who believe in democracy, *provided that they work.* Our system of government is supposed to be a democracy but it fails to provide mechanisms for participation except for voting and writing to elected representatives. Both are shams, because voters are manipulated and letters are ignored. Hiring a lobbyist to represent a pressure group may be more effective than writing letters, but it leaves government in the hands of the few.

In contrast, nonviolent issue campaigns involve many people directly in practical solutions of their own problems. Thousands of citizens participated in various civil rights demonstrations during the 1960's. And they achieved concrete, if limited, results. Most who participated were ennobled by the very act of standing up for themselves, and they learned more about their government and economy than they ever learned in school. If lobbyists, administrators, or elected officials win victories for people, citizens are forever made dependent upon them for further progress. When people act together in an issue campaign like the civil rights movement, citizen organizations emerge. They are no longer dependent on someone else to solve their problems; they can do it themselves. A permanent, watchful citizenry is born, jealous of their rights and experienced in the tactics of direct action.

Nonviolent issue strategies are practical, as well as participatory. They are aimed at specific, achievable goals. They mobilize enough people to make it difficult for an enemy to refuse. Good rhetoric and high sounding purposes never hurt an issue campaign, but the key job is to translate general goals into specific demands and sympathy into direct action. By getting the sulfur dioxide pollution reduced in Chicago, CAP was able to build resources for even bolder battles.

Neither vague goals nor vague promises from public officials are a substitute for concrete victories by people themselves. People cannot live on hope alone. They must have evidence that their efforts have an effect. Nonviolent issue campaigns may have long-range goals, but the success of a particular campaign is measured by short-run, specific victories.

Issue strategies avoid violence and the repression that almost always follows. In the American revolution and some other revolutions for independence, violence may have been necessary. Yet when a new regime is installed by violence, as in Russia in 1917, a civil war and repression of all dissent may result. If a dissident movement fails, as did the socialists in the Weimer Republic, repression sometimes ends in a fascist regime. Until nonviolent strategies become impossible, they are preferable to violent strategies because fewer people are killed and important gains can be made. The fabric of society, although stretched by the tensions of nonviolent conflict, can provide a base for a better society. Riots are unproductive; violent confrontations only draw attention to problems while leaving them unresolved. But nonviolent issue campaigns provide immediate solutions to some problems and lay a foundation for long-term institutional change. Instead of repression they bring an accommodation, which both grants concrete demands and gives power for the first time to many citizens who have been excluded from decision-making.

Issue strategies have the further advantage of allowing immediate action on specific problems. While this technique cannot instantly eliminate major social problems like racial discrimination, they can open up particular segregated facilities in a hurry. This speed is important. Moreover, as we pointed out in the previous chapter, an issue campaign can pave the way for an administrative or electoral strategy. Thus, an issue campaign on the Chicago schools could thrust new administrators into power or provide campaign issues for candidates in a mayoral election.

Finally, issue strategies are particularly useful to minorities. The intensity of a group's concern can be focused more successively in an issue campaign than in an electoral campaign, where all votes count the same. Nonviolent issue campaigns are effective for people who have been powerless and for people who have just complaints against an economic and political system which has taken them for granted.

Issue campaigns also have weaknesses. Surprisingly, one problem arises with those community groups who win their battles. Alinsky was often asked if he felt guilty about starting the Back of the Yards Council. This group in Mayor Daley's neighborhood had originally fought the oppressive conditions around the stockyards. Once these citizens became organized and attained power, some critics have charged that they became racists, supporters of the less than liberal city administration, and corrupt in handling their finances. The truth of these charges is not our concern here. The question remains: once a group is organized, will they repress others as they were once repressed? There is, of course, no guarantee that this will not occur, but it is unrealistic to bypass a useful strategy to lift a particular group out of their misery because it doesn't also produce the brotherhood of man.

Building any group and planning any action is always a gamble. To act in history is always to act on faith—faith that more good than evil will result. The effect of a strategy can be calculated to some degree. But to know what will happen to an organization a decade from now or to foresee the historical result of a demonstration undertaken today is beyond anyone's capabilities. We can try to guide the course of history, but the outcome of an action will remain uncertain—and probably always mixed.

A second problem with nonviolent issue campaigns is that while they may bring immediate victories, they are less effective in dealing with broad problems. For example, it is difficult to be sure that the antiwar movement helped to end the Vietnam War. Even if it did, certainly it is hard to claim that the movement had any great effect on the foreign policy which gets us into wars. Demonstrations and nonviolent issue campaigns are a beginning, but other strategies must be employed to change permanently government policies.

For the powerless, for those who care deeply about an issue, for those concerned with justice, for those who face issues which must be acted on immediately, nonviolent issue campaigns are an important lever for change. Whatever the weaknesses of this strategy, the ability of people to act together on their problems, to confront directly their oppressors is a great advantage. Nonviolent issue campaigns are a valuable weapon in the arsenal for change. No group need remain silent. No problem need go unexposed. Neither private power nor government authority need go unchallenged.

PART V

A Time For Change

The Signing of The Declaration of Independence, Courtesy Yale University Art Gallery.

Chapter 8

Strategies for Change

> *To every thing there is a season,*
> *and a time to every purpose under the heaven:*
> *A time to be born, and a time to die;*
> *A time to plant, and a time to pluck*
> *up that which is planted;*
> *A time to kill, and a time to heal;*
> *A time to break down, and a time to build up; . . .*
> *A time to rend and a time to sew;*
> *A time to keep silence and a time to speak . . .*
>
> Ecclesiastes 3:1-7

We believe ours to be a time for change. Since the Second World War, much that has been built up in America's first two centuries has changed. We are no longer a rural society but an urban one. We are no longer an isolated nation but a major imperialist power. Times and beliefs and authorities and mores have changed. Ivy no longer grows on university walls. People leave their spouses for other lovers. Drugs destroy many of our generation. Government officials regularly lie to us. Those who were slaves are free but not yet equal in our society. What was sacred is now profane. What was stable is now in flux. What were revolutionary institutions two centuries ago are reactionary institutions today. Our society continues to fall apart.

Where old institutions have broken down, it is time to build up again. Now that the silence of the fifties and the hysteria of the sixties is past, it is time to talk quietly with one another as to what kind of America we will build for ourselves. We can plant

161

new seeds of hope where the land has been cleared, swept clean of old growth.

We are not neutral. Our own goals are to speed the end of repression and enlarge both freedom and responsibility. These are the seeds we would plant. We do not believe that working within the system through political parties, lobbying, or administrative influence will bring our ends. Revolutions, riots, and confrontations seem equally unproductive. We conclude that greater freedom, justice, and equality can only result from new strategies, ones which involve more people directly in deciding their own destiny. New approaches require new spokespeople, new strategies, and new organizations. We write this book to encourage others to join us in the struggle for change. By sharing our dreams and our experiences, we may deepen your commitment, your knowledge, and your ability to help in the reconstruction of America.

There are few schools for strategists and no almanacs to tell when to plant and when to pluck up. We hope our book may help some of you to become strategists. Others of you may begin to understand better the tasks which you have already undertaken. Still others at work in scattered towns and cities around the country will know that you are not alone in the vineyard, for we toil with you.

Strategists depend on their own experiences and on those of others to teach them the art of organizing. In this book we have discussed two strategies which have been put into practice in Chicago and another that has yet to be tried. We encouraged you to think about the strengths and weaknesses of each. In addition to reporting our own experience, we have tried to demonstrate how to analyze strategic problems—what questions to ask and what answers to reject.

At the end of this book is a series of readings to help you to continue your study of strategies. We are not so much trying to sell a single strategy as to encourage the skills needed to assess accurately any situation and to choose an effective course of action. We are offering more than a particular ideology. We want to help you develop the ability to plan and execute your own political actions successfully. Change is coming, whether we will it or not. Either we train ourselves to control it or we place ourselves at the mercy of others bold enough to implement their plans for change.

There are certainly many important strategies other than the ones we have presented. For instance, Ralph Nader's investigative and legal strategies which involve intensive research, citizen pressure, and appearances before regulatory agencies, legislative committees, and the courts are certainly legitimate and complementary.[1] Citizen lobbying, as conducted by John Gardner's Common Cause, is certainly a useful approach in that it mobilizes thousands of people at once to pressure legislators.[2] Nader, Gardner, and many others not mentioned here serve in the legions of nonviolent, citizen-based reform movements.[3]

Reformers cannot afford to become fixed on any single strategy. Time and circumstances dictate different solutions to varying problems. Moreover, several complimentary approaches, operating at the same time and in pursuit of the same general goals, may reinforce each other, making success much more likely. If you choose an election strategy, look on those who pursue administrative and issue strategies as partners. A good example of complimentary strategies was the anti-pollution battle in Chicago. In this case loosely coordinated and parallel strategies forced Commonwealth Edison to change its policies, whereas a single strategy might have failed. Each situation must be analyzed afresh to determine which strategy or combination of strategies is most likely to win. What worked before may not work again. What failed before, when modified to meet a new circumstance, may prove successful.

Our approach is to break down the process into three essential steps: 1) define the situation accurately; 2) evaluate a range of alternatives; and 3) develop new tactics and new institutions.

A good strategic analysis begins with an assessment of the situation. The strategies presented here were developed only after the realities of our electoral system, our bureaucratic society, and our public and private institutions were studied. Effective strategies conform to the facts of the situation—the fact that there are over half a million elected officials, that large bureaucracies dominate most of a citizen's life, and that powerful institutions and officials perpetuate harmful policies. No matter which course re-

formers choose, they must face the facts of a situation, while remaining idealistic enough to see the potential for changing the
status quo. Strategists must have the vision to know what must be
changed along with the practical wisdom to know how to change it.

Having defined the situation correctly, the next step is to evaluate alternatives. Traditional strategies usually fail because they
are no longer realistic; too often the reality changes but the strategies do not. For example, writing a letter to a legislator in order
to change the school bureaucracy is futile because mail seldom·
determines the votes of lawmakers. Even if they agree with your
letter, they no longer control the schools. Riots and revolutions
are also unlikely to work in a bureaucratic society. As Alinsky
put it, when the other side has all the guns, we are foolish to
choose a violent tactic. In every case it is important to pinpoint
exactly why a previous strategy will not work in the situation we
now face.

The final step is to create a strategy which is both realistic and
involves participation, equality, and justice. It is our experience
that new movements are always needed to execute new strategies.
New institutions are the main vehicles for change. Old institutions
usually are too rigid and too tradition-bound either to transform
themselves or to bring about change. Finally, our strategies and
institutions must practice the principles we are urging society to
adopt. They must be realistic, nonviolent, and participatory.
*Creating these new institutions as both examples and vehicles of
change is the supreme task.*

Propositions for Effective Strategies

> *. . . there are rules for radicals who want to change their
> world; there are certain concepts of action in human
> politics that operate regardless of the scene or time.*
>
>   Saul Alinsky

On the basis of our experience in Chicago and our analysis
of various strategies, we suggest eleven guides for action. It is all

well and good for us to say that a situation must be properly defined, that inadequate strategies should be carefully analyzed, and that new approaches should conform to certain basic principles. But we also believe that there are some hard, practical facts which must be considered:

1. *There is a need for some full-time staff.* Only full-time staff can provide the communication with and coordination of hundreds of members, numerous groups, and disparate activities. Some members of the movement must be able and willing to devote all of their time to building and strengthening the organization. Staff alone cannot make a successful movement, but neither can a successful movement be created without full-time personnel. Someone has to channel the energies of volunteers and help both leaders and members to use their limited time effectively.

2. *The staff must be professional and possess specific skills.* America is run by those who possess the required skills and knowledge for the key positions in this industrial society. Amateurs generally lose if faced with experts on the side of the status quo. In addition to the typing, filing, and clerical skills necessary to any organization, the movement requires professional skills in organization, use of the media, and fund-raising. Some of these skills may be possessed by volunteers but the paid staff must have real skills. Some strategies also require special expertise in the the electoral process, the law, or the operation of large bureaucracies.

3. *Effective strategies for fundamental change require significant amounts of money.* Funds are needed to pay the salaries of the full-time staff and for communication—typewriters, stationery, stamps, telephones, mimeograph machines, printed brochures, and posters. Money is required to rent space for the office staff and sometimes for meetings. Publicity in newspaper ads, billboards, press releases, photographs, and use of news wire services all have to be paid for. Poorly financed, part-time, amateurish efforts generally fail. While the establishment will always have greater financial resources than reform movements, we must raise enough money to pay a professional staff, provide office space, and communicate with potential supporters.

4. *We need the active support and participation of a relatively*

small percentage of the total population. All citizens in an electoral
district do not have to be cranked up for fundamental change.
To "raise the consciousness of the masses" would require impossible efforts and resources. The movement may, in fact, change
the attitudes of a majority of citizens over a long period of time,
but a strategy with that immediate goal is destined for failure.
Let's face it, most people are not concerned most of the time about
politics. Most people become involved only when an issue or an
election involves their self-interest. So, a relatively small group
of activists can usually carry the day against the more apathetic,
less informed public.

Given this situation, our principal aim is to defeat that other
relatively small group which is on the other side of the fence. They,
too, are well trained and organized but for different priorities.
Thus, politics, even in a democracy, is primarily an intense struggle
among a relatively few partisans.

We are not suggesting strategies which two or three friends can
execute. Successful methods require mobilizing and training hundreds of active workers and attracting at least minimal support
from thousands of people.

5. *Strategies for fundamental change rely primarily on the
professional middle class.* For some issues, such as civil rights
and minimum wages, working class people and other nonprofes-
sionals are vital. However, only those in the professional, middle
economic strata generally have the skills, financial resources, and
institutional positions required for extensive social change. Reliance upon the professional middle class does not mean that laborers, the unemployed, or the poor are precluded from important
roles and positions in the movement for change. But strategies
which fail to attract and to use effectively the professional middle
class are probably doomed. No matter which other groups participate or which goals are sought, the middle class will be the
backbone of the campaign. In addition to the professional middle
class, we hasten to add that *a campaign must bring together all
those concerned with an issue, regardless of race, economic level,
or occupation.* Those protecting the status quo almost instinctively
adopt a strategy of divide and conquer. Historically, they often

win. To win reforms, a movement must unite people across class and racial divisions.

The situation today makes unified action by whites and non-whites difficult to achieve. Furthermore, unions further pit those in different jobs against each other. Yet, in fact, the major issues and problems now facing the United States cut across occupations, economic levels, and racial groupings. It thus becomes critical for those who agree on specific issues to unite. Reformers must not allow themselves to be pitted against each other.

7. *Activists must be willing to participate in a variety of different projects.* Someone who participates in an election campaign is in no way disqualified from joining a nonviolent issue campaign or an administrative fight. Individuals can work on a variety of issues in different ways, gaining in the process a deeper understanding of the difficulty and the potential for change.

Everything cannot be done at once. All wrongs cannot be righted by a single organization or campaign. Thus, it is important for both individuals and the movement as a whole to select carefully and flexibly those particular battles which will attract strong support. Particularly in these confusing times, flexibility and a good sense of timing are crucial.

8. *Activists must participate in various positions as both leaders and followers.* Although there is a need for organization, specialized skills, and discipline, long term effectiveness in a basically volunteer movement is best attained when positions of responsibility are shared. Rotation of leadership positions develops new skills throughout the membership, allows former leaders some time off, and provides a quiet interval for those who begin to lose their creative edge and need to think issues through again. In a strong movement, a precinct worker in one campaign may serve as a campaign manager in the next and then as a poll watcher the following year. It is healthy to rotate leadership roles so that every participant has a chance to lead. We are not basing our hopes on saints who work 24 hours a day, 365 days a year, but on experienced citizens who are periodically willing to sacrifice some comfort for both the responsibility and satisfaction of participation.

9. *An effective strategy is one that wins.* Social movements need victories—visible progress toward goals. Although a few hardy soldiers can be sustained by their own personal commitment, broad support requires that specific goals be won—and be won early. To keep alive a group like IPO we had to elect Bill Singer alderman in 1969. To create the broader civil rights movement, Dr. King had to win the Montgomery bus boycott. Alinsky sustained his community groups by concrete victories, which then became the base for greater efforts.

By actually winning an election, by actually taking over power within bureaucracies like the Chicago school system, or by winning an issue battle with a major corporation, movement participants can see the fruits of their labors. Their successes attract new members. Situations must be defined so that such wins are possible with enough hard work. Concrete victories, not martyrdom and losses, create fundamental change.

10. *Strategies increase their effectiveness by providing psychological rewards for participants.* As Alinsky pointed out, "People hunger for drama and adventure, for a breath of life in a dreary, drab existence.... Through the organization and its power [the citizen] will get his birth certificate for life . . . he will become known. . . things will change from the drabness of a life where all that changes is the calendar."[4]

Concrete victories, of course, provide important psychological rewards. But more than success is needed. An effective strategy must encourage active participation, not passive membership. The IPO in Chicago, for example, through its Ward and General Assemblies allows members to determine policies and to control the organization. By requiring participation and making it effective, IPO gives its members a sense of efficacy. By its very structure, IPO members are recognized as valuable and gain a sense of power.

A strategy for change brings people out from isolation into community, from apathy to involvement, from subservience to responsible citizenship. With the early Greeks, we believe that joining actively in political life is part of human development—without it we are less than human.

11. *Effective strategies use existing power to achieve new*

goals. Strategies must be constructed in light of the realities of power. Alinsky organizations, for example, use institutional jujitsu to pit powerful institutions against each other. Similarly, if power resides with stockholders, then Alinsky organizations obtain stock proxies and attend stockholder meetings. In the same way administrative strategists use the power of insiders as a base for change. Electoral techniques use the power of voters and independent political institutions to bring change. Successful strategies use existing power to achieve new goals. Power must be discovered and molded to our purposes, it cannot be created from nothing. Strategists harness currents of history and use this power for their own ends. Our job is not to create power but to direct existing power to build a new America.

To conclude then, effective strategies for fundamental change require professional, full-time staff; enough money to provide essential resources; the active support from members of the professional middle class; and generalized support across race, economic, and occupational lines. The movement must be flexible in its selection of targets and must have members willing to play a variety of roles in different campaigns. Both concrete victories and psychological rewards are essential. Existing power must be harnessed to achieve freedom, justice, and equality. A movement might possess all of these characteristics and still fail, but without most of them, it is unlikely that we can succeed.

Institution-Building

We believe that those who are affected by the decisions of government must be consulted by those who govern. It is the right of a citizen to have access to the instruments of power; it is his duty to learn to use them effectively and wisely. . . .

The Independent Precinct Organization is a means to achieve this program for the community at large. We will serve as well to make visible a political community which is at once energetic and humane. All who have a

*stake in our decisions will participate in making them;
all who participate will share the responsibility for implementation. By fostering responsible citizen participation in public affairs, by promoting fresh, responsive political leadership, by demonstrating in our ways of work
the wisdom of popular democracy, we seek to bring
about a new political order in our community.*

Independent Precinct
Organization Charter

It is not enough to dream of change. It is not enough to act
uprightly as individuals. Without new institutions there can be
no radical, substantive change. Old institutions have become too
fossilized to change themselves. To fight for new goals through
established institutions is to carry the impossible burden of dead
structures and entrenched authorities. Those who would bring
fundamental change must build new institutions to serve as the
vehicles for change or else court defeat. Without institution-
builders, then, no strategy of change can succeed, no permanent
victories can be won.

The strategies we have advocated in this book all require new
groups to undertake them. Independent electoral campaigns call
for an Independent Precinct Organization. Administrative strategies call for a new movement of insiders and outsiders. The Civil
Rights movement requires a Southern Christian Leadership Conference. An anti-pollution battle requires a Campaign Against
Pollution. Such organizations are painstakingly put together by
strategists who combine a theoretical understanding of institution-
building, a concrete knowledge of the reality they face, deeply
felt personal beliefs, an understanding of the problems which
move those they would organize, and a humane concern for the
people who might join a new institution. Of all the skills of a
strategist, this ability to create new institutions is most crucial to
fundamental and lasting change.

Each strategist, facing a unique situation, develops his or her
own method of building new institutions. However, we have some
general advice to offer. We believe that a strategist begins with
a special mix of philosophical ideas and practical experience which

result in what King called "an idea whose time has come."

We have stressed throughout this book the importance of defining the situation accurately but favorably. We have also maintained that such definitions do not come from ivory tower contemplation; rather, they are born of an interaction between goals and experience. We must continually ask how we can best apply our ideals in real situations. Partly, our questions can best be answered by a pragmatic analysis of prior experience. If only one or two of the principles which support the status quo can be reversed and stood on their head, then a new reality can be achieved. *Therefore, to build a new institution we must understand precisely the existing ones.*

As an example of the marriage of experience and goals, let us consider attacking the Chicago Democratic machine by setting up an Independent Precinct Organization. At its simplest level the machine uses patronage jobs and payoffs to buy the precinct captains and votes which win elections. This in turn provides the jobs and spoils necessary to run the machine. We can, however, stand machine politics on its head by recruiting an army of volunteers motivated by psychological rewards. The rewards include letting the volunteers, not slatemakers, choose the candidates who best represent their ideas and concerns and providing volunteers the sense of excitement and fulfillment which comes from participating in winning campaigns. If these candidates can be elected, they can then use their power to dismantle and discredit the machine. If we understand the machine and if we understand volunteers, we can create effective new institutions by simply substituting the guiding principles of volunteer organizations for those of the machine.

Certainly, IPO was created from a marriage of idealism and experience. It was born from the experience of a common failure. Those of us who founded IPO had worked in the 1968 McCarthy-for-President campaign in Chicago's 9th Congressional District. After working for months, organizing hundreds of volunteers, and raising thousands of dollars, we still failed to elect the McCarthy delegates to the Democratic National Convention. We asked ourselves why we had failed. On the one hand, we had failed because a single six month campaign cannot match a political machine which had existed for generations. We concluded that it was foolish to disband at the end of each campaign only to start all over again at the next election.

One principle on which IPO was founded was our conviction that only a permanent, year-round organization can compete against an entrenched political machine. But not just any permanent organization would suffice. The Independent Voters of Illinois (IVI) had existed for years on the north side of Chicago as little more than a liberal discussion group. Meetings were supposed to be "fun" and guest speakers usually provided the program. IVI meetings were often social occasions, not opportunities for action. IVI had become an ingrown group of liberals talking to each other.

Another principle of the IPO was that we would be a precinct-based organization with members in every precinct committed to work both in electoral and issue campaigns. The concept of membership demanded much from IPO members but gave them the power to control the organization in return. Membership in IPO required monthly work and dues; in return, members decided which candidates and issues IPO would back. Campaigns were undertaken only if the candidates received a two-thirds vote. No special speakers entertained the members. Meetings were called primarily to make decisions, which committed the members to carry them out. Instead of a social club, IPO became a political action group.

Thus, in our quest for a pragmatic institution which could fully embody our goal of participatory politics, we began with an analysis of the political institution which had defeated us. We searched for a method of overcoming an entrenched political machine in a way which would allow for participatory politics. We concluded that if we provided every voter with information about qualified candidates running on appealing issues, we would find a large number of "plus" voters for our candidates. To compete with the patronage workers in reaching the voters we needed an army of precinct workers. To coordinate and train this army of volunteers, we had to have experienced personnel, which were the IPO members. Thus, a year round, precinct-based, psycho-

ɔgically motivated IPO defeated the Chicago Democratic machine
n several wards and in various elections.

The machine will defeat any handful of untrained volunteers,
no matter what candidate they support. But the number of patronage jobs is limited. If the machine is opposed by three or four
times as many volunteers under experienced campaign leadership,
t can be beaten. The machine can be defeated only if it is out-
organized, only if independents reach more voters with a better
candidate and better issues, only if the patronage precinct cap-
ain can be challenged directly by IPO members in the local precincts. On the other hand, IPO members of the caliber needed
o win elections can be attracted only if they have a voice in de-
ermining the government under which we live. The plane of democratic idealism intersects the plane of practical politics at the
point where a new institution can be built.

In our experience, the first stage in creating an organization
uch as IPO is the clear statement of an "idea whose time has
come." Frequently, this has taken the form of a brief proposal
which outlines the principles and proposed structure of the new
organization. This paper then serves as a discussion point for a
small group of leaders who have the time, the talent, and the inclination to implement it. Just one person can convince a dozen
leaders who, in turn, can organize hundreds of members. Thus
began the Christian Church. Thus begins every new organization
with an idea which provides relief for people's needs. (The Appendix on institution-building provides most of the key documents in
the creation of IPO including the original paper, "A Proposal for
a Permanent Precinct Organization.")

Building institutions is dynamic, not static. It requires a sense
of history and an intuitive understanding of the potential of any
particular situation. Institution-builders are like the birds which
sing before the dawn. They herald a new opportunity just at the
moment when people are willing to accept change. At the proper
historical moment, new forms meet a real need on the part of
many people. Thus, a pioneer in this area sees what others cannot
see, and convinces others that this is a new "idea whose time has
come."

As we have tried to indicate, a great idea by itself does not build organizations, nor win victories. Neither is discussion of a theoretical paper with friends enough to change the status quo and transfer power. What is required is an idea, a strategist, and several leaders willing to work hard to implement the idea. IPO was begun by a dozen of us who met one evening to discuss a seven-page paper. At the end of the meeting we each wrote a check for $25 to fund our fledgling organization. A few days later we rented a headquarters and called a large meeting of several hundred former McCarthy and Kennedy campaigners. This meeting endorsed three Democratic and two Republican candidates, for whom we worked in the November 1968 election.

One of the authors (Simpson) served as Executive Director of IPO without pay for eighteen months, working about five or six hours a day in addition to his other job. His wife became full-time office manager of the IPO headquarters with no pay for the first six months. Of the original founders, eight served as precinct coordinators, area chairmen, and finance chairmen of various political campaigns. Most also served on the executive committee of IPO for the first several years until its existence was relatively secure.

Every new institution needs not just a single leader but a cadre of leaders dedicated to the new organization. They must agree on its general form and purposes and be willing to work actively for at least several years. We begin with an idea and a personal commitment. Next we communicate that commitment to people with the skills and personal strength to serve as leaders of the new group. This is the beginning of a new institution.

A good idea and a few loyal followers are not the whole story either. A new institution will succeed only to the extent it can serve as a means of power and expression for many citizens—it must be rooted in their discontent. The institution is only a vehicle for change; there must be people who want to use such a vehicle for it to be effective. Strategists must develop a special sense of where power lies and an ability to motivate others to make the sacrifices necessary to attain power.

There are two approaches to creating organizations for social change. Alinsky suggested that a good beginning is to pick your enemy carefully, in short, someone with power. In Chicago for the last twenty years, Mayor Daley and his machine have frequently been the target. In the South the civil rights movement organized against southern bigots like "Bull" Connors. Whichever enemy is chosen, organizations willing to oppose them automatically seem powerful and more legitimate simply because of the strength of their foes. Their courage alone brings a group respect and a certain legitimacy.

The other approach begins with a positive cause such as racial justice, participatory democracy, or freedom. This is not to suggest that viable new institutions can be founded on slogans; they can't. The issue must be specific—the right to sit at *this* lunch counter or the ability to elect *that* candidate to public office. Frequently, even if there is a specific enemy, there must also be a positive thrust in a movement for change. Both give explicit form and substance to a new group.

An "idea whose time has come," good leaders, a clear-cut enemy, and a positive purpose provide a sound foundation for a new institution, but they alone cannot sustain it. Nothing short of victories can do that. In the end, a successful and permanent institution is one which undertakes real battles and wins. From each battle and each opponent we learn new techniques, attract new supporters, train new leaders, and make concrete changes in the world around us. From the diverse members who join a successful group, we develop a new vision of what can be done. As long as some of our early battles end in victory and as long as we continue to win from time to time, the organization will continue to grow despite some defeats. Even these will provide a base from which to launch new attacks, if the battles were against tough enemies.

Institutions live in cycles just like people. First we must win, then as we expand and take on stronger opponents, we may lose for a time until we grow strong enough to replace the elected officials, the administrators, or the businessmen who have been in power. Many organizations fail because they never win their first battles. Other organizations lose their vision or their will during the period when they are attempting to expand to broader issues or to a broader constituency. This is why wise strategists carefully pick the initial battles and work hard to sustain the organization during its expansion period.

Having spelled out in some detail the work which goes into creating new organizations, let us also consider the special virtue and reward of institution-building. A good organization is not only a means to an end, it is an end in itself. The purpose of the Independent Precinct Organization was to create participatory politics. Every time we endorse a candidate or an issue, IPO members have decided the question. We live in a democracy of our own making. We experience first-hand the joys and pains of responsible decision-making. We know what it means to participate in government, just as the members of the Southern Christian Leadership Conference know they have dignity, equality, and personal freedom when they stand up for their rights, whether or not the society immediately grants their rights. In the same way, members of Alinsky community organizations who have been powerless all their lives have, for the first time, real power—power to force slumlords to fix their buildings, to force industrial plants to stop pollution, and to force politicians to stop procrastinating. In the same way, a movement fighting for quality education has already gained the essence of a real education—the ability to reason and decide for ourselves what is right. A new institution is not utopian, it is here and now. While we fight to transform American society and government, we have already transformed our own lives.

Now Is the Time For Change

> *We say we are for the Union. The world will not forget that we say this. We know how to save the Union. The world knows we do know how to save it. We—even we here—hold the power and bear the responsibility. . . . Other means may succeed; this could not fail.*
> Abraham Lincoln

Citizens who join our movement for change give up petty concerns. We no longer calculate our worth by salary and status. We no longer sit alone at home glued to television sets. We are not bossed by government officials, party hacks, or the rich. We govern our own communities. We determine the outcome of elections. We decide what businesses may and must do. We act as a check on bureaucrats. By joining together, we discover our strength as a group and our abilities as individuals. We act courageously, we speak forcefully, we decide our future for ourselves. We are the seeds of change. We are a better, more self-conscious, freer people, quite able to govern ourselves. Whatever the outcome of particular battles, we live full lives. While the success of our movement is not preordained, it has much promise. While there are many burdens, it provides us with a lively life while making freedom, justice, and equality possible for others.

Thus, our faith in the future is grounded in our personal experience of the present. We are already what we would have our society become. There has been a time to tear down, but now is the time to build up. And we who dare can be the instruments of this change. We can be the founders of new, participatory institutions. It is our charge to revitalize and enlarge the meaning of democracy, and no greater challenge befalls any generation. Through study, reflection, and experience we become effective citizens. As effective citizens we reshape our society and give a rebirth to freedom. We refound the American republic as a government of, by, and for all the people.

Now is the time for change. Now is the time for us to quit our private concerns. Now is the time for us to become public men and women. In the Bostons, Chicagos, Bloomingtons, Atlantas, Seattles across this land we plant seeds of change in the form of new institutions and in the new people who are shaped by our institutions. This is how we found a new America. We begin, not in Washington, but at home. We begin, not at the top, but in the fertile soil. Now is the time to plant, for too much evil already grows in our country. If we are to return to waving grain and azure skies, it can only be by the sweat of our brow and the work of our hands.

Now is the time for change. It cannot be put off. The hands of the clock will not reset. We act or we fail to act. We give birth to a beautiful new America or we live out our lives in the end of a decadent civilization. We accept the burdens of freedom or the yoke of tyranny. We become free men or slaves.

Now is the time for change. We can no longer say we do not know what needs to be done. We know, the world knows, and history will know. Other means might succeed but these strategies for change could not fail.

Change is never easy. Victories are never cheap. For a new America, we must pay a price. But the price of cowardice and laziness is greater. We hold the power and we must bear the responsibility. Now is the time for change.

Appendix

A Documentary History of Institution-Building

Institution-building is never easy and there are no clear rules to follow. However, we include in this appendix some of the relevant documents about the creation of two new institutions, the Independent Precinct Organization and the 44th Ward Assembly. Both were begun in Chicago. IPO began in September 1968 (although some discussions were held earlier) and the 44th Ward Assembly in the fall of 1971 (although the first Assembly meeting of the entire body was not held until January 1972). Both proceeded from an idea committed to a brief paper, discussed among potential leaders, rewritten, introduced to a larger meeting, and carried out by a cadre of leaders and several hundred members of the new institutions. Both required money, leadership, and hard work. Both were successful.

These documents include the original paper which was used to spark discussion and leadership commitment, the resulting charter of the organization, and some descriptions of the organization as it functioned. They provide less than a complete blueprint for institutions you may want to build but they reveal a good bit about the process we followed successfully in Chicago.

"The Roots of IVI" by Mary Herrick gives the background of the formation of IPO's predecessor and parent organization. The Independent Voters of Illinois is a statewide organization and affiliate of Americans for Democratic Action (ADA), but its local roots were in Hyde Park on the south side of Chicago. On the

179

north side where IPO began, the IVI chapters were little more than liberal social clubs.

"A Proposal for A Permanent Precinct Organization of the 9th District IVI" by Dick Simpson was written during the summer of 1968 as a proposal for transforming IVI into a precinct-based, year-round, local independent organization capable of defeating the political machine which had governed the north side without a single independent being elected for over one hundred years. The principles set forth in this original proposal are echoed and developed in the "IPO Charter" which follows. This is the amended and current charter governing IPO today.

Paula Jo Dubeck's Ph.D. dissertation, *Membership Experiences and Voluntary Organization Maintenance* (Northwestern University, 1973), provides a background description of IPO during its first years which remains basically true today.

The principles of IPO applied to electoral politics and allowed for a new instrument in the place of political parties. The creation of IPO, however, did not change the structures of government. For this task a new organization named the 44th Ward Assembly was formed. The first document, "Creating a 44th Ward Assembly," is the original position paper or proposal which generated the necessary support and leadership to begin. It can best be compared to "The 44th Ward Assembly Charter" as amended in 1973 to demonstrate again the consistency between the original proposal and the actual structure of the institution.

Not included here but of interest to serious students of the Ward Assembly is a dissertation by Greta Salem, *Citizen Participation: Opportunities and Incentives* (Ph.D. dissertation; University of Maryland, 1974).

The Roots of IVI*

IVI did not spring out of Jove's head all of a sudden. Nor was it the only effort Chicago had made to unite citizens sick of corruption and misgovernment.

The early Municipal League which fought the "gray wolves" of the city council of the 1890's and the Yerkes looting of the streetcar lines, and the uprising against Big Bill Thompson in the early 20's were not organized thoroughly enough to last. But IVI grew out of a variety of already existing nuclei.

The largest of these were the Fifth Warders, who had elected Charles Merriam alderman in the first decade of the 1900's, supported him in two mayoral campaigns, and elected some aldermen in later years, notably Paul Douglas in 1939. They had elected some legislators as well. Walter Johnson, Dick Meyer, Mick Greenebaum and James Luther Adams were active Hyde Parkers in the first IVI board.

The gross and ruthless exploitation of the schools by the Kelly regime, which destroyed the junior high schools, fired a thousand teachers without notice, gave principals two schools to operate rather than one, paid teachers on time only eight times in four years on a salary cut of 23 percent, based promotions on political connections, cut curriculum and enormously increased class size, had given rise to the Citizens Schools Committee which fought these changes in ward organizations in more than a dozen wards. John Lapp, Beulah Berolzheimer, Ethel Parker, and I were deeply concerned with this issue and brought it, and a structure, with us to IVI.

The increasing pressure of the Kelly machine on organized labor had developed strong, politicized labor leaders like fiery Lillian Herstein, member of the Chicago Federation of Labor executive board. Frank McCulloch had organized the unemployed in the

*IVI Independent Day Dinner Book (1974), Mary Herrick

181

30's. Both brought their organizing skills to IVI.

Edgar Bernhard, the sturdy and steady civil libertarian who had steered the ACLU through its troubles, was an invaluable wise stabilizer in the early days. John Lapp was not only an officer of the Citizens Schools Committee, but president of the City Club. Leo Lerner's keen sense of timing and news values were an obvious professional asset.

The first real effort, even before formal organization of IVI's predecessor, "Voters for Victory," in 1944, was against the far right movement to ignore what was going on in Europe in 1940 and early 1941. Courtenay Barber monitored the meetings of "We the Mothers" and an openly Nazi candidate for Congress in a western suburb, and got many of us to alert others.

In 1944, IVI supported Curtis MacDougall for Congress and Emily Taft Douglas for Congresswoman-at-large. She defeated William Stratton (later Governor) who had franked out masses of material to keep us out of war at all costs.

James Luther Adams and I were co-chairmen of the Fifth Ward IVI, which set right to work to organize by precinct and block and to get enough bellringers to reach the people. On election day, we manned polling places as far as we could reach.

One primary election—Earl Dickerson was running for Congress and Paul Douglas for the Senate—I watched all night at 29th and Wentworth, in the bailiwick of a well-known gangster who sat in the polling place all afternoon. One of the election judges had already served a jail sentence. I sat next to the other judge where I could see the ballots.

After I had challenged some dozens of ballots, the precinct captain said he would get me a promotion in the school system if I'd go home right then. Finally, at 6:00 A.M. I checked with the one clerk who would talk with me, called IVI with the count, and departed to meet the 7:30 bell at school. At least those votes got tallied.

Someone should write a real book on the history of IVI. It would help many people understand how we got the way we are, how patronage really works, and would encourage this generation to look further ahead, plan more comprehensively and work even harder! The time may be here for a really big change.

—Mary Herrick

A Proposal for a Permanent Precinct Organization of the 9th District IVI

Neither local nor national problems are being resolved to our satisfaction. The war continues in Vietnam and discrimination continues at home. The schools, jobs, and housing in our district are insufficient and inadequate. Both local and national government continue to be a government over the people rather than *of the people*. In short, many of us feel powerless—unable to force our leaders to do what we believe they should do.

Although there may be important questions about programs and demands, the essential proposals of liberals and radicals and poor people are reasonably well known. The problem is that they seldom have the power to get their demands met. Several different approaches are possible, but one of the most direct is the attempt to change policies and leaders through organized political power at the ballot box. However, our political system is so constructed that major changes cannot be wrought by a reform group at a single election. Furthermore, much of the nitty-gritty of politics occurs between elections. To get our demands met then *we must go into politics on a permanent basis.*

In the 9th Congressional District of Illinois there are 442 precincts with usually 450-600 voters each. In the majority of these there are permanent Democratic and Republican precinct captains who attempt to turn out the vote for their respective parties. (Until we can match them with an *Independent* precinct captain working for liberal policies and people, our influence on the government will remain marginal.) Moreover, independent precinct workers are needed 1) to help people with problems which government could solve if proper action were taken (such as in-

183

dividuals who should receive social security benefits or street
which need to be fixed), 2) to keep citizens informed as to wha
is being done (or more often not being done) in government an
3) to provide the opportunity and encouragement that will le
people take significant political action. The precinct worker i
vitally important because he goes to people's homes with the rele
vant political information—they do not have to attend meeting
or listen to long-winded speeches, etc.

There are many techniques and purposes of precinct work and i
will take many experiments before we can develop an ideal mod
of operation. But one thing is clear—it is the one sure, long
term way to political power. While an individual election may b
decided by the news media or some other way, there is a grea
residue of votes available to those who will contact the voters an
explain to them what to do and why.

Goal and Program

Our goal is nothing less than political reform—the creation o
extension of a *New Democracy*. This is very different from govern
mental reform although such reforms may also be needed. Ou
goal is not primarily to change the city charter or state constitu
tion but to change the political system. If changes in charters o
constitutions are necessary, fine, but they are not our first targe
The current two-party system must be changed if a new democrac
is to come into being. The new democracy is both substantive an
procedural. On the one hand we desire to see liberal program
enacted and on the other we seek to give the individual citizen
greater role in the governing process. Making both of these prac
tical realities will not be easy. Further defining what program
and what procedures we want will be one of the on-going tasks o
the permanent organization.

To work towards these goals we must develop an on-going pro
gram with the following components:
1. Social gatherings which highlight information on Chicag
   politics, problems and possible action. (The start has bee
   made with the bi-weekly gatherings at the North Park Hote
   Monthly coffees should also start to be organized in th
   highrise areas along the lake. The importance is the regu

larity with which they meet, the relevance of the information conveyed, and the enthusiasm which can be built by an exciting discussion of issues and projects.)

2. Provision of assistance to individuals and neighborhoods. (This includes referral to government agencies, assistance in obtaining jobs, help with special problems, forcing action by government agencies on street cleaning and other neglected duties. This has always been and will continue to be the job of a precinct worker.)

3. Determination of views of citizens on important issues. (Techniques will have to be developed here. Petitions, mock elections, mail campaigns are one method. Constant telephone calls by hundreds of people to an offending agency, picketing and other methods of participation will need to be explored. The main key is organization of the effort with a clear knowledge that if a certain level of participation is reached, success is guaranteed. If the issue should be lost, an appeal process to a higher authority where we can win must already be planned.)

4. Provision of information through written media. (Regular releases or columns in the *neighborhood* newspapers should be given on the basis of thorough investigation into local problems and decisions of the city and state. Carefully written position papers should be drafted on long-range issues.)

5. Sponsorship of public meetings and hearings. (Candidates for office should be forced to debate in public under our regular sponsorship. Elected officials at all levels should be forced to attend public hearings on their activities. Although we will have to cooperate with many groups to make such meetings possible, we should be willing to initiate them.)

6. Running and endorsing candidates. (As often as possible we should run our own candidates. When a really outstanding candidate from one of the regular parties is running, we should consider endorsement. We should only endorse a candidate that we know the vast majority of our organization want to work for. We can state a preference for one

candidate over another but an endorsement should mean absolute commitment. We cannot afford to lose many campaigns at this stage. Nor can we afford to win them with mediocre candidates.)

Structure of the Permanent Precinct Organization

The organization and effort which I have been describing will take months, if not years, to build. It will need to grow up alongside the current IVI structures and programs. Even after it comes into existence, much of the current IVI structure would remain. Within the precinct organization itself, the structure would look something like the following:

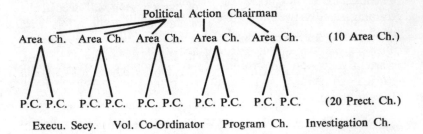

Political Action Chairman

Area Ch.   Area Ch.   Area Ch.   Area Ch.   Area Ch.   (10 Area Ch.)

P.C. P.C.   P.C. P.C.   P.C. P.C.   P.C. P.C.   P.C. P.C.   (20 Prect. Ch.)

Execu. Secy.   Vol. Co-Ordinator   Program Ch.   Investigation Ch.

The structure thus contains both functional and direct political components. All members would be required to join IVI and to give a set amount to the operation such as a dollar a week. The Political Action Chairman is, of course, an officer in the IVI chapter and many of the IVI officers likewise have a special position (such as program chairman or area chairman) in the campaign structure. Some jobs such as investigations, public relations, etc. would be the same in both the chapter and campaign structures.

How To Begin

We must begin from our strength in the 43rd ward and build out as quickly as possible to the 9th district and then to the whole north side of Chicago. We must count on our friends in the 2nd district to do likewise for the south side. With existing IVI chapters and the contacts through the McCarthy campaign this should not be difficult to do. The main thing is start slowly with carefully selected leaders and experiment until we develop truly effective techniques, structures, and leaders.

Although there are some things that can be done now, the real beginning must wait until after the McCarthy campaign has reached its conclusion or at least until after the convention. The real beginning point lies in developing a rigorous weekend training session which would be attended by five to ten potential area chairmen. The training would involve a programmed textbook, the simulation of a campaign, and a series of interviews with politicians. We will not be able to work on these until fall and will be lucky if we can put together a training session and contact participants individually by October. We may have to wait until the November election is over but hopefully we can begin before then. Several training sessions would be held in the months following, and as soon as we had a minimal active group of fifteen or twenty trained, all the techniques would be tried in various precincts in the 43rd ward. Events and opportunities may, of course, overtake us and cause us to revise these plans but this is the way we will eventually have to begin.

Obligation and Motivation of Members

Each member in the permanent precinct organization must join for at least a one year period. During that time he must work in the precinct where he lives, although he may have other responsibilities in the organization. Unless he is a low-income person, he must pay the original IVI membership dues plus $1.00 a week. He must pledge to spend an average of five hours a week on IVI activities such as canvassing, planning events, etc.

Obviously no one will join the organization who is not very dedicated to its goals and confident of its leadership. Instead of the usual payoffs the city offers to keep its precinct workers, we offer the possibility of great commitment and such an investment of oneself that loyalty is assured.

—Dick Simpson

Independent Precinct Organization Charter

I. PURPOSE

We believe that those who are affected by the decisions of government must be consulted by those who govern. It is the right of citizens to have access to the instruments of power; it is their duty to learn to use them effectively and wisely. We seek to elect to public office men and women who will serve with wisdom and imagination, while remaining responsive to those who gave them office. We seek to build a citizenry confident in its capacity to select its leaders and to take part in the making of public policy.

The Independent Precinct Organization seeks to achieve this program for the community at large by means of a broadly based, precinct level political structure. We will serve to make visible a political community which is at once energetic and humane. All who have a stake in our decisions will participate in making them; all who participate will share the responsibility for implementation. By fostering responsible citizen participation in public affairs, by promoting fresh, responsive, and progressive political leadership, by demonstrating in our ways of work the wisdom of popular democracy, we seek to bring about a new political order in our community.

II. MEMBERSHIP

A. *Membership* in the Independent Precinct Organization is open to any individual and is attained by fulfilling the the responsibilities of membership for two consecutive months. These responsibilities are:

1. A regular sustained expenditure of time on activities

of the organization.

    2. A regular monthly payment of dues in an amount set by the individual.

B. *The Ward Membership Chairperson,* or the general IPO Membership Director, in the case of members-at-large, is responsible for evaluating the membership status of a member and for suspending that membership should the person fail to continue fulfilling the responsibilities of IPO membership. Any decision regarding membership may be appealed to the Ward Executive Committee or to the IPO Executive Committee.

C. *A Person Who Joins A Ward Organization* that has been organized for two months or less is a member as soon as a membership application and dues payment for one month have been received.

III. THE GENERAL ASSEMBLY

A. *The General Assembly* consists of all members of the organization. The General Assembly determines the leadership, candidates, and policies of the organization as a whole.

B. *There Shall be at Least One Meeting* of the General Assembly per quarter. All Assemblies and meetings of the IPO are open to all persons at all times. *A quorum* is required at all assembly meetings to conduct business. A quorum for the General Assembly shall be one-fifth of the membership.

C. *At Least One Week's Notice* is required for any General Assembly meeting.

D. *Selection of Candidates and Policies* or programs to be supported by the organization as a whole requires a two-thirds majority of those voting.

E. *Meetings of the General Assembly* are scheduled by the Executive Director and the Executive Committee. A member may call a meeting of the General Assembly by presenting to the Executive Director a petition with the signatures of 10% of the membership. The Executive Director must then schedule a General Assembly meeting for the earliest date which allows for proper notice of the meeting, or for a later date if agreeable to the petitioning member.

F. *Administrative Officers*

1. *The IPO General Assembly Administrative Officers* consist of the Executive Director, the Associate Executive Director, the Chairperson of the General Assembly, the Membership Director, the Electoral Action Director, and the Community Action Director.

   a. These officers are elected for six month terms by the General Assembly and may succeed themselves. Elections for these offices are to be held semiannually. A simple majority is required for election.

   b. In the event of vacancy of the office of Executive Director, the Associate Executive Director shall fill that office until an election can be held. In the event of other vacancies, The Executive Committee shall choose a replacement until an election can be held.

   c. Removal from office or censure requires the presentation to the Executive Committee of a petition signed by ten percent of the membership. The matter shall then be placed on the agenda for the next General Assembly meeting. A two-thirds majority of those voting is required for removal or censure.

2. *The responsibilities and duties of the Executive Director* shall include;

   a. Implementing the policy of the organization as established by the General Assembly, promoting the organization's development, and acting as its spokesperson.

   b. Convening and chairing meetings of the IPO General Assembly Administrative Officers.

   c. Presenting an integrated budget for the entire organization to the Executive Committee for approval.

  d. Establishing procedures for controlling the funds of the organization to insure their safe and proper application.
  e. Maintaining the historical record of IPO including the recording and dissemination of all resolutions passed by IPO assemblies, charter, or by-law amendments and revisions, and all similar decisions or actions which will affect future policies or programs of IPO.
  f. Appointing or hiring such office staff, committee chairpersons, or assistants, with the advice and consent of the Executive Committee, as are necessary to effectively discharge the duties of office.
3. *The responsibilities and duties of the Associate Executive Director* shall include;
  a. Assisting the Executive Director in the development of the organization.
  b. Assuming the duties of the Executive Director when the Executive Director is incapacitated or absent.
4. *The responsibilities and duties of the Chairperson of the General Assembly* shall include making arrangements for meetings of the General Assembly, Executive Committee, and district assemblies, including the chairing of the meetings.
5. *The responsibilities and duties of the Membership, Electoral Action and Community Action Directors* shall include:
  a. Directing the activities and serving as chairperson of the IPO Membership, Electoral Action and Community Action Commissions.
  b. Submitting periodic reports of the activities of office and of the Commissions to the Executive Director, as the Executive Director may require.
G. *Administrative Committees*
  1. *The IPO Executive Committee* consists of the Executive Director, the Associate Executive Director, the Chairperson of the General Assembly, the Coordi-

nator of each ward, one representative elected by each Ward Assembly, and the Directors of the Commissions.

a. *A quorum* of a majority of its members shall be required to conduct business and it shall meet no less than once a month.

b. *The responsibilities and duties of the Executive Committee* shall include:

   (1) Implementing the decisions of the General Assembly.

   (2) Approving the budget.

   (3) Approving expenditures.

   (4) Approving the procedures for the collection and disbursements of funds.

   (5) Appointing a search committee which shall be representative of all wards and which shall seek candidates to fill the following positions:

   Executive Director
   Associate Executive Director
   Chairperson of the General Assembly
   Directors of the Commissions

   The persons holding offices elected by the General Assembly may not serve on the search committee. The search committee, wherever possible, will seek at least two candidates for each position. These candidates shall be presented to the General Assembly by the Executive Committee. Nominations shall be made from the floor of the General Assembly.

   (6) Recommending to the General Assembly by-laws to this Charter.

   (7) Approving any appointments made by the Administrative Officers.

   (8) Admitting new Ward Assemblies. A two-thirds majority of Executive Committee members is required for admission.

(9) Reporting to the General Assembly all major decisions of the Executive Committee including fund allocation, expansion, etc.

   c. *Any member may appeal* to the General Assembly any decision made by the Executive Committee. A two-thirds majority of those voting is required to overturn any decision under appeal.

2. *Such committees as may be necessary* for fulfilling the duties of office may be appointed or formed by each IPO officer.

H. *Commissions*

1. *An IPO Commission* consists of the elected IPO Director and comparable ward-level membership, Electoral Action, or Community Action officers. The IPO Director will serve as Chairperson.

   a. *The responsibilities and duties of the Membership Commissions* shall include developing and coordinating membership programs and activities.

   b. *The responsibilities and duties of the Electoral Action Commission* shall include locating potential candidates for public office, coordinating endorsement sessions, maintaining liaison with elected officials, and investigating possibilities for electoral reform.

   c. *The responsibilities and duties of the Community Action Commission* shall include investigating the social and economic problems of the community and developing proposals for political means of dealing with them.

2. *A Commission may undertake informal discussion* with representatives of political parties and community organizations as part of its work; it may commit the name, workers and funds of IPO to other groups only with the consent of the General Assembly or of a District or Ward Assembly.

IV. THE WARD ASSEMBLY

A. *A Ward Assembly Consists* of all IPO members who work in that Ward's precinct organization or who reside

in the Ward and regularly work on the staff, a committee, or commission of IPO. The Ward Assembly determines the Ward. A member of a Ward Assembly who
does not reside within that Ward may not serve as an
elected officer of that Ward Assembly.

B. *Selection of Candidates and Policies* or programs to be
supported by the Ward as a whole requires a two-thirds
majority of those voting.

C. *At Least One Week's Notice* is required for any Ward
Assembly meeting.

D. *There Shall Be at Least One Meeting* of each Ward Assembly per quarter. *A Quorum* is required at all assembly meetings to conduct business. For Ward Assemblies,
a qurum shall be one-fifth of the members, or ten members, whichever is greater.

E. *Meetings of a Ward Assembly* are scheduled by the Ward
Coordinator and Ward Executive Committee. A member
of the Ward Assembly may call a meeting of that Assembly by presenting to the Ward Coordinator a petition
with the signatures of five members or ten percent of
the Ward membership, whichever is greater. The Ward
Coordinator must then schedule a Ward Assembly meeting for the earliest date which allows for proper notice, or
for a later date if agreeable to the petitioning member.

F. *A Ward Decision* deemed by an IPO member to be
contrary to the IPO Charter or bylaws may be appealed
to the IPO Executive Committee. If a majority of the
Executive Committee considers the Ward decision to be
in conflict with the IPO Charter or bylaws, the matter
shall be brought before the next General Assembly,
where a two-thirds majority of those voting shall be
required to overturn the original decision of the Ward
Assembly.

G. *Ward Administrative Officers*
   1. *The Ward Administrative Officers* consist of the
   Ward Coordinator, Ward Membership Chairperson,
   Ward Electoral Action Chairperson, and Ward Community Action Chairperson.

2. *Ward officers are elected* for six month terms by the Ward Assembly and may succeed themselves. Elections for these positions are held semi-annually. Election of officers requires a simple majority vote.

3. *In the event of a vacancy,* the Ward Executive Committee shall choose a replacement until an election can be held.

4. *To remove from office or censure* requires a petition with the signatures of five members or ten percent of the membership, whichever is greater, to be presented to the Ward Coordinator. The matter shall then be placed on the agenda for the next meeting of the Ward Assembly. A two-thirds majority of those voting is required to remove or censure.

5. *The responsibilities and duties of the Ward Coordinator* shall include:
   a. Implementing the policies of the ward, as established by the Ward Assembly, and acting as spokesperson for the Assembly.
   b. Chairing the Ward Assembly and Ward Executive Committee meetings.

6. *The responsibilities and duties of the Ward Membership Chairperson* shall include:
   a. Evaluating membership status and participation.
   b. Assuming primary responsibility for the expansion of ward membership.

7. *The responsibilities and duties of the Ward Electoral Action Chairperson* shall include:
   a. Locating potential candidates for public office and coordinating all ward endorsement sessions.
   b. Maintaining liaison with elected officials.

8. *The responsibilities and duties of the Ward Community Action Chairperson* shall include investigating and bringing to the Ward Assembly recommendations for community action programs to be undertaken by that ward.

H. *Ward Administrative Committees*
   1. *A Ward Executive Committee* consists of a Ward

Coordinator, Ward Electoral Action Chairperson, Ward Community Action Chairperson, and Ward Membership Chairperson.

a. *Responsibilities and duties of the Ward Executive Committee* include:

(1) Implementing IPO policies within the Ward as ,established by the Ward Assembly.

(2) Approving Ward expenditures.

(3) Approving appointments made by the Ward Coordinator.

(4) Seeking candidates to fill the following positions:

Ward Coordinator
Membership Chairperson
Electoral Action Chairperson
Community Action Chairperson
Representative to the IPO Executive Committee

Wherever possible, at least two candidates will be sought for each position. Nominations shall be made from the floor of the Ward Assembly.

(5) Reporting to the Ward Assembly all pertinent actions of the Ward Executive Committee.

(6) Appointing area chairpersons and encouraging them to attend Ward Executive Committee meetings. At least one special meeting of area chairpersons shall be held quarterly.

(7) Implementing a permanent IPO precinct structure.

b. *Any member may appeal* to his Ward Assembly any decision made by the Ward Executive Committee. A two-thirds majority of those voting is required to overturn any decision under appeal.

2. *Such committees as may be necessary* for fulfilling the duties of office may be appointed or formed by each ward officer.

V. THE DISTRICT ASSEMBLY

A. *When An Electoral Action Campaign* or community action program affects an area larger than a ward but smaller than the area in which IPO is organized, the affected Ward Assemblies, or parts, thereof, may meet and act together as a "district" body. Meetings may be called by a Ward Executive Committee and are subject to the same notice requirements as Ward Assembly meetings.

B. *Recommendations for Candidates for Public Office* and for policies or programs will be brought before a "district" assembly in the same manner as before a Ward or General Assembly. A "district" assembly decision that may be in conflict with the Charter or bylaws is similarly subject to overrule by the IPO Executive Committee and General Assembly.

C. *For "District" Assemblies, a Quorum* shall be at least 25 members, or a greater number if otherwise specified in the IPO bylaws.

VI. ENDORSEMENTS

A. *The Endorsement of Candidates for Public Office* or of policies and programs requires a two-thirds majority of those voting. Endorsement must be by the highest level IPO Assembly in the affected electoral or community action area. Endorsement by any IPO Assembly shall be commitment by the members of the Assembly to work in support of that endorsement.

B. *The Electoral Action Officer* shall bring to the Assembly recommendations for candidates and electoral action policies or programs. Recommendations of other community-wide citizens' committees shall also be presented by the Electoral Action officer.

C. *The Community Action Officer* shall bring to the Assembly recommendations for community action policies and programs.

D. *Additional Nominations* or proposals for policies and programs may be made from the floor of the Assembly.

VII. CHARTER REVISION
   A. *A Majority Vote* of the General Assembly is required to form a Charter Revision Committee. Such a vote must be taken at least once every three years.
   B. *Revisions of This Charter* shall be presented to the General Assembly by the Charter Revision Committee. The Executive Committee shall provide for the formation of a Charter Revision Committee which shall have at least one member selected by each ward.
   C. *Amendments to This Charter* may be presented by any member at a meeting of the General Assembly.
   D. *Any Suggested Revisions* or amendments must be published to the membership one month prior to the General Assembly meeting at which the vote is to be taken.
   E. *A Two-Thirds Majority* of those voting is required to adopt revisions or amendments.

VIII. ADOPTION OF BY-LAWS
   A. *General By-laws May Be Adopted* implementing the provisions of this Charter. They shall be presented at a meeting of the General Assembly and can be amended in the same manner. Such by-laws will go into effect when passed by a majority of those voting. Notice of proposed by-law changes must be included with notice of the General Assembly meeting.
   B. *Wards May adopt Their Own By-laws* insofar as they do not conflict with the IPO Charter or general by-laws. Such by-laws shall be presented at a meeting of the Ward Assembly. They will go into effect when they are passed by a majority of those voting at the Ward Assembly and are filed with the IPO Executive Committee. Conflicts between Ward by-laws and the IPO Charter or by-laws will be resolved by the IPO Executive Committee in accordance with Article IVF.

IX. PARLIAMENTARY AUTHORITY
   All Rules of Order not provided for by this Charter or by IPO by-laws shall be in accordance with Robert's Rules of Order (Paperback Edition, with a Guide and Commentary by Rachel Vixman. Pyramid Books, 1972).

The Independent Precinct
Organization
The Research Site

A single organization was selected as the research site for this study. The following discussion presents a background of the organization.

The Independent Precinct Organization (IPO) in Chicago is described by its founders as "an experiment in independent politics." Its goals are to involve community people in the choice and election of their public officials, as well as in community decisions which affect them. A grassroots precinct organization is the structure used to attain these goals; IPO members contact neighborhood people about candidates running for office (those endorsed by IPO) and about issues of local community interest.

IPO was founded in September 1968, after the 1968 Democratic National convention. The nucleus of founders had worked together in (Eugene) McCarthy's campaign for Democratic nomination for president. And through this work, they gained experience with organizing people on a precinct-by-precinct basis. With IPO they hoped to capture the enthusiasm and energy of people from the McCarthy campaign and channel this into constructive community action.

Geographical location. IPO is located on the north side of Chicago and its members live in the 42nd, 43rd, 44th, 46th, and 48th Wards of the city;[1] this area also encompasses the 11th and

[1] The city has since been redistricted. Also, at the beginning of research, IPO was organized in the 42nd through 46th Wards; during research it expanded into the 48th Ward.

12th State Congressional Districts of Illinois. Within this geographical region, there are 136,150 registered voters distributed across 312 precincts.

IPO purpose. The beginning paragraphs of the IPO Charter state the aims of IPO in the community:

> . . . It is the right of a citizen to have access to the instruments of power; it is his duty to learn to use them effectively and wisely. . . . We seek to build a citizenry confident in its capacity to select its leaders and to take part in the making of public policy.

> . . . By fostering responsible citizen participation in public affairs, by promoting fresh, responsible political leadership, by demonstrating in our ways of work the wisdom of popular democracy, we seek to bring about a new political order in our community.

The goals relating to operating procedures within IPO also reflect this orientation:

> All who have a stake in our decisions will participate in making them; all who participate will share the responsibility for implementation. . . .

IPO, then, seeks to practice participatory democracy within and attempts to effect citizen participation in the larger political community. Increased public involvement in decision-making is made through the election of officials who are "responsive to the needs of the community" and by educating the public on issues, so they can make intelligent decisions about community problems.

Membership. Official requirements for IPO membership are the commitment of both time and money to the organization. Time contribution serves to fulfill the IPO goal of contacting community people about political and community events which affect them; time is contributed primarily through campaign work, although some members volunteer time as office workers. Money contribution serves to maintain IPO by supplying funds for operating costs of the organization; money is contributed in the form of monthly dues.

Although time is a requirement for membership, it is not systematically checked by the organization; members are expected to fulfill their time contribution and IPO has instituted no mechanism by which to determine whether or not this is done. The amount of time contributed to a campaign ranges from less than an hour to a full forty-hour week. *The median amount of time contributed to these campaigns by IPO members was an average of 6 hours per week, in the four weeks preceding the primary and general elections.* Finally, there are members, known to the IPO leadership, who have not contributed time to IPO through campaigns or other activities; however, their names have not been removed from the membership list.

The commitment of money to IPO, in the form of monthly dues, is the major source of monetary support for the organization. The amount of dues pledged is specified by each member when he signs a membership form for IPO. Theoretically, there is no "minimum" pledge which is required of members; however, most officers, when asked about dues, specify the minimum monthly dues at $.50. The dues which have been pledged to IPO range from $.50 to $12.50 per month; members of religious groups are excused from dues. *At the time of research, the average monthly dues pledged to IPO was just under $2.25, and the median dues pledged was $2.00 per month.*

Dues payment is the only membership requirement which is systematically checked by IPO; it is enforced informally when voting takes place at meetings. Although a member is not to vote on IPO decisions unless his dues are currently paid up at the time of a meeting, enforcement of this rule depends on the member; if he has not paid dues, he is expected not to vote.

Membership assembly meetings. IPO has, officially, two types of membership assemblies: Ward assemblies and the General Assembly. Members of IPO belong to the General Assembly and to one of the Ward Assemblies.[2] Ward assemblies are sub-units of IPO, organized within city Ward boundaries; there are five such IPO assemblies.

[2] There were six persons who were classified "out of district"; they had no particular ward affiliation.

The Charter states that the Ward assembly "determines the leadership candidates, and policies or programs for the Ward."[3] Because the Ward assemblies are locally based units, members can concentrate on their own community problems. To plan and coordinate such efforts, each Ward elects four officers; (1) Ward Coordinator, (2) Community Action Commission representative, (3) Electoral Action Commission representative and (4) a Membership Committee representative.

When IPO decisions involve the participation of all IPO members, a General Assembly meeting is called. A decision that would require the participation of all IPO members in the endorsement of a candidate whose campaign would cover all IPO-organized wards. Thus, IPO's decision to endorse Adlai Stevenson III for U. S. Senator (Summer, 1970) was made at a General Assembly meeting. The General Assembly elects five officers to coordinate activities affecting the overall IPO organization. These are (1) the Executive Director, (2) Chairman of the General Assembly, (3) Chairman of the Community Action Commission, (4) Chairman of the Electoral Action Commission, and (5) Chairman of the Membership Committee. The latter three officers head the major sub-committees of the Executive Committee which is responsible for organizational planning.

Recently, IPO organized assemblies within the boundaries of two State Congressional Districts—the 11th and the 12th Districts. These assemblies endorsed candidates for the Illinois State Constitutional Convention (Con-Con), and it was within these boundaries that campaign efforts were coordinated. The two IPO District assemblies were instituted to meet specific organizational needs, and are not part of the formal structure of IPO. Also, there are no official officers for District assemblies; instead, officers of the Wards within Districts coordinate their efforts to manage District assemblies.

Planning and decision making. IPO differentiates between two bodies of members in the allocation of planning and decision making responsibility. The first of these, the Executive Committee, has the responsibility for planning and coordinating activities

[3] IPO Charter, p. 2.

for IPO. The second is the general membership which is responsible for making final decisions about plans and activities for IPO. Thus, plans made by the Executive Committee must be approved by the general membership before any IPO-supported action can be taken.

—Paula Jo Dubeck
Membership Experiences and
Voluntary Organization Maintenance

Creating a 44th Ward Assembly

Purpose: To Be A New Instrument of Government

The primary reason for the Ward Assembly and its basic purpose is to determine those policies and priorities that are in the best interests of all the citizens of the Ward. It is to allow for this determination that the Assembly is to be partly representative, partly participatory: that full deliberation will be encouraged within a fixed agenda; and that all voices will be heard in this public gathering. The policies and priorities that result will be both advisory and binding upon the alderman. Most of all, the Assembly is the *place* where these decisions can be made by the community and in which every citizen can participate effectively in the process of governmental decision-making.

The 44th Ward Assembly and groups like it create a new instrument of local government. Combining the principles of representative and direct democracy, the Ward Assembly is an institution which embodies the hope of men of good will that democratic government is still a possibility in our century. It is meant to foster the development of citizens with important responsibilities and privileges once again. For these reasons the creation of the Ward Assembly and the outcome of its deliberations is an event of high seriousness. If it is successful, there is much reason for hope. If it fails, we shall have to settle for much less from our government and from ourselves.

Membership:

Since the purpose of the Assembly is to serve partly as an advisory and partly as a governing council for the entire ward, it is necessary to mirror the composition of the ward to allow for the expression of quite diverse opinions, and to foster widespread and long-term participation. To reflect the diversity of the ward and to make its decisions binding and effective, it needs to have some attributes of a representative assembly. To reflect the intensity and breadth of public feeling and to make its deliberations significant, it needs to have some attributes of a town-hall meeting. To achieve this particular hybrid, the Assembly shall have different kinds of membership. But participation in the Assembly will be open to all people residing in the 44th ward regardless of their legal citizenship, voting status, or age.

One set of *voting members* shall consist of two elected representatives from each precinct. These representatives shall be chosen at a *precinct meeting* held within each precinct (normally at one of the neighbor's homes), and all residents shall be invited by flyers left at each home. *Or* the representatives may be any citizen with the signatures of 25 or more voters from a precinct nominating him/her as representative. These precinct elections shall be held (or nominating petitions turned in) by the first Ward Assembly meeting in September. And each representative so nominated shall serve a one year term until the following September. If a vacancy occurs, it may be filled by a precinct meeting at any time. No precinct shall have more than two representatives to represent them no matter which means of selection is used.

The second set of voting members shall consist of one representative chosen from each organization with more than twenty-five members who live in the ward. These representatives may be chosen by any method consistent with the organization's own rules and procedures. They shall serve as long as the organization is satisfied. If any vacancy occurs, or if the organization desires to change its representative, it may choose a new representative at any time.

The assembly shall also consist of two important groups without vote. Any citizen of the 44th ward shall be a non-voting member. Citizens who reside in the ward, regardless of their age or whether they are legally registered to vote, shall have the privilege of speaking and debating before the Assembly provided that they are speaking on the topic at hand or during the appropriate section of the meeting. They may speak as long as they like unless a specific limitation on the period for debate is established by a two-thirds vote of the voting members.

Aldermanic staff members who are not 44th ward citizens shall be *observers*. As such they shall have the right only to present reports on areas in whch they carry responsibilities or to present information on the subject under debate. They shall have the right to observe all the discussions of the ward assembly, however, unless the topic under discussion is whether or not they have performed their duties adequately. Other observers are also welcome at the Assembly meetings even if they do not live in the ward. However, they may be excluded if there is insufficient space or by vote of two-thirds of the voting members if some item under discussion warrants secrecy.

Chairman:

The Alderman of the 44th ward shall serve as chairman of the Assembly. He shall have no vote in the Assembly. But he shall put the questions to be voted upon before the group and shall rule on points of order. He may, however, be overruled in his parliamentary decisions by a two-thirds vote. Unlike the chairmen of other groups, he may speak and discuss the issues with the Assembly. It is the Alderman's willingness to be bound by the deliberations of the Assembly that give it power. He is ultimately the one who must vote Yes or No in the City Council and who must carry out the priorities established by the Ward Assembly. Unless he is confident of the Assembly process and unless the Assembly is confident of the intentions of the Alderman, the proceedings become a farce. With mutual confidence the decisions become the basis of a full political community.

Process:

Assembly meetings will be held once a month at a regular date established by the assembly. Emergency meetings can be called either by the Alderman, or by any ten voting members, or by petition of any hundred voters in the ward. An emergency meeting will only consider the specified topic for which the meeting was called. The Assembly shall be in official session and a quorum declared only if at least twenty-five percent of the precincts and community organizations are represented by at least one representative. Although the meeting will be generally conducted in

English, translation will be provided if minority groups want to make presentations to the Assembly in their native language provided that they notify the Alderman's office at least one day before the meeting. It is hoped that the Assembly will encourage minority participation.

When possible, reports to the Assembly shall be written as well as oral. All issues and questions related to these reports and any additional concerns or issues brought up by members of the Assembly shall be decided by consensus of all members (voting and non-voting) whenever possible. When controversial issues arise that cannot be decided by consensus of the entire Assembly, the vote shall be taken from among the voting members after full discussion. Any measure which received two-thirds or more votes of the voting members of the assembly *shall be binding upon the Alderman.* It will not prevent him from voicing contrary opinions in public, but it will bind him both in his vote in the City Council and on the programs undertaken in the ward requiring the resources of the Aldermanic office. Any measure which fails to receive two-thirds of the votes will be advisory but not binding.

Thus, in addition to generally advising the Alderman and discussing community issues, the Assembly will have two broad powers:

a.) Programs undertaken by the aldermanic office will be submitted to the assembly, in order that the assembly may determine which programs should receive priority.

b.) All legislation and resolutions sponsored by the Alderman, except those dealing with routine matters, will be submitted to the assembly for approval as will other crucial legislation which is to be voted on at future City Council meetings.

Agenda:

The agenda shall be the same for all meetings except emergency meetings to discuss a single topic. It will be:

    I.   Call of the roll and quorum determined present.

    II. Meeting declared open by Alderman.

    III. Legislative report, deliberation and decisions by assembly.

    IV.   Community projects report, deliberation and decisions by assembly.

    V.   Service report, deliberation and decisions by assembly.

    VI.   Office and financial report, deliberation and decisions by assembly.

    VII.   Additional issues or concerns passed by members of the assembly.

    VIII.   Additional business proposed by non-members of the assembly.

    IX.   Meeting declared closed by Alderman.

Creation:

Members of the Ward Assembly having been duly chosen to represent precincts and community organizations, the Ward Assembly shall come into being with the formal signing of two covenants. The Alderman will sign a covenant at the first meeting of the new Ward Assembly each year declaring his willingness to be bound by the Assembly on important questions on which at least two-thirds of the voting members are agreed. Voting members will also sign a covenant declaring their willingness to carry out their duties as representatives.

The first order of business of each assembly will be to agree to at least a temporary set of by-laws or rules which may later be changed by a two-thirds vote of the voting members.

When these two acts have been completed, the Alderman shall declare the 44th Ward Assembly to have been officially formed within all the powers and procedures already described.

—Dick Simpson

The 44th Ward Assembly Charter

I. PREAMBLE

In the United States in the 1970's, people have come to feel increasingly powerless. This is especially true for people living in large cities. Overcrowding, the fast pace of city life and the remoteness of elected representatives from their constituents shut out most people from decisions that vitally affect their lives and erode their trust in the process of government.

We, the people of the Forty-Fourth Ward of the City of Chicago, seek to turn in a new direction. We seek to restore a sense of trust and mutuality in public life. We seek to create a forum for the broadest possible exchange of views among the people themselves and between them and their Alderman. We seek to open up the political process within our ward to all its people. To this end, we establish this body in a spirit of mutual respect and collaboration among ourselves and with our alderman.

II. NAME

The name of this body shall be the 44th Ward Assembly.

III. PURPOSE

The purpose of the 44th Ward Assembly shall be as follows:

A. To direct and to advise the Alderman as to how he shall cast his vote in the City Council.

B. To direct and to advise the Alderman as to what new legislation he shall sponsor in the City Council.

C. To establish priorities for programs-to be undertaken by the Alderman for the benefit of the Ward and to take supportive action to reinforce such programs.

D. To make possible free and responsible debate on all the issues that affect the welfare of residents of the Ward.

IV. COVENANT

In return for the willingness of the members to participate in the deliberations of the Assembly, the Alderman will sign a covenant at the first meeting each year declaring his willingness to be bound by the Assembly on important questions as provided in ARTICLE VII.

V. MEMBERS

A. All residents of the 44th Ward, regardless of citizenship, age, or whether they are registered to vote, may participate in the activities of the Ward Assembly.

B. There shall be two kinds of voting members.

1. *Precinct representatives*

a. Each precinct of the Ward may have two representatives who must live in the precinct they represent and who shall be elected at a well-publicized meeting of residents of the precinct. At the same time, the residents may elect a first and second alternate delegate who shall be entitled to vote in the absence of the regular delegate or delegates. In the event of a vacancy, the first alternate shall fill such vacancy and become a regular delegate; the second alternate shall fill any subsequent or additional vacancy. If less than 25 residents of the precinct attend the meeting the representatives chosen shall submit petitions signed by 25 residents of the precinct.

b. A precinct representative shall serve for a term of one year or until his earlier resignation, non-residency in the precinct or failure to attend three consecutive meetings.

c. If a vacancy occurs, it shall be filled by the alternate. In the absence of an alternate, any resident of the precinct may succeed to the post upon presentation of a petition signed by 25 other residents of the precinct.

2. *Organization representatives*

a. One representative and alternate may be chosen from each organization with at least 25 members residing in the Ward and from each major committee of an organization with at least 25 committee members residing in the Ward if the committee performs a function independent of that of its parent organization. The term and method of selection of organization representatives shall be determined by their organizations.

b. An organization that desires representation shall apply to the Steering Committee which will recommend action to the Assembly at the next regularly scheduled meeting. The representative of the organization shall become a voting member at the meeting following the meeting at which his eligibility is approved.

3. Conflicts concerning eligibility of precinct and organization representatives shall be initially considered by the Steering Committee which will make recommendations to the Assembly.

A person may vote only as a precinct or as an organization representative.

VI. OFFICERS AND COMMITTEES

A. The presiding officer shall be the Alderman of the 44th Ward. He may participate in the debate without vacating the chair. In the absence of the Alderman, the presiding officer shall be appointed by the Steering Committee.

B. There shall be a Steering Committee which shall consist of the Alderman; ten representatives elected by the Assembly of whom at least five shall be precinct representatives; and the Chairman of the standing committees. The Steering Committee shall elect a Chairman and a Secretary.

C. There shall be three standing committees: Finance, Social Issues and Services. They shall study issues for consideration by the Assembly, prepare background material with the help of the Ward Office, and present the issues to the Assembly.

VII. MEETINGS
A. The Assembly shall hold at least ten regular meetings each year on a regular date established by the Assembly.
B. Emergency meetings can be called by the Alderman, by any 200 residents of the Ward, by notice to all voting members. An emergency meeting will consider only the specified topics for which the meeting was called.
C. A quorum shall be twenty-five percent of the voting members. The Assembly may deliberate without a quorum but its decisions shall be advisory only.
D. Important questions on which the Assembly can bind the Alderman shall be decided by a two-thirds vote. Important questions shall be: the Alderman's vote in the City Council; legislation to be sponsored by him in the City Council; and programs to be undertaken by him for the benefit of the Ward.
E. The assembly will be conducted according to *Robert's Rules of Order, Revised* where it does not conflict with this Charter or any standing rules adopted by the Assembly.

VIII. AMENDMENTS
This Charter may be amended by a two-thirds vote if the amendment was submitted in writing at the last regular meeting.

IX. ADOPTION
This Chapter shall be adopted by a majority vote, a quorum being present.

Notes

CHAPTER 1

1. E. E. Schattschneider, *The Semi-Sovereign People* (New York: Holt, Rinehart and Winston, 1960), p. 68.
2. Stokely Carmichael and Charles Hamilton, *Black Power* (New York: Random House, 1967), pp. 104-105.
3. Other authors have made similar distinctions. See Schattschneider, *The Semi-Sovereign People*, Chapter 2; and Michael Walzner, *Political Action: A Practical Guide to Movement Politics* (Chicago: Quadrangle, 1971), pp. 25-27.

CHAPTER 2

1. William Mitchell, *Why Vote?* (Chicago: Markham, 1971), p. 52.
2. Herbert Alexander, *Political Financing* (Minneapolis: Burgess, 1972), p. 5.
3. Alexander, *Political Financing*, p. 39.
4. *Ibid.*, pp. 24 and 33.
5. Schattschneider, *The Semi-Sovereign People*, Chapter VI, pp. 97-113.
6. V. O. Key, *Politics, Parties, and Pressure Groups*, Fourth Edition (New York: Thomas Y. Crowell Company, 1958), Chapter XXI.
7. Angus Campbell, et al., *The American Voter* (New York: John Wiley and Sons, 1960), p. 174, Table 4-1.
8. For evidence on these points see: Warren Miller and Donald E. Stokes, "Constituency Influence in Congress," *American Political Science Review*, Vol. LVII (March, 1963), pp. 45-56; John Kenneth Galbraith, *The New Industrial State*, Second Edition, Revised (Boston: Houghton Mifflin, 1971), Chapters XXVI-XXVII; Charles Cnudde and Donald McCrone, "The Linkage Between Constituency Attitudes and Congressional Voting Behavior: A Causal Model," *American Political Science Review*, Vol. LX (March, 1966), pp. 66-72.
9. For an analysis of revolutionary strategies in modern societies see: Karl Marx and Frederick Engels, *Communist Manifesto*

(New York: International Publishers, 1969), first published in 1848; Hannah Arendt, "Thoughts on Politics and Revolution," *New York Review of Books* (April 22, 1971), pp. 8-20; Herbert Marcuse, *An Essay on Liberation* (Boston: Beacon Press, 1969); Herbert Marcuse, "The Problem of Violence and the Radical Opposition," *Five Lectures* (Boston: Beacon Press, 1970), pp. 83-108; and Murray Bookchin, "Listen, Marxist!" *Post-Scarcity Anarchism* (San Francisco: Ramparts, 1971), pp. 171-220.

10. Michael Harrington, *Toward A Democratic Left* (Baltimore: Penguin Books, 1969), 274. First published by Macmillan, 1968.

11. For a brief history of American political parties, see William Nisbet Chambers, *Political Parties in a New Nation: The American Experience 1776-1809* (New York: Oxford University Press, 1963). For a summary of party functions and how they are performed by both existing parties and reform clubs, see James Q. Wilson, *Amateur Democrat* (Chicago: University of Chicago Press, 1962), especially Chapters I and XII. For one argument on the need for party reform and the consequence of unrelieved pressure politics, see David Broder, *The Party's Over* (New York: Harper and Row, 1971), especially pp. 179-180.

12. Walter Dean Burnham, *Critical Elections and the Mainsprings of American Politics* (New York: W. W. Norton, 1970), pp. 119, 120, 130, 131.

13. Thucydides, *History*, Book II, Chapter VI, Section 40, translated by Alfred E. Zimmern in *The Greek Commonwealth* (London: Oxford University Press, 1911), p. 204.

14. Neil Shadle, "New Politics in the 43rd Ward" (Unpublished paper, October, 1970).

CHAPTER 3

1. For a detailed handbook of independent campaigns, see Dick Simpson, *Winning Elections: A Handbook in Participatory Politics* (Chicago: Swallow Press, 1972). For a film which actually shows a campaign, see William Mahin and Dick Simpson, "By The People: Independent Politics, Chicago 1969" (New York and Oak Park, Illinois: Radim Films, 1970), 81 min. b/w 16mm soundfilm.

2. Harold Gosnell, *Machine Politics: Chicago Model* (Chicago: University of Chicago Press, 1968), Chapter VIII, pp. 156-181. First published, 1937.

3. See Reinhold Niebuhr, *The Nature and Destiny of Man: Vol. II, Human Destiny* (New York: Charles Scribner's Sons, 1943), p. 155; Harry Davis and Robert Good (eds.) *Reinhold Niebuhr on Politics* (New York: Charles Scribner's Sons, 1960), p. 135;

and all of Reinhold Niebuhr, *Moral Man and Immoral Society* (New York: Charles Scribner's Sons, 1932).

4. Robert Michels, *Political Parties: A Sociological Study of the Oligarchical Tendencies of Modern Democracy* (New York: Dover Publications, 1959). First published in English in 1915.

5. David Bazelon, *Power in America: The Politics of the New Class* (New York: The New American Library, 1967) argues that professionals are indeed a new class in America which, because of their skills and position, may come to govern America.

6. An example of the type of local campaigns which are being run across the country can be found in Chester Atkins, *Getting Elected: A Guide to Winning State and Local Office* (Boston: Houghton Mifflin, 1973), Chapter 11, pp. 163-190.

7. James Q. Wilson, *Amateur Democrat* (Chicago: University of Chicago Press, 1962), pp. 342.

8. *Ibid.,* pp. 342-343.

9. Robert Pranger, *The Eclipse of Citizenship* (New York: Holt, Rinehart and Winston, 1968), p. 102.

CHAPTER 4

1. David M. Potter, *People of Plenty* (Chicago: The University of Chicago Press, 1954), p. 166.

2. See, for example, Adolph A. Berle and Gardiner C. Means, *The Modern Corporation and Private Property,* Revised Edition (New York: Harcourt, Brace & World, 1968); Adolph A. Berle, *Power Without Property,* (New York: Harcourt, Brace & World, 1959).

3. For some comments on the world-wide development toward bureaucracy and management, see James Burnham, *The Managerial Revolution* (Bloomington: Indiana University Press, 1941). J. Leiper Freeman, *The Political Process: Executive Bureau-Legislative Committee Relations* (New York: Random House, 1965) presents a statement of policy-making at the sub-system level identifying bureau chiefs, senior members of congressional committee, and interest groups as the principal participants.

4. In other words, formal "subordinates" have real power. Consider, for example, the following statement by Paul Diesing, *Reason in Society: Five Types of Decisions and Their Social Conditions* (Urbana: University of Illinois Press, 1962), pp. 181-182. "By 'power' I mean the ability to inflict unpleasant consequences at will. In some childrens' gangs the unpleasant consequences may be a beating. In more formal organizations consequences such as dismissal or demotion, fines, jail, or vetoes are at the disposal of the formal leader, and the threat of these consequences forces people to listen to him. But the most usual kind of

power is the contribution a person makes to an organization's activities. The more important a person's contributions are, the more dangerous their removal would be, and the fear of removal forces people to listen to his views. The contributions a person can make depend on the needs of the organization—money, influence over votes or customers, administrative skill, labor, special knowledge or information, high status or prestige, patronage, and so on. Once an organization has become dependent on a person's contribution, the threat of withdrawal is usually enough to force admission into the organization's decision structure."

5. Chester I. Bernard, "A Definition of Authority," in Robert K. Merton, *et. al.* (eds.), *Reader in Bureaucracy* (New York: The Free Press, 1962), pp. 180-185.
6. Karl E. Weick, *The Social Psychology of Organizing* (Reading, Massachusetts: Addison-Wesley Publishing Company, 1969), p. 5.
7. Although "[the] calculability of behavior in bureaucracy rests on the premise that official policy will be faithfully carried out by subordinates . . . research has indicated [that] this policy is often modified or nullified in its passage through the administrative hierarchy." Merton, *et. al.*, (eds.), *Reader in Bureaucracy*, p. 179.
8. Harold L. Wilensky, "The Influence of the Staff Expert," in Cyril Rosemann, *et. al.*, (eds.), *Dimensions of Political Analysis*, (Englewood Cliffs, New Jersey: Prentice Hall, Inc., 1966), p. 244.
9. Arthur M. Schlesinger, Jr., *A Thousand Days: John F. Kennedy in the White House* (Boston: Houghton Mifflin Company, 1965), p. 685.
10. Such a recruitment procedure does not mean that *all* bureaucrats are competent nor that patronage and other types of hiring have been *completely* eliminated. Indeed, most persons have had enough contact with bureaucrats in government agencies and businesses to document that not all bureaucrats are recruited on the basis of professional training and tested competence. Nevertheless, the real-life consequences of these deviations from the normal recruitment pattern must not be overstated if we wish to understand the unique strength and stability of bureaucratic society. The dominant characteristics of the large bureaucracies are not patronage, stupidity, and failure but rather hiring on the basis of competence, intelligence, and success. The ability of the large organizations to complete their complicated tasks— in a word, their ability to succeed—is made possible *only* if the general norm is the recruitment of trained, competent personnel.
11. Hans H. Gerth and C. Wright Mills, "A Marx for the Managers," in Merton, *et al.*, *Reader in Bureaucracy*, p. 171.

12. **As Alvin W.** Gouldner has suggested, the bureaucratic organization as a whole should not be considered as having its own end. Rather it "is ... necessary to specify the ends of different people, of the typical ends of different strata within the organization. Such a refocusing suggests that these vary, are not necessarily identical and, may in fact be contradictory." Alvin W. Gouldner, "On Weber's Analysis of Bureaucratic Rules," in Merton, *et al., Reader in Bureaucracy,* p. 50.

13. David Rogers, *110 Livingston Street, Politics and Bureaucracy in the New York City School System* (New York: Random House, 1968), p. 13.

14. For a more extensive discussion of the effect of status and income, see George H. Crowell, *Society Against Itself* (Philadelphia: The Westminster Press, 1968), Chapters 7 and 8.

15. Chicago Board of Education, *Facts and Figures: Chicago Public Schools, (1972-1973),* pp. 62, 75, 83.

16. Chicago Board of Education, *Annual School Budget 1973,* p. xv; "Cash Crisis Seen for Schools," *Chicago Tribune* (July 10, 1975), p. 5.

17. "Legislative Unit Probes Deficiencies," *Chicago Tribune* (June 8, 1970), p. 1.

18. See, for example, "Tests Show Pupils Here Fall Further Behind," *Chicago Tribune* (May 5, 1972), p. 8; "47% of the 8th Graders Here Lag in Reading." *Chicago Tribune* (June 7, 1973), p. 3.

19. Real Estate Research Corporation, *Projections of Population and School Enrollments by Community Areas for the City of Chicago 1970 and 1975,* (April, 1968), p. viii-6.

20. The central administration employs 14 persons and spends $149,826 to keep track of school attendance. Each of the 27 district offices employs truant officers; District 12, for example, employs six at a cost of $59,750. *Annual School Budget 1973,* pp. 20, 723.

21. Chicago Board of Education, *Increasing Desegregation of Faculties, Students, and Vocational Educational Programs* (August 23, 1967), p. A-10.

22. *Annual School Budget, 1973,* p. 16 and "490 Armed Guards Patrol Public Schools in Chicago," *Chicago Tribune,* (March 26, 1972), Section N, p. 3.

23. "... organized labor [is] perhaps the single biggest factor in the unique survival of the big city organization in Chicago. Labor provides Daley with his strongest personal support and contributes great sums to his campaigns. ... Thousands of trade union men are employed by local government. ... Chicago always pays the top construction rate, rather than the lower maintenance scale, although most of the work is maintenance. ... His policy

is that a labor leader be appointed to every policy-making city board or committee." Mike Royko, *Boss* (New York: Dutton, 1971), pp. 67-68. See also the series of articles on the cost of custodial personnel in the *Chicago Sun-Times,* beginning July 7, 1971, p. 1.

24. It is usually enlightening to examine the budgets of larger organizations. The size of the larger operations usually precludes keeping a separate, private set of books because of the expense and time involved. Therefore, budgets of large organizations when properly understood, often reveal their true nature.

25. Administrative costs have superceded instructional costs in the Chicago schools for some time. "An Office of Education study ... showed Chicago in 1935-36 to be the lowest in instructional costs per capita of the ten largest cities and the highest in non-instructional costs." Mary J. Herrick, *The Chicago Schools: A Social and Political History* (Beverly Hills: Sage Publications, 1971), p. 228.

26. *Annual School Budget, 1973,* p. xliv.

27. See, for example, *Annual School Budget, 1973,* pp. 5-39.

28. *Facts and Figures, 1972-1973,* p. 126. Emphasis added.

29. *Facts and Figures, 1972-1973,* p. 126. Emphasis added.

30. Such a situation is not unique to Chicago. One community group in New York, the United Bronx Parents, has taken the position that their schools do *not* need more money but rather that existing school money should be spent differently; in particular, that funds be transferred to the local boards. Eveline Antonetty, executive director of the group, said, "If you give one more dime to that decaying maze you might as well be burning your money.' " The group contends that "... only one-third of the $1.9 billion 1970-71 budget goes to the local districts for direct instructional services." "Urban Fiscal Crisis Hits New York City Schools," *Guardian* (April 3, 1971), p. 6.

31. James D. Koerner, *Who Controls American Education? A Guide for Laymen* (Boston: Beacon Press, 1968), p. 137.

32. When interviewed, Jim Shiflett, an activist member of one community group that has numerous dealings with the Chicago schools, said that the school system is a very large bureaucracy which is wound up in itself and feeds upon itself. Its attentions and efforts, he said, are spent on itself. Its primary concern is with its own preservation rather than with problems on the outside. Many others who have had experience with the Chicago schools agree with Shiflett's analysis.

33. Koerner overstates the case when he singles out the superintendent as the one with "unconscionable" power. Koerner, *Who Controls American Education?,* p. 141. Superintendents are more

powerful than their boards, but bureaucrats in large systems are the ones whose power prevails over all others.

34. Henry S. Resnik, *Turning on the System, War in the Philadelphia Public Schools* (New York: Pantheon Books, 1970), p. 22.
35. Koerner, *Who Controls American Education?*, pp. 173-174.
36. *Ibid.*, p. 154.
37. National School Public Relations Association, *Education U.S.A.*, Washington, D.C. (February 12, 1973).
38. Koerner, *Who Controls American Education?*, p. 147.
39. After spending about 100 pages on the overcrowding, poor buildings, terrible curriculum, and political corruption of the Chicago Schools, Herrick informs us that the new Chicago Teachers' Federation founded in 1887, ". . . set out its first year of existence to find out why they were not getting better salaries." And speaking of the effect of the Chicago Teachers' Union in the 1930's she states that the gains of the union ". . . did not aid in solving *the problem closest to the teachers themselves*— the restoration of pay cuts." Herrick, *The Chicago Schools*, pp. 99-100 and 249. Emphasis added. Miss Herrick has been active in the Chicago teachers union.
40. Rogers, *110 Livingston Street*, pp. 195-196.
41. On the New York teachers' union and decentralization, see Sol Stern, " 'Scab' Teachers," *Ramparts* (November 17, 1968), pp. 17-24.
42. "Urban Fiscal Crisis Hits New York City Schools," *Guardian* (April 3, 1971), p. 5.
43. "Teachers Strike in Newark," *Guardian* (February 27, 1971), p. 7.
44. Direct action tactics are partially explained in Morton Oppenheimer and George Lakey, *A Manual for Direct Action* (Chicago: Quadrangle Books, 1964); see especially p. 26.
45. "South Shore's Informal School," *Chicago Sun-Times* (January 18, 1971), p. 38.
46. Information on the Parents School is from an interview with Jean Thomases, a former teacher at the school.

CHAPTER 5

1. John H. Schaar and Sheldon S. Wolin, "Where We Are Now," *New York Review of Books* (May 7, 1970), p. 3.
2. Hannah Arendt, "Thoughts on Politics and Revolution," *New York Review of Books* (April 22, 1971), p. 10.
3. Staughton Lynd, "Organizing the New Politics: A Proposal," *Ramparts* (December, 1971), p. 15.
4. E. E. Schattschneider, *The Semisovereign People* (New York:

Holt, Rinehart and Winston, 1960), p. 74.

5. Sidney Lens, *Radicalism in America* (New York: Thomas Y. Crowell Company, 1969), p. 367.

6. Michael Harrington, *The Other America, Poverty in the United States* (Baltimore, Maryland: Penguin Books, 1962), p. 156. George H. Crowell, in *Society Against Itself* (Philadelphia: The Westminister Press, 1968), p. 79, put the argument this way: "Our hope for initiative in social action, short of outbursts of revolutionary violence from frustrated, disadvantaged, lower class people, must rest largely upon people of the higher class who are sensitive to existing alienation and injustice among men . . . there are many such people in the United States. There are people who recognize that their real, long-range self-interest lies in the elimination of injustice however this may affect their own immediate interests."

7. David Rogers, *110 Livingston Street, Politics and Bureaucracy in the New York City School System* (New York: Random House, 1968), p. 393. It is, of course, still problematic if those available insiders who wish fundamental change have a sufficient leverage of power to bring it about. Many dissident insiders, for example, are at lower levels of organizational power. Such dissidents within the Democratic Party have not had enough power to alter fundamentally that political party. The argument presented here is that needed changes can be brought about with acceptance of new definitions and the creation of new movements (not coalitions) that join insiders with outsiders.

8. A further step in the development of an effective administrative strategy necessitates relationships among individuals in different institutions. This follows from the fact that administrators in the Chicago schools, for example, receive both help and hindrances from administrators in other institutions such as various federal and state agencies dealing with education. The movement must start somewhere, but the connections among various bureaucracies requires the coordinated efforts of individuals not only within institutions but also among them. For a discussion of the connections among various bureaucracies, see Gordon Tullock's discussion of "allies" in *The Politics of Bureaucracy* (Washington, D.C.: Public Affairs Press, 1965), pp. 48-50.

9. Lewis Mumford, "The Moral Challenge to Democracy," *Virginia Quarterly Review,* Vol. 35 (Autumn, 1959), pp. 574-575. Mumford's slip recommending that one speak "truth to power" rather than "power to power" is the consequence of applying the basic individualistic moral imperative to social situations. One of the classic statements of this problem in Reinhold Niebuhr, *Moral Man and Immoral Society* (New York: Charles Scribner's Sons, 1932).

10. "U.S. Employees Set An Antiwar Rally," *New York Times* (March 31, 1969), p. 8.
11. Rogers, *110 Livingston Street*, p. 393.
12. Within the schools and similar organizations, structural manipulations of various sorts have been tried and in most instances found wanting. The New York school administration, for example, established subunits in the bureaucracy (Human Relations was one of them) supposedly as vehicles for change and innovation. But these units have received limited resources, and their influence has been minimal. In addition, they are insulated from the rest of the system and often made the scapegoat for problems that are not solved by the school system.

    In this instance, what is true of the New York school bureaucracy is true of bureaucracies generally. Because the primary goal of every organization is its own existence, stability, and status, it segregates and thereby weakens pressures for new policies and programs. Those in power will not support on their own initiative a truly radical structural change nor establish a subunit that is truly innovative. They will not foster viable alternatives to the existing procedures and policies and, from their point view, why should they?

    On these points, see Rogers, *110 Livingston Street*, pp. 344, 348; Victor A. Thompson, *Bureaucracy and Innovation*, (University, Alabama: University of Alabama Press, 1969), p. 22.
13. "Youth Corps Head Explains His Role," *New York Times* (July 31, 1968), p. 28.
14. Herbert Simon in *Administrative Behavior, A Study of Decision-Making in Administrative Organizations*, Second Edition (New York: The Macmillan Company, 1957), pp. 116-117, has argued that promotion is not a strong incentive for all individuals. There is some evidence for that aspect of administrative strategy which requires bureaucrats not to be dominated in their actions by the inducement of promotion. According to Simon, "There is a great variation among individuals in the extent to which opportunities for promotion act as incentives for participation. Promotion is, of course, both an economic and a prestige incentive. . . . It would be a mistake . . . to assume that these desires [for advancement] provide a strong incentive in all individuals."
15. Crowell, *Society Against Itself*, p. 103.
16. Karl E. Weick, *The Social Psychology of Organizing* (Reading, Massachusetts: Addison-Wesley, 1969), p. 36.
17. The following is Bernard's statement on this point: "If a directive communication is accepted by one to whom it is addressed, its authority for him is confirmed or established. It is admitted as the basis of action. Disobedience of such a communication

is denial of its authority for him. Therefore, under this definition the decision as to whether an order has authority or not
lies with the persons to whom it is addressed and does not reside in 'persons of authority' or those who issue these orders
... Even though physical force is involved, ... authority nevertheless rests upon the acceptance or consent of individuals. ... Our
definition of authority ... no doubt will appear to many whose
eyes are fixed only on enduring organizations to be a platform
of chaos. And so it is—exactly so in the preponderance of attempted organizations. They fail because they can maintain no
authority, that is, they cannot secure sufficient contributions
of personal efforts to be effective or cannot induce them on terms
that are efficient. In the last analysis the authority fails because
the individuals in sufficient numbers regard the burden involved
in accepting necessary orders as changing the balance of advantage against their interest, and they withdraw or withhold the
indispensable contributions." Chester I. Bernard, "A Definition
of Authority," in Robert K. Merton, *et al.*, eds., *Reader in
Bureaucracy* (New York: The Free Press, 1962), pp. 180-181.

18. "... if an instruction is disregarded, an executive's risk of being
wrong must be accepted, a risk that the individual cannot and
usually will not take unless in fact his position is at least as good
as that of another with respect to correct appraisal of the relevant situation. Most persons are disposed to grant authority because they dislike the personal responsibility which they otherwise accept, especially when they are not in a good position to
accept it. The practical difficulties in the operation of organizations seldom lie in the excessive desire of individuals to assume
responsibility for the organization actions of themselves or others,
but rather lie in the reluctance to take responsibility for their
own actions in organization." Bernard, in Merton, *et al.*, eds.,
Reader in Bureaucracy, pp. 184-185.

19. Barons have assets which improve their power relationships with
their formal superiors, such as independent wealth, powerful
personal connections, technical expertise, a strong personal following among other members of the hierarchy, and internal
strength of character. Tullock, *The Politics of Bureaucracy*, pp.
113-116.

20. Francis E. Rourke, *Bureaucracy, Politics, and Public Policy*
(Boston: Little, Brown and Company, 1961), p. 11.

21. "Youth Corps Head Explains His Role," *New York Times* (July
31, 1968), p. 28.

22. Crowell, *Society Against Itself*, p. 103.

23. Jason Epstein, "The Politics of School Decentralization,' *The
New York Review of Books* (June 6, 1968), p. 28.

CHAPTER 6

1. See, for instance, Floyd Hunter, *Community Power Structure* (Chapel Hill: University of North Carolina Press, 1953); Robert and Helen Lynd, *Middletown* (New York: Harcout, Brace, 1929); William Lloyd Warner, *et al., Democracy in Jonesville* (New York: Harper, 1949).

2. See, for instance, Robert Dahl, *Who Governs?* (New Haven: Yale University Press, 1961); Robert Agger, Daniel Goldrich, and Bert Swanson, *The Rulers and the Ruled* (New York: Wiley, 1964); Nelson Polsby, *Community Power and Political Theory* (New Haven: Yale University Press, 1963); Robert Presthus, *Men at the Top* (New York: Oxford University Press, 1964).

3. Edward Banfield, *Political Influence* (New York: The Free Press of Glencoe, 1961).

4. Mike Royko, *Boss: Richard J. Daley of Chicago* (New York: Dutton, 1971). In addition to Banfield and Royko, other sources on Chicago politics include Pierre de Vise, *Chicago's Widening Color Gap* (Chicago: Interuniversity Social Research Committee, 1967); Bill Gleason, *Daley of Chicago* (New York: Simon and Schuster, 1970); Ovid Demaris, *Captive City* (New York: Pocket Books, 1970), first published by Lyle Stuart, 1969; Harold Gosnell, *Machine Politics: Chicago Model* (Chicago: University of Chicago Press, 1937); Peter Knauss, *Chicago: A One-Party State* (Champaign, Illinois: Stipes, 1972); Lloyd Wendt and Herman Kogan, *Bosses in Lusty Chicago* (Bloomington, Indiana: Indiana University Press, 1967), first published by Bobbs-Merrill, 1943; Clark C. Kissinger and Paul Booth, "Welcome to Chicago: Meet the Men Who Own It," *Ramparts*, (September 7, 1968), pp. 24-30.

5. Tom Hayden, *Rebellion in Newark* (New York: Random House, 1967), p. 69.

6. Although the most immediate cause of a riot is a specific event of some sort, not even a brutal and offensive event will cause a riot unless other factors are present. Thus, the more basic causative factors are those which create and sustain an environment and set of attitudes which provide the context out of which a particular event can become a riot.

7. Numerous newspaper accounts, magazine articles, and books have analyzed these confrontations from various perspectives. A few examples from this literature are: (1) on the confrontations at Columbia (1968), see "Report of the Fact-Finding Commission Appointed to Investigate the Disturbances at Columbia University in April and May, 1968," *Crisis at Columbia* (Cox Commission Report) (New York: Vintage Books, 1968); Dan-

iel Bell, "Columbia and the New Left," and Roger Star, "The Case of the Columbia Gym," in Daniel Bell and Irving Kristol, eds., *Confrontation, The Student Rebellion and the Universities* (New York: Basic Books, Inc., 1968), pp. 67-127; Ellen Kay Trimberger, "Columbia: The Dynamics of a Student Revolution," in Howard S. Becker, ed., *Campus Power Struggle* (New York: Aldine Publishing Company, 1970), pp. 27-58. (2) On the Democratic National Convention (1968), see *Rights in Conflicts, The Violent Confrontations of Demonstrators and Police in the Parks and Streets of Chicago During the Week of the Democratic National Convention,* a report submitted by Daniel Walker, Director of the Chicago Study Team, to the National Commission on the Causes and Prevention of Violence (New York: Bantam Books, 1968). (3) On Kent State see I. F. Stone, *The Killings at Kent State: How Murder Went Unpunished* (New York: New York Review, 1971); Bill Warren, ed., *The Middle of the Country, The Events of May 4th as Seen by Students and Faculty at Kent State University* (New York: Avon Books, 1970); Phillip K. Tompkins and Elaine Vanden Bouth Anderson, *Communication Crisis at Kent State, A Case Study* (New York: Bordon and Breach, 1971); *The Report of the President's Commission on Campus Unrest* (Scranton Report) (Washington, D. C.: U. S. Government Printing Office, 1970), pp. 233-410. The Scranton Report also contains a helpful annotated bibliography of sources and bibliographies on many aspects of the student protest movement, pp. 476-518.

One of the better ways to study these confrontations is through film accounts. See especially *Columbia Revolt* (Lawrence, Kansas: Kansas Media Project, 1968); *Conventions: The Land Around Us* (Chicago: University of Illinois at Chicago Circle, 1969).

8. This was not the pattern, however, at the University of Chicago in 1969. Students occupied buildings and created problems for authorities, but President Levi did not call in the police to remove the students. *New York Times* (April 27, 1969), p. 65. See also Bell's comment on "what might have been" if the police had not been called in the Columbia confrontations. Daniel Bell, "Columbia and the New Left," in Bell and Kristol, (eds.), *Confrontation,* pp. 102-105.

9. "The activists [at Columbia University, 1968] believed that the use of police to clear the buildings would radicalize the campus and bring many more students and faculty to their side. This did happen after the first police action. According to the Barton survey, faculty support for the sit-ins increased by 17 percent and student support by 19 percent. Timberger, in Becker, (ed.) *Campus Power Struggle,* p. 45.

10. One of the earliest, full treatments of the role of interests in American politics is Arthur F. Bentley, *The Process of Government*, (Bloomington, Indiana: The Principia Press, 1949) first published in 1908. According to William T. Bluhm, [*Theories of the Political System, Classics of Political Thought and Modern Political Analysis*, Second Edition (Englewood Cliffs, N.J.: Prentice-Hall, 1971) pp. 358-388], a theoretical forerunner of Bentley is the 17th century theorist, James Harrington. A more recent presentation of American politics from this theoretical orientation is David B. Truman, *The Governmental Process, Political Interests and Public Opinion* (New York: Alfred A. Knopf, 1951). On the more specific topic of lobbying at the state level, see Harmon Zeigler and Michael Baer, *Lobbying: Interaction and Influence in State Legislatures* (Belmont, California: Wadsworth Publishing Company, 1969) and the numerous studies cited therein. Arnold M. Rose, *The Power Structure, Political Process in American Society* (New York: Oxford University Press, 1967), pp. 70-76, cites many of the key studies on lobbying.

11. Martin Luther King, Jr., *Why We Can't Wait* (New York: Signet, 1963), pp. 30, 40.

12. *Ibid.*, pp. 83-84.

13. Saul D. Alinsky, *Reveille for Radicals* (New York: Random House, 1969), p. x. First published in 1946.

14. Saul D. Alinsky, *Rules for Radicals*, (New York: Vintage Books, 1971), pp. 162-163.

15. *Ibid.*, p 225.

16. See, for example, Richard B. Gregg, *The Power of Nonviolence* (Nyack, New Jersey: Fellowship Publications, 1959), pp. 141-175.

17. King, *Why We Can't Wait*, p. 78.

18. *Ibid.*, p. 44.

19. Alinsky, *Rules for Radicals*, p. 126.

20. Saul Alinsky, a conversation with Marion K. Sanders, "The Professional Radical, 1970," *Harper's Magazine* (January, 1970), pp. 36-42.

21. Alinsky, *Rules for Radicals*, p. 130.

22. *Ibid.*, p. 97.

23. *Ibid.*, pp. 27-28.

24. Michael Lipsky, "Protest as a Political Resource," *American Political Science Review*, LXII, No. 4 (December 1968), p. 1147.

25. For more detailed information, would-be organizers and community spokesmen are advised to study Dr. King's *Why We Can't Wait* and Saul Alinsky's *Rules for Radicals*. Two films

further illustrate nonviolent issue strategies as they have been practiced: William Mahin's and Dick Simpson's *In Order to Change* (Chicago: Vision Quest, 1974), Color, 16mm, 74 minutes, which shows the pollution battle in Chicago; and Canadian Broadcast Company, *Saul Alinsky Goes to War* (New York: Contemporary Films/McGraw Hill, 1968), B/W, 16 mm, 57 minutes, which covers a variety of Alinsky organizations and campaigns. Finally, tactical details of a nonviolent demonstration can be learned from Martin Oppenheimer and George Lakey, *A Manual for Direct Action* (Chicago: Quadrangle, 1964).

CHAPTER 7

1. Alderman William Singer then represented Chicago's 43rd Ward. He rose to national prominence when he challenged the Mayor's delegates to the 1972 Democratic National Convention. The "Singer 59" were seated and the Mayor's delegates were thrown out of the convention. Alderman Singer ran for Mayor of Chicago in 1975 but was defeated.
2. In forming a group, there are basically two alternatives—organize within a single community or around a single issue. Either the community boundaries or the nature of the issue define who should join.
3. Alinsky, *Rules for Radicals*, pp. 77-78.
4. *Ibid.*, pp. 116-117.
5. *The Troublemakers* (New York: Grove Press, 1967) B/W, 16 mm, 54 minutes.

CHAPTER 8

1. Ralph Nader and Donald Ross, *Action for a Change* (New York: Grossman, 1971). See also, Donald K. Ross, *A Public Citizen's Action Manual* (New York: Grossman, 1973).
2. John Gardner, *In Common Cause* (New York: Norton, 1972).
3. In our view, the problems of contemporary, technological society and the deterioration of traditional political institutions require moving beyond many of the strategic suggestions of Nader and Gardner. Nader and his associates advocate "whistle blowing" on corporate and governmental injustices, but they cannot protect those who dare openly to oppose their organizational superiors. Most whistle blowers lose their jobs. (Ralph Nader, *et al.*, (eds.) *Whistle Blowing, The Report of the Conference on Professional Responsibility* (New York: Grossman, 1972). A change may be made in automobile construction, a product

may be taken off the market, but the large organizations continue to be run by the same people pursuing essentially the same objectives. Gardner still pins his hopes on the traditional two party system and a reformed Congress, not seeing the need to develop new institutions for a new age. Our purpose, however, is not to criticize those like Nader and Gardner who seek a more humane America but to suggest what seem to us to be better ways to achieve the same goal. Only history will finally determine which methods succeeded.

4. Alinsky, *Rules for Radicals*, pp. 120-121.

Bibliography

In addition to the material listed in this bibliography we have produced other films and books which may be of special interest. For those of you particularly interested in electoral strategies, you may wish to use in combination a film by William Mahin and Dick Simpson, "By The People" (81 minutes, black and white, 16 mm. distributed by Radim Films, 1034 Lake Street, Oak Park, Illinois 60301) and Simpson's book, *Winning Elections: A Handbook in Participatory Politics* (Chicago: Swallow Press, 1972). For those interested in an analysis of the deficiencies and disintegration of traditional politics and the need for new descriptions and citizen actions which focus on administration, you will want to read Beam's book *Usual Politics: A Critique and Some Suggestions for an Alternative* (New York: Holt, Rinehart and Winston, 1970). For those concerned with issue strategies, you will want to view the film on the Chicago anti-pollution campaign by William Mahin and Dick Simpson, "In Order to Change" (74 minutes, color, 16 mm. distributed by Vision Quest, 7715 N. Sheridan, Chicago, Illinois 60626).

Our brief comments on the other books listed in this bibliography are not meant to do justice to the wide range of ideas and insights contained in each. We have limited our remarks, for the most part, to just those aspects of the books which deal directly with electoral, administrative, and issue strategies.

I. General

Bookchin, Murray. *Post-Scarcity Anarchism*. San Francisco: Ramparts Press, 1971.

In this collection of essays the author's primary focus is technology and he encourages activists to develop strategies which can utilize technology to bring about the decentralization of large urban areas and to reduce degrading work. In "Listen, Marxist!" he documents the limits of Marxist analysis and strategy—only by harnessing the potentialities of modern technology, affluence, and the creative role of the youth movement can contemporary strategists help to build a better America according to Bookchin.

Bondurant, Joan V. *Conquest of Violence, the Gandhian Philosophy of Conflict.* Revised Edition. Berkeley: University of California Press, 1965.

Every strategist interested in effective nonviolent action should become familiar with the philosophy and techniques of " 'the greatest revolutionary' India has yet produced." In this book the precepts basic to the Gandhian technique (satyagraha) are analyzed, historical instances of satyagraha in action are discussed, and in the last two chapters Gandhi's thoughts and actions are evaluated within the context of western political theory. A useful bibliography on nonviolence and Gandhi is also included.

Carmichael, Stokely, and Charles V. Hamilton. *Black Power, The Politics of Liberation in America.* New York: Vintage Books, 1967.

In addition to its significance as the first full statement of the meaning of "black power," this book is also important as a rejection of traditional liberal approaches to the problems of racism, poverty, and urban decay. Carmichael and Hamilton argue that fundamental change is needed and that new institutions must be built which have a power base constructed from an independent, unified, and militant community. They stress the strategic importance of acting upon an accurate description of the situation and the need for new definitions. "Those who have the right to define are the masters of the situation." This book provides complementary analysis and supporting evidence for some of the key strategic concepts described by E. E. Schattschneider, *The Semi-Sovereign People*.

Crowell, George H. *Society Against Itself*. Philadelphia: The Westminister Press. 1968.

A major contribution of Crowell's essay is his identification of the basic values and social pressures in American society which inhibit effective social action; the most powerful being the commitment to job and family. By understanding how cultural values and orientations in support of the status quo eliminate incentives for social action, strategists may be able to develop techniques for circumventing these forces. Crowell argues that established volunteer organizations and part-time efforts will not suffice to remedy the problems of this age. He argues that by "initiating social action through the job" (inside action) adequate resources can be marshalled for significant change.

Goldwin, Robert A. *On Civil Disobedience; American Essays, Old and New*. Chicago: Rand McNally, 1969.

This collection of essays includes Thoreau's famous treatise ("Civil Disobedience") which advocates civil disobedience as the means for creating "*at once* a better government." Included also are six essays by contemporary writers; some write in defense of civil disobedience, others argue that it is an unjustifiable and counterproductive tactic. Strategists should be aware of Thoreau's position and the case which can be made against civil disobedience—these essays present both sides of the issue.

Lakey, George. *Strategy for a Living Revolution*. San Francisco: W. H. Freeman and Company, 1973.

George Lakey, activist and scholar, believes that we

have only a few decades remaining to enact fundamental change or else mankind is ended. The strategy he outlines is nonviolent and, since our most basic problems are worldwide in scope (pollution, war, hunger), he argues that an effective strategy must be transnational. Convinced that established liberal institutions, lobbying, and electoral politics are inadequate, Lakey develops a revolutionary strategy of five steps; cultural preparation, building organizational strength, direct action, noncooperation, and the creation of strong parallel institutions.

Rejai, Mostafa. *The Strategy of Political Revolution.* New York: Anchor Press, 1973.

Rejai surveys the literature on revolution and presents a definition of political revolution which distinguishes revolution from riot, rebellion, and coup d'etat. He identifies five aspects of a revolutionary strategy: leadership, ideology, organization, the role of terror and violence, and the manipulation of the international situation. Rejai applies his definition of revolution and his concept of revolutionary strategy to three historical examples (Boliva-1952, North Vietnam, France-1968) and concludes with a comment on the possibility of revolution in the United States today.

Revel, Jean-Francois. *Without Marx or Jesus, The New American Revolution Has Begun.* New York: Doubleday & Company, 1971.

Without Marx or Jesus is a bit dated with its emphasis upon dissent in the 1960's and, in some instances, it is an oversimplified celebration of the virtues of the American order. Yet, strategists for fundamental change in America can learn from this book because, in addition to presenting some basic and realistic strategic principles, Revel's argument is a healthy antidote to those who continuously fail to see the extensive possibilities in America for not just a national but even a worldwide revolution. Revel points out the errors of traditional left-ist movements and discusses the requirements for revolution in a technologically advanced world—requirements which are met only in America.

Schattschneider, E. E. *The Semi-Sovereign People, A Realist's View of Democracy in America.* New York: Holt, Rinehart and Winston, 1960.

This book is an excellent theoretical statement of many principles basic to any type of strategy. Schattschneider points out, using numerous examples from American politics, that successful strategists "blot out" existing issues and make their own issues the focus of public debate, control the scope of conflict to their advantage, and either use or modify existing rules so that benefits accrue to them rather than to their opponents. *The Semi-Sovereign People* is one of the best introductions and a good resource for the study of political strategies.

Sharp, Gene. *The Politics of Nonviolent Action.* Boston: Porter Sargent, 1973.

Beginning with an analysis of power which documents the reliance of rulers upon the contributions and compliance of subordinates and citizens, Sharp provides a theoretical basis for the effectiveness of nonviolent action. In Part II he identifies 198 different methods of nonviolent action. Each is discussed briefly and examples from various historical periods are cited for every method. Part III develops the underlying philosophical and strategic principles of nonviolence. The numerous historical examples are clear evidence that nonviolent methods can be effective and the theoretical analysis in Parts I and III furnish guidance for those pursuing various types of nonviolent action.

Theobald, Robert. *An Alternative Future for America II.* Chicago: The Swallow Press, 1968.

Theobald is convinced that the present cultural order

has collapsed and that the youth and others on the periphery of society are the basis for change. Technology, he says, provides us with the tools to create a better world. The primary means for mastering technology and for constructing a more humane social order are communication, dialogue, and cooperation.

Walzer, Michael. *Political Action, A Practical Guide to Movement Politics.* Chicago: Quadrangle Books, 1971.
Walzer packs a lot of basic, realistic advice into this brief essay on citizen politics. Rejecting militancy, sectarianism, and terrorism he believes that only pressure and electoral politics which remain focused on single issues, tactical flexibility, and incremental change are effective strategic options. *Political Action* is a handbook of pragmatic, general advice on a wide range of issues—finding a constituency, coalitions, meetings, etc. As a one-two punch against the status quo, a reading of Walzer followed by an examination of a more detailed study (for example, Simpson, *Winning Elections,* or Huenefeld, *The Community Activist's Handbook*) provides a strategist with some training and ideas for effective political action.

II. Electoral Strategy

Agranoff, Robert, (ed.), *The New Style in Election Campaigns.* Boston: Holbrook Press, 1972.
This reader covers campaign management, information systems such as public opinion polling, and manipulation of the mass media (especially television). An introductory essay by Agranoff describes the decline of political parties and the rise of candidate-centered, technologically-oriented campaigns. It is a thought-provoking collection rather than a handbook for employing this new style of campaigning. It updates much of the material

in the Nimmo and Perry books also cited in this bibliography.

Anderson, Walt. *Campaigns: Cases in Political Conflict.* Pacific Palisades, California: Goodyear, 1970.
An historical treatment of fourteen campaigns ranging from the Lincoln-Douglas campaign up to the New Hampshire campaign of Eugene McCarthy, *Campaigns* points up the differences in campaigns in various regions and at various times in our history, as well as emphasizing candidates, oratory, issues, and events which influenced the outcome.

Atkins, State Senator Chester, with Barry Hock and Bob Martin, *Getting Elected: A Guide to Winning State and Local Office.* Boston: Houghton Mifflin, 1973.
One of the best complete guides for candidates who would combine the techniques of volunteer campaigns with running in regular party primaries, *Getting Elected* is particularly helpful for someone deciding whether or not to run. The principles behind each of the campaign activities from public relations to canvassing are well explained. Vignettes about six progressive candidates running for local office for the first time in different parts of the country (including the Simpson aldermanic campaign in Chicago) reassure the reader that it can be done. Certainly this is a guide well worth reading for strategists just getting into electoral politics. The fact that Atkins himself was elected to the Massachusetts State Senate lends considerable credibility to his recommendations.

Bullitt, Stimson, *To Be a Politician.* Garden City, New York: Doubleday, 1961.
The book is divided into four sections covering politics as a profession, campaigns, qualities present in the best politicians, and the need for leadership from among the leisure class. Stimson's treatment of campaigning in-

cludes a thoughtful consideration of changing methods and of the continued need for organizations such as political parties. It is not a nuts-and-bolts discussion, but a general overview of the process.

Chamber of Commerce of the United States. *Action Course in Practical Politics.* Washington, D.C.: Chamber of Commerce, 1959.
Eight pamphlets are provided for eight separate sessions in which various aspects of practical politics can be studied and discussed. The bias is toward participation through the normal political party channels. The pamphlets cover the following topics: 1) The Individual in Politics, 2) Political Party Organization, 3) The Political Precinct, 4) The Political Campaign, 5) Political Clubs, 6) The Political Leader's Problems, 7) Political Meetings, and 8) Businessmen in Politics.

Dubeck, Paula. *Membership Experiences and Volunteer Organization Maintenance.* Ph.D. Dissertation, Northwestern University, 1973.
The only dissertation yet written on the Independent Precinct Organization tests a series of hypotheses about IPO members, their role in organization decision-making and their work in political campaigns. It is particularly important for strategists considering founding such an institution as part of their electoral strategy. Ms. Dubeck concludes that the perceived internal democracy of IPO was important in bringing support for IPO efforts by the membership. By identifying various conditions under which participation can be rewarding for members, she focuses on an important question for all strategists and institution-builders.

Fetridge, William Harrison. *The Republican Precinct Worker's Manual.* Chicago: United Republican Fund of Illinois, 80 East Jackson Blvd., 1968.
Fetridge, who served as campaign manager of Robert

Merriam's campaign for Mayor of Chicago in 1955 and as chairman of the Midwest Volunteers for Nixon-Lodge in 1960, has put together an extremely readable manual in the form of a dialogue between a new party volunteer and an elder statesman of the party. It answers many of the questions likely to occur to an inexperienced worker.

Knapp, Robert *A Manual for Precinct Workers.* Chicago: Labor Education Division, Roosevelt University, 1969. First published by Independent Voters of Illinois.
A step-by-step guide for independent precinct workers, covering all stages of a campaign from gathering petition signatures until after the election. Brief but most helpful for new workers.

Lamb, Karl and Paul Smith. *Campaign Decision-Making: The Presidential Election of 1964.* Belmont, California: Wadsworth, 1968.
Although not about an independent politics campaign, *Campaign Decision-Making* raises important issues about the inherent relationship between campaign structure and campaign rhetoric or ideology. Advocates of "new politics" should be acutely aware of the defects of the Goldwater campaign of 1964, as well as the normal campaign methods of presidential candidates. This book provides important information and theories about both.

Levin, Murray. *Kennedy Campaigning.* Boston: Beacon Press, 1966.
Based upon Edward Kennedy's campaign of 1962 for senator of Massachusetts, Levin's book explores the Kennedy style of campaigning, campaign organization, use of television, allocation of resources, and method of creating news.

Manso, Peter, (ed.). *Running Against the Machine.* Garden City, New York: Doubleday, 1969.

These readings are taken from speeches and position papers by Norman Mailer and Jimmy Breslin in their campaign for mayor and president of the City Council of New York in the 1969 Democratic primary. They ran a philosophical campaign based on a "left-conservatism" platform of making New York the 51st state and returning power to the neighborhoods. Although Mailer and Breslin are two of the best known authors in America, their political campaign was never taken seriously by the press. Nonetheless, it stands as one alternative—a campaign with issue positions quite divergent from "accepted opinions"—and as such is worthy of careful study.

Mathewson, Joe. *Up Against Daley, The New Politics in Illinois.* La Salle, Illinois: Open Court Press, 1974.
Called by some reviewers the unauthorized biography of the Independent movement in Chicago, *Up Against Daley* tells at least part of the not very well known story of the success of that movement in a machine-controlled city. Since Mathewson's book was published the fortunes of Independents have ebbed somewhat with the loss of the Singer mayoral campaign of 1975 (which Mathewson accurately predicted), but the book does introduce the reader to the real people in the movement from precinct volunteers to independent elected officials and to Mayor Daley as well. The book describes the human element of political battles and theoretical section on "the third force" has important strategic implications.

McGinniss, Joe. *The Selling of the President 1968.* New York: Pocket Books, 1970. First published by Trident Press, 1969.
This volume updates the normal material on electioneering to include attempts to manipulate the media to a candidate's advantage. In this case, McGinniss provides an inside story of the attempt to use the media to elect Nixon as president in 1968. It is not a handbook, but it does give detailed descriptions and contains an appendix

of several scripts for various political commercials.

Murphy, William T., Jr. and Edward Schneier, *Vote Power*. New
York: Doubleday, 1974. First published as a handbook for the
Movement for a New Congress by Prentice Hall, 1970.
This second edition is considerably improved as a handbook to help elect liberal congressmen. It concentrates
upon how to choose campaigns, the role of volunteer
campaign workers, and how to remain politically effective after the campaign is over. This single text is probably not detailed enough to serve as the sole handbook
for a campaign but it is a very useful adjunct to any
others you will read. *Vote Power* also includes appen-
dices on marginal congressional districts and registration
laws in the fifty states.

Nimmo, Dan. *The Political Persuaders*. Englewood Cliffs: Prentice Hall, 1970.
Treatment of new techniques of profiling the electorate
and projecting the candidate through the mass media.
Nimmo also presents considerable information about
professional campaign managers and the successes and
failures of such techniques in recent years. *Political
Persuaders* is very similar to Perry's *The New Politics*.

Parkinson, Hank. *Winning Your Campaign: A Nuts-and-Bolts
Guide to Political Victory*. Englewood Cliffs: Prentice Hall, 1970.
A realistic guide to modern campaign practices and
most particularly to the public relations aspects such as
announcing candidacy, holding press conferences, writing press releases, and campaign scheduling. It is written
primarily for potential candidates, offering advice both
under what conditions one should run and how to run
an successful campaign. Probably the best handbook for
regular party candidates available.

Parkinson, Hank. *Winning Political Campaigns With Publicity*.

Wichita, Kansas: Campaign Associates Press, 1973. Parkinson's second campaign handbook concentrates on all the necessary techniques of a news-making, public relations campaign. A particularly essential book for a candidate who may not understand the media, the campaign manager who wants to sharpen his or her tools, and the volunteer or professional public relations person working their first big campaign. The book focuses generally on tactics and mechanics but inadvertently raises strategic questions for the reader as to the implications and possible abuses of this kind of campaigning.

Perry, James. *The New Politics.* New York: Potter, 1968. An early account of the effect of professional campaign managers using new computer technology along with television to sell candidates to the voters. The two characteristics of this style of politics are that appeals are made directly to the voters and that the techniques used to make the appeals—polling, computers, television, direct mail—should be sophisticated and scientific. Perry provides a good general description of the techniques, but only limited suggestions for running campaigns.

Reum, Walter and Gerald Mattran. *Politics From the Inside Up.* Chicago: Follett, 1966. (Paperback edition by Dutton). A humorous book detailing twenty-five rules on how to build a successful political career. It includes how to join the party, which party to join, how to conduct your campaigns, what to do once elected, and how to be elected to higher positions. Not only is it a most readable book, but the suggestions on how to succeed reveal the way a political party actually works instead of the usual "good government" explanations of how they should work.

Shadegg, Stephen C. *How to Win an Election, The Art of Political Victory.* New York: Taplinger Publishing Co., 1964. Shadegg, a professional campaign manager who has successfully engineered many politicians into office (e.g., Barry Goldwater), presents electoral tactics aimed at swaying the "Indifferents," the undecided voters. Supporting his arguments with numerous personal experiences, Shadegg shows how citizens can be manipulated and exploited, and how various gimmicks, "corny" and "emotional" literature, and public opinion polls can be used to translate indifferent citizens into electoral victories. Some of his guidelines about the use of mass media, direct mailings, and candidate identification are realistic and helpful to any strategist who wants to win. However, by describing what it takes to win traditional electoral campaigns, Schadegg has documented the bankruptcy of traditional electoral politics and, inadvertently, has shown the need for a new electoral politics which treats citizens honestly.

Simpson, Dick. *Winning Elections: A Handbook in Participatory Politics*. Chicago: The Swallow Press, 1972.
Based upon experiences garnered from electoral victories against traditional party organizations and the Daley machine in Chicago, Simpson provides strategic guidelines for the success of Independent politics. This handbook explains the basic principles of Independent politics and presents step-by-step instructions for building the effective, participatory organizations required for a new type of electoral politics. It provides the nuts-and-bolts instructions for those who would pursue the independent politics strategy we advocated.

Stavis, Ben. *We Were the Campaign*. Boston: Beacon Press, 1969.
This is one of the best books on the McCarthy campaign in terms of the details of campaign organization and day-to-day decision-making. It is also successful in distinguishing between the McCarthy campaign and earlier efforts, and in telling the story of the campaign from the perspective of student volunteers. Stavis also discusses the internal campaign struggles and problems.

III. Administrative Strategy

We are not aware of any published literature about administrative strategies. The following books document the dominance of bureaucracy and explain the major characteristics of this prevalent institutional structure. Hopefully, the information in these studies will help in the development of an effective administrative strategy.

Berle, Adolph A. and Gardiner C. Means. *The Modern Corporation and Private Property. Revised Edition.* New York: Harcourt, Brace & World, 1968.

First published in 1932, Berle and Means provide early documentation of the separation of ownership and control in modern corporations; a development which has continued until the present time. The key to understanding corporate power is not who owns corporate property, but rather who has control—Berle and Means argue that most large corporations are management-controlled. *The Modern Corporation and Private Property* is one of the best statements of the change from traditional capitalism to corporate capitalism and should be studied by any strategist who wishes to affect corporate structures and policies.

Bower, Joseph L. *Managing the Resource Allocation Process: A Study of Corporate Planning and Investment.* Boston: Division of Research, Graduate Schools of Business Administration, Harvard University, 1970.

Based upon four case studies of the capital investment process in a large corporation, Bower shows that the expenditure of huge capital resources is almost completely controlled by the initiatives and contributions of subordinates in lower echelons. Proposals for expenditures made by lower level officials are seldom changed by those at the top. Modern corporations are management-controlled—as Berle and Means have shown—and because this control is often exercised at lower echelons, an effective administrative strategy must focus on those below the top of the hierarchy.

Burnham, James. *The Managerial Revolution*. Bloomington: Indiana University Press, 1960. First published in 1941.

Written over three decades ago, *The Managerial Revolution* remains a powerful and relevant argument explaining the rise of managers throughout the modern world. According to Burnham, both capitalism and socialism have been superseded by managerialism. Managers have become predominant in modern society because they, rather than capitalists or workers, possess the needed skills to actually run industry and government. Although Burnham's thesis has been refined and improved upon by more recent studies, *The Managerial Revolution* is still an accurate statement of modern society and worth careful study.

Etzioni, Amitai. (ed.), *Complex Organization, A Sociological Reader*. New York: Holt, Rinehart and Winston, 1961.

This collection of readings discusses aspects of bureaucracy crucial for creating an administrative strategy—organizational goals, organizational structures, and how organizations and organizational policies change. The excerpts and essays focus on a wide range of organizations (factories, prisons, government agencies, trade unions, universities, and others), thus providing the reader with information about the bureaucratic character of most aspects of modern life.

Freeman, J. Leiper. *The Political Process, Executive Bureau-Legislative Committee Relations*. Revised Edition, New York: Random House, 1966.

According to Freeman, major power in American national government is exercised by subordinate groups in the executive branch (the bureaus), and by sub-units within the legislative branch (the committees). Except in crisis situations, policy is made by lower echelon bureaucrats as they cooperate with and are supported by senior members of congressional committees and interest group leaders. Increasingly, policy making has become the prerogative of specialists and staff personnel.

Galbraith, John Kenneth. *The New Industrial State*. Second Edition, Revised. Boston: Houghton Mifflin, 1971.
Galbraith argues that the whole economic and governmental order has changed and that traditional economic and political theories are not adequate to explain the new industrial state. The imperatives of technology have created large interlocking organizations in which groups of specialists within the Technostructure prevail over all others in the exercise of power. *The New Industrial State* is one of the most interesting and well-written statements explaining the significant changes that have occurred in contemporary American society.

Gittell, Marilyn. *Participants and Participation, A Study of School Policy in New York City*. New York: Frederick A. Praeger, 1967.
A case study of the New York city school system which describes the dominant role of professional bureaucrats and the declining influence of the Board of Education and the Superintendent, even in such crucial areas as budget-making and curriculum development. An informative bibliography on the political and administrative aspects of school systems is also included, as well as additional sources on the New York school system.

Jacoby, Henry. *The Bureaucratization of the World*. Berkeley: University of California Press, 1973.
Jacoby has written a highly readable, yet broad-gauged and scholarly essay on the world-wide growth of bureaucracy and its permeation into all aspects of modern life. He incorporates in his analysis some of the studies cited in this section of the bibliography and, by documenting the ubiquity of bureaucracy, his book becomes one of the best starting points for those interested in administrative strategy.

Koerner, James D. *Who Controls American Education? A Guide for Laymen.* Boston: Beacon Press, 1968.
Koerner's study of primary and secondary educational institutions describes how educational policy is controlled. Examining the influence of government agencies, teacher organizations, local school boards, and other groups, he concludes that educational experts control American education. He presents some guidelines for how laymen can get the best use out of experts without caving in to them, but he has no concrete strategic suggestions for how laymen can regain control from the professional educators in education.

Mace, Myles L. *Directors: Myth and Reality.* Boston: Division of Research, Graduate School of Business Administration, Harvard University, 1971.
The data for this study were accumulated from personal interviews and the major conclusion is that boards of directors of large corporations do not really exercise much control. The strategic implication is clear: if you want fundamental change, don't waste your time pressuring or replacing members of the boards.

Merton, Robert K. *et al.* (ed.) *Reader in Bureaucracy,* New York: The Free Press, 1952.
One of the best collections of articles and excerpts covering a wide range of issues important to the construction of an administrative strategy. The following topics, among others, are discussed: theoretical conceptions of bureaucracy, control and ownership in modern corporations, and the role of subordinates in granting authority to superiors.

Resnik, Henry S. *Turning on the System: War in the Philadelphia Public Schools.* New York: Pantheon Books, 1970.
This book documents a major effect in 1967 to reform the Philadelphia school system through new appointments at the top of the structure. The would-be reform-

ers failed. Resnik's book is a case study documenting the inability to bring about fundamental change in a large bureaucracy through new appointments at the top, even if the new appointees wish to change things and work hard.

Rogers, David. *110 Livingston Street, Politics and Bureaucracy in the New York City Schools.* New York: Random House, 1968.
The bureaucratic nature of the New York City school system is well documented in this book. Early chapters discuss the efforts of various community groups to affect the schools and Chapters VII-XII describe the power of various units in the bureaucracy; the school board, the superintendent, headquarters staff, and professional educators. Chapter XIII considers "alternative reform strategies," none of which can, with any assurance, "substantially reverse the downward trend of the past." Rogers advocates decentralization and strong city-wide leadership to obtain piece-meal and politically attainable reform programs.

Weber, Max. *From Max Weber: Essays in Sociology.* Translated, edited, and with an introduction by H. H. Gerth and C. Wright Mills. New York: Oxford University Press, 1946.
This collection of essays and excerpts from Weber's works includes his now classical statement of the characteristics of bureaucracy (Chapter VIII). Weber's description of bureaucracy, published in the early 1900's, is still the touchstone for those who continue to write about administration, bureaucrats, and large organizations.

IV. Nonviolent Issue Strategy

Alinsky, Saul D. *Reveille for Radicals.* New York: Vintage Books, 1969. First published in 1946.

Written by probably the most successful community organizer of our day, *Reveille for Radicals* discusses the general principles for building an effective "people's organization." Alinsky tells what it takes to be an organizer—the sort of disposition and orientation required; the sort of work the organizer must do and what organizers must not do if they are to succeed. Alinsky recounts many of his own organizing experiences to demonstrate the need for flexible and creative pressure tactics which adapt to new situations.

Alinsky, Saul D. *Rules for Radicals, A Practical Primer for Realistic Radicals.* New York: Vintage Books, 1971.

As in his earlier book, *Reveille for Radicals*, Alinsky discusses organization-building and the qualities required of an effective organizer. Of additional importance for any strategist is his analysis of means (tactics) and ends (goals), and his thirteen rules of power tactics. These rules are an important guide for effective pressure action against established institutions and policies. *Rules for Radicals* is Alinsky's mature reflection on community organizations, confrontation, and organizing. It should be read by all strategists whatever their persuasion.

Boyarsky, Bill and Nancy. *Backroom Politics: How Your Local Politicians Work, Why Your Government Doesn't and What You Can Do About It.* Los Angeles: J. P. Torcher, Inc., 1974.

This book is best as a description of the nation's ills and the horrors of local and state government. It tells of citizen victories around the country but spends only one chapter describing the strategies and techniques in any detail. For a description of the problem, the ineffectiveness of many traditional techniques, and a discussion of the weaknesses of the government, the press, etc., it is generally helpful. It is also reassuring that there are some victories to report from those employing the strategies we have advocated here.

Gardner, John W. *In Common Cause.* New York: W. W. Norton & Company, Inc., 1972.
John Gardner started *Common Cause* in 1970; it has grown to 200,000 members, and was effective in its support of the constitutional amendment granting the 18 year old vote and the campaign-spending legislation of 1972. *Common Cause* is a citizen's lobby group which sustains on-going, professional lobbying techniques to pressure politicians on specific problems. In this book Gardner makes a case for re-establishing the link between citizens and their elected representatives as the strategy for meeting the problems of contemporary America. Although recognizing that problems exist in the private corporate sphere, Gardner argues that citizens should pressure the government to correct these ills through new legislation and better regulation.

Huenefeld, John. *The Community Activist's Handbook: A Guide to Organizing, Financing, and Publicizing Community Campaigns.* Boston: Beacon Press, 1970.
Huenefeld does not discuss basic strategic principles but he does provide step-by-step details on how to get an organization started, how to run a meeting, how to raise money, how to get publicity, and how to increase the membership of the organization. His guidelines are for those who wish to focus on local government and he provides realistic suggestions for effective leadership and control.

King, Jr., Martin Luther. *Stride Toward Freedom: The Montgomery Story.* New York: Harper & Row, 1958.
Stride Toward Freedom is King's personal account of the successful Montgomery bus boycott, 1955-56. No reader will finish this book untouched by the faith and suffering of King and the 50,000 blacks of Montgomery. King describes many of the day-to-day problems, decisions, and actions of this dramatic effort but, more im-

portantly, he conveys his own personal insights, courage, commitment, and the hope and feelings of the thousands involved. This powerful chronicle of a truly significant event in American history is clear evidence that fundamental social change is not just the result of strategic and tactical engineering but also requires an initiating spark, creative and committed leadership, and the enthusiastic support of thousands who remain strong throughout the long struggle.

King, Jr., Martin Luther. *Why We Can't Wait*. New York: New American Library, 1963.

Martin Luther King was not only a man whose life and words exemplified the best aspects of the Christian faith; in addition, he was a sophisticated strategist. From the early 1950's until his death in 1968 he led the civil rights movement in one of the most effective efforts for fundamental change in recent American history. *Why We Can't Wait* is a case study of one of the major events in that struggle; the civil rights campaign in Birmingham, Alabama, 1963. A number of tactical issues —sit ins, filling up the jails, boycotts—are discussed and evaluated. A key factor in King's approach in his affirmation of the strategic value *and* moral necessity of nonviolence. This book not only discusses effective pressure tactics but also provides a philosophical-religious defense for nonviolent direct action.

Michael, James R. (ed.) *Working on the System, A Comprehensive Manual for Citizen Access to Federal Agencies*. New York: Basic Books, 1974.

Prepared by Ralph Nader's Center for Study of Responsive Law, this large reference book (950 pages) is a collection of reports, essays, and documents about twelve major regulatory commissions in the federal government. Advocating public pressure against government agencies, *Working on the System* provides information and data to help citizens find points of access into these agencies. Various types of action are discussed, ranging from individual complaints to full-scale intervention in protracted trial-type hearings.

Nader, Ralph and Donald Ross. *Action for a Change, A Student's Manual for Public Interest Organizing*. New York: Grossman Publishers, 1971.
This book is primarily a manual for setting up Public Interest Research Groups (PIRG's) on university campuses. PIRG's organize students with paid professional staffs for action against government agencies and corporations. Nader and Ross argue that students can best contribute to social change through scientific and legal research and that such research is most effective when used in the public arena by the full-time, paid staffs of the PIRG's. The primary social action of the PIRG's is advocacy in administrative and legislative bodies, and in courts of law. PIRG's are an example of a pressure against strategy and the operating formula is: student energy, plus professional skills, equals major change.

Nader, Ralph., *et al.*, (eds.) *Whistle Blowing: The Report of the Conference on Professional Responsibility*. New York: Grossman Publishers, 1972.
Ralph Nader and his associates recognize the needed contributions of inside professionals as participants in strategies for change. This book is a series of case studies of engineers, doctors, inspectors, government employees, and military personnel who blew the whistle on corporate and governmental injustices. Whistle blowing is a pressure strategy which aims to correct specific wrongs primarily by creating outside public pressure against corporations and government agencies. Included are guidelines for effective whistle blowing which results in concrete policy changes.

Oppenheimer, Martin, and George Lakey. *A Manual For Direct Action, Strategy and Tactics for Civil Rights and All Other*

Nonviolent Protest Movements. Chicago: Quadrangle Books, 1964. This book is focused primarily upon the pressure tactics of the 1960's civil rights movement but some of the strategic insights easily apply to other issues and situations. The discussion of the importance of the situation (Chapter 2), the presentation of guidelines for democratic and effective organizations (Chapter 4), and the brief list of various types of direct action (Chapter 7) are helpful for those beginning their study of strategies.

Ross, Donald K. *A Public Citizen's Action Manual.* New York: Grossman Publishers, 1973.
Ross discusses a wide range of specific problems and issues in the areas of consumer protection, health care, women's rights, taxation, and suggests methods of citizen action to fight these problems. Numerous examples of citizen pressure against business and government are mentioned and many helpful sources of information on pricing, civil rights, safety standards, consumer protection, etc., are listed throughout the book. In addition, Ross indicates how to get citizen's action groups started and how to keep them running.

Sanders, Norman K. *Stop It! A Guide to Defense of the Environment.* San Francisco: Rinehart Press, 1972.
In Part I Sanders discusses aspects of organizing and the tactics he has found helpful in fights against polluters. Specifically, he explains how citizens can use public hearings, referendums, initiatives, and litigation in the courts to defend the environment. According to Sanders, litigation is not a sufficient tactic and he advocates political action (pressuring incumbent legislators and electing new environment-conscious officials) and educational programs to sensitize the citizenry about the environment and its defense. Much of the analysis in this brief book is based upon Sanders' own experience as an activist in California. Part II is a collection of case studies documenting successful fights against varied polluters.

Acknowledgments

This book has been seven years in the making. It grew from a seminar on Strategies for Change held at the University of Illinois at Chicago Circle in 1968. Seminar participants included, among others, Alderman A. A. Rayner, David Wallace from Operation Bread Basket, John Kearney from Independent Voters of Illinois, Edwin Bell from the City Council Finance Committee, Tom Gaudette from Organization for a Better Austin, Paul Booth from Citizens Action Program, and Scott Simpson from Independent Precinct Organization. This diverse group did not agree on the contradictory strategies and commitments which surfaced in the seminar and would not necessarily agree with what we have advocated here. Yet this book is at least a partial consequence of the discussions, disagreements, and commitments of those who participated in the seminar.

The book also reflects seven years of experience with the Independent Precinct Organization, Citizens Action Program, and dozens of electoral and issue campaigns in Chicago. Thousands of participants in these efforts have taught us what works, what doesn't work, and, most of all, the spirit necessary to sustain a movement for change.

Our students at the University of Illinois at Chicago Circle have discussed and debated much of the material in this book for many years now. Not only in our special Strategies for Change course, but in our regular courses, questions of political philosophy and political action frequently focused on the issues we discuss here. Those prior discussions have clarified the arguments in this book.

Our publisher and our editors deserve special thanks. Mort Weisman, president of Swallow Press, has been an active participant in independent electoral campaigns. His contributions to independent politics in Chicago and his sustained interest in this book have been solid encouragement throughout. Durrett Wagner, who edited an earlier draft, carefully guided us in creating a better manuscript. Susan Houston, the final editor, who has been active with civic groups and independent campaigns, eliminated hundreds of errors, awkward phrases, and unclear passages. With all this assistance, any errors which remain can but be our own.

This book has been retyped by the typing staff of the Political Science Department at Chicago Circle many times and we are most grateful to the department for its assistance.

251

Finally, Our families have been patient—most of the time—with the lost evenings and vacations which we spent at our typewriters. Without a full family commitment to strategies for change neither this book nor our past and future actions would be possible.

The changes needed today require a self-conscious, coordinated movement; and such a movement requires leaders. Our efforts will have been worthwhile if this report of our reflections and experiences can help develop these leaders.

Index